Canoeing
Mississippi

Canoeing
Mississippi

Ernest Herndon

University Press of Mississippi
Jackson

www.upress.state.ms.us

09 08 07 06 05 04 03 02 01   4 3 2 1
⊗
Library of Congress Cataloging-in-Publication Data

Herndon, Ernest.
    Canoeing Mississippi / Ernest Herndon.
       p.   cm.
    Includes bibliographical references and index.
    ISBN 1-57806-221-7 (cloth : alk. paper)—ISBN 1-57806-222-5 (pbk. : alk. paper)
       1. Canoes and canoeing—Mississippi—Guidebooks.   2. Mississippi—Guidebooks.
    I. Title.
    GV776.M7 H47   2001
    917.6204'64—dc21

                                                                              00-064657

British Library Cataloging-in-Publication Data available

This book is dedicated to my wife, Angelyn, who has the grace and wisdom to let me take long trips into the woods; my longtime camping buddy Scott Williams of Prentiss, who not only paddles and sails boats but builds them; and Charles Dunagin and Jack Ryan, my bosses at the McComb Enterprise-Journal newspaper, who allowed me to float rivers and write about them both in the newspaper and for this book.

Contents

Canoeing Mississippi

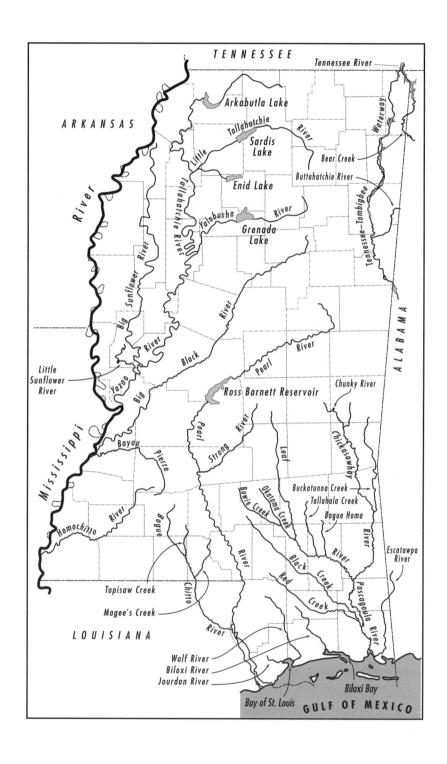

TENNESSEE

Tennessee River

ARKANSAS

Arkabutla Lake

Tallahatchie River

Sardis Lake

Bear Creek

Little

Buttahatchie River

Enid Lake

Tallahatchie River

Yalobusha River

Grenada Lake

Big Sunflower River

River

River

Black River

Pearl River

Tennessee–Tombigbee Waterway

ALABAMA

Little Sunflower River

Yazoo River

Big

Ross Barnett Reservoir

Chunky River

Mississippi

Bayou

Pierre

Pearl River

Strong River

Leaf

Chickasawhay

River

Homochitto River

Bogue

Bowie Creek

Okatoma Creek

Buckatunna Creek

Tallahala Creek

Bogue Homa

River

Escatawpa River

Topisaw Creek

Chitto

River

Red

Black Creek

River

Pascagoula River

Magee's Creek

River

Creek

LOUISIANA

Wolf River
Biloxi River
Jourdan River

Biloxi Bay

Bay of St. Louis

GULF OF MEXICO

1. The Rivers of Mississippi

An Overview

Mississippi is blessed with rivers. Yet there are plenty of Mississippians who have no concept of the number and variety of the state's streams, and plenty of non-residents who imagine them all to be muddy, stagnant sloughs harboring clouds of mosquitoes and swarms of snakes. They may not be aware of the sandy streams of southwest Mississippi, the rock-walled creeks in the northeast, the blackwater brooks of the southeast, the gem-clear streams of the Gulf Coast, or the lustrous Pearl and its sparkling tributaries—in addition to those murky rivers of the Delta, which actually harbor some pleasant surprises too.

Picture the state: roughly rectangular, with a boot heel on the bottom right and the Mississippi River forming a crooked 400-mile border on the left. Let's start in the lower left corner and work clockwise. The wide, shallow, sandy Homochitto River runs west into the Mississippi south of Natchez. Bayou Pierre, known for its colorful clays, parallels the Homochitto to the north. Big Black River, which is as muddy as they come, slices southwest across the state into the Mississippi below Vicksburg. At Vicksburg, the Yazoo pours its silt-laden contents into the Mississippi, comprising the waters of Big Sunflower, Yalobusha, Tallahatchie, and Coldwater Rivers, among others. These largely agricultural streams may have given rise to the stereotypes of mud and mosquitoes, but even they have segments worth exploring, such as the reaches where they border national forest or wildlife refuge.

North-central Mississippi harbors the headwaters of two creeks that become canoeable in Tennessee: the Wolf and the Hatchie. The Wolf (distinct from the Wolf River on the Coast) empties into the Mississippi at Memphis. The Hatchie swings farther north, passing through two national wildlife refuges en route to the Mississippi. (Southwest Mississippi likewise gives rise to a pair of rivers that become properly floatable in another state. The Amite, which sheds its logjams at the Louisiana line when its two forks merge, empties into Lake Maurepas. The Tangipahoa, which widens enough to be pleasantly canoeable at the Louisiana town of that name, flows into Lake Pontchartrain.)

The Tennessee River clips the northeast corner of Mississippi as it loops from Alabama into Tennessee headed for the Ohio River. In the 1980s, a massive U.S. Army Corps of Engineers project linked the Tennessee with the Tombigbee River, which runs southeast past Columbus and into Alabama to the Gulf of Mexico below Mobile, so for all practical purposes the Tennessee-Tombigbee Waterway is one system. Bear Creek, a delightful stream that slices through Tishomingo State Park, crosses from Alabama into Mississippi and back before entering the Tennessee. Another prime canoeing tributary, Buttahatchee River, flows into the Tenn-Tom just north of Columbus.

That brings us to the Pascagoula River system, the state's canoeing mecca and one of the finest river systems in the nation. Near Meridian, Chunky River courses between rock cliffs into the Chickasawhay River, an impressive waterway more than 150 miles long; the Buckatunna is another good tributary. The Chickasawhay merges with the Leaf, which comes in from the northwest, to form the Pascagoula. Like the Chickasawhay, the Leaf is a brawny, deep-woods river. Its tributaries include the gentle Bowie, the whitewater Okatoma, and sinuous Tallahala and Bogue Homa Creeks. The Pascagoula River muscles through massive wildlife management areas not far from national forest and national wildlife refuges, a remarkable aggregation of public wildlands. It's fed by tannin-stained Black and Red Creeks from the west and Alabama's Escatawpa River from the east before sprawling into the Mississippi Sound at the city of Pascagoula.

The swamps of the Pascagoula and the Pearl to the west form the ragged edges of a sandy apron of terrain on the Gulf Coast. Seaming this apron are the many-faceted Wolf and the short but lovely Biloxi and Jourdan Rivers, as well as languid Davis Bayou. Offshore, within sea kayaking range, stretch a host of wild barrier islands.

The Pearl River runs more than 400 miles from northeast Mississippi near

Philadelphia through Ross Barnett Reservoir, past the state capital and down the southern half of the state into the labyrinthine Honey Island Swamp. Its tributaries include the sleepy Strong and gorgeous Bogue Chitto Rivers as well as sweet little creeks like Topisaw and Magee's.

There are countless other creeks as well: short, shallow, logjammed, and/or seasonal, usually enjoyed by local residents who go when conditions are best and don't mind battling logs and shoals for a mess of fish and a day of adventure. Then there are the lakes: oxbows, state fishing lakes, state parks, national forest lakes, national wildlife refuges, reservoirs, and water parks. There are dozens of these flatwater destinations, man-made and natural, developed and remote.

All told, canoeing Mississippi is a massive project.

I started my own "project" when a friend introduced me to the Bogue Chitto River in the late 1970s. Since then I've been caught in a flash flood on the Homochitto, gotten lost in Honey Island Swamp, hauled bass out of Bear Creek, battled headwinds on the Tennessee-Tombigbee Waterway—and generally had a ball enjoying the incredible beauty and diversity of Mississippi's waters. I've also been chagrined at the problems: erosion, litter, pollution, channelization, crowds, lawsuits. It's crucial that we become more aware and appreciative of these rivers and take measures to prevent further degradation.

This book is for armchair travelers as well as paddlers planning a trip. Many river guidebooks are rich in logistical data but offer little else. As a reader I want to know more: history, folklore, geology, wildlife, ecology, plus some good adventure stories. I've tried to include all that here, inspired as much by Mark Twain's *Life on the Mississippi*, say, as by modern guidebooks. At the end of each river description I have listed the essential facts for quick reference when planning a float. The information is as up to date as I can make it, but things like park fees and bridge access are always subject to change. When possible, phone ahead at the numbers given to check current fees, conditions, or access points. If readers encounter any changes that need reporting in future editions, send them to me care of University Press of Mississippi, 3825 Ridgewood Road, Jackson, MS 39211-6492.

2. Equipment and Techniques

Boats

Mississippi doesn't have a strong canoeing tradition like some North Woods states. Somehow, as we evolved from Native American log dugouts to plank pirogues and aluminum johnboats, canoes fell by the wayside. In the North, by contrast, the transition went from birchbark to wood-and-canvas to modern canoes. Drive around Michigan or Minnesota these days and you'll see canoes everywhere; drive around Mississippi and you'll see mainly johnboats. However, a few hardcore southern fishermen have always appreciated canoes for their ability to get them into narrow or shallow waters. In the 1970s canoeing boomed as its recreational potential was belatedly discovered. Nowadays it's wildly popular on a handful of streams like Black Creek, Bogue Chitto, and Okatoma, which are the right size and speed to make floating easy and exciting, plus have outfitters handy. But travel more remote or less stereotypically canoeable rivers like the Chickasawhay, Big Sunflower, or Bayou Pierre and you may not encounter another human, much less a paddler.

Not that Mississippi paddlers are confined to canoes. Our hospitable waters accommodate most any type of small boat—canoe, pirogue, johnboat, whitewater kayak, sit-on-top kayak, sea kayak, inner tube. This is partly due to the variety of environments. The state has little creeks like Magee's, midsized streams like Bowie, wide rivers like the Pearl, as well as lakes, swamps, marshes, and even the wide-open Mississippi Sound.

Canoes are the most versatile of the small boats, at home anywhere from creeks to lakes. Lighter, shallower pirogues are better suited for narrow creeks since they slide over barely submerged logs and portage easily if you have to go around. Whitewater kayaks and sit-on-tops, since they pivot with each stroke of the paddle, prefer crooked streams to long, open stretches. Straight-tracking sea kayaks, on the other hand, thrive on big water, whether Ross Barnett Reservoir or the Mississippi Sound. Slow-moving johnboats fare best on streams with a good current to help them along.

Since many Mississippi rivers lack canoe rentals, paddling enthusiasts often wind up buying a boat of their own. There are hundreds of canoe styles available, quite a contrast with a few decades ago when the basic aluminum model was the main thing going. Advances in materials and technology have revolutionized the business so there is a design for every purpose.

A typical buyer's guide in a paddling magazine lists these categories: recreational/casual, cruiser, tripper, wilderness tripper, touring, whitewater, downriver, pack, utility, solo sport, sport combination/sportsman, combination tourer, specialty, decked, competition cruising, outrigger, racing/competition. From the Mississippi perspective, such divisions seem unnecessary, to say the least. Just how specialized does a boat design have to be to float a gentle waterway like, say, Red Creek? For most canoers—or canoeists, as some would have it—plain old recreational-style crafts are just fine. That's because recreation, or family, canoes tend to reach a good compromise in design elements.

For instance, a good all-around canoe for Mississippi has slight rocker, which is a compromise between extreme rocker and no rocker. Rocker refers to how much the bow and stern rise from the center of the boat. Picture the rocker on a rocking chair. A canoe shaped like that pivots quickly so it can handle the sudden changes required for paddling whitewater—which Mississippi doesn't have, with a few minor exceptions. Such extreme rocker is a disadvantage on our languid streams, where you don't want the boat to swivel every time you dip the paddle. A rockerless canoe, on the other hand, will track straight across a wide lake but is hard to turn on a crooked creek. Therefore, slight rocker is a good compromise, and is found in most general-purpose canoes.

There are other differences in hull shapes. Turn a canoe upside down and view it from one end and you'll be able to tell whether the bottom is flat, slightly arched, or slightly V-shaped. Generally speaking, a flat bottom has more initial stability—that is, it feels more stable at first—but less secondary stability, which means it may roll over more easily than the other two styles. Semi-arch and semi-V, meanwhile, feel a bit tippy at first but perform better in rough conditions since they can roll to the gunwales (or edges) and still recover. Such distinctions might make a difference on whitewater torrents or vast windswept lakes but matter little on Mississippi's easygoing waters.

A few other basics of canoe design: Tumblehome refers to sides that curve in, while flare indicates sides that angle out from the boat. Recurve stems are ends that curve back toward the center of the boat, while plumb stems rise straight, and others angle outward. Tumblehome sides and recurve stems suggest the classic look associated with birchbark vessels, but none of these traits makes a noticeable difference in performance on our forgiving waters.

Size is a tricky topic too. Shorter isn't faster when it comes to boat design. A 15-foot-by-36-inch canoe is slower than a 17-by-36. And a wider boat is slower than a narrow one of the same length and design. Generally speaking, 34–36 inches is a reasonable width. For length, a 16-footer is a good compromise for solo with gear or tandem day-tripping, while a 17-footer is better for two people with camping equipment.

Materials can likewise confuse. The buyer's guide lists proprietary composite layup, composite layup, fiber-reinforced plastic, Royalex, R-84 Royalite, aluminum, polyethylene, polypropylene, Kevlar, skin on frame, wood/canvas, wood, and wood/epoxy. Any of these will do in Mississippi. Each does have its advantages and drawbacks, however.

Fiberglass is affordable and serviceable but can crack when it slams into rocks, of which we have few in Mississippi; cloth fiberglass is more durable than chopped, and worth the extra expense. Although aluminum is considered old-fashioned these days, it's rugged and functional, the main drawback being that it's cold and noisy. Foam-core plastic materials like Royalex are heavy but virtually indestructible, a good choice for rough use on logjammed, gravel-shoaled streams. Polyethylene sheet plastic, found in the cheapest boats, is flimsy and flexible but still serviceable. Wood is beautiful but sure to get scratched on logs and gravel. Kevlar is ultra-tough but expensive and hard to repair. Royalex, fiberglass, and aluminum are the most commonly used and practical materials because they're tough and relatively inexpensive.

Incidentally, a few people use inflatable boats since they're portable and in some cases cheaper. They will do, but I don't particularly recommend them. A rubber raft would take forever to get down our slow streams. Inflatable canoes are faster than rafts but still sluggish and subject to puncture, as I discovered when I

Pirogues, like these two homemade wooden models, evolved from dugout canoes.

sank one in the snake-infested Wolf River of west Tennessee. A hidden stob sliced the bottom open, and the boat sank under us as we paddled frantically to shore. We had a long slog out of the swamp, which in places was chest-deep.

Canoes can be alarmingly expensive—new ones start at around $600 and go to $3,000 and up—so the best bet is to scan the want ads or visit canoe rentals after the summer season when they sell extra boats. My philosophy is to go for the deal, not the ideal. I'm not sure an ideal design exists, and even if it does, so what? In tropical countries people negotiate savage rapids in 36-foot log dugouts. They're heavy, narrow, shallow, tippy and reluctant to turn, but they get the job done and ensure plenty of adventure.

It was from such dugouts that pirogues evolved. The word *pirogue* is a French derivation of a Spanish derivation of a Caribbean Indian word for dugout canoe. Relics of centuries-old Native American dugouts have been found on the Homochitto River. South Louisiana Cajuns developed the boat into a craft all their own. Nowadays, Cajuns often strap their pirogues upside down on top of motorboats; they speed across the swamp, then switch to the pirogue for hard-to-get-to backwaters. But there are plenty of folks who use the lightweight vessels for plain old canoeing.

A typical pirogue is 14 feet long, 21 inches wide at the bottom and 34 at the gunwales. With a center height of 11 inches it's a low rider, as in an inch of freeboard when fully loaded. Made of chopped fiberglass, it weighs 40–55 pounds and costs from $250 up. Wooden pirogues are hard to come by these days because of the cost of materials and longer construction time, though plans are available for home-built plywood models. Pirogues are at their best when paddled down narrow, twisty creeks or poled across shallow swamps. Their small size and slight draft allows them to go places so tight even canoes fear to tread. They're at their worst in any sort of rough conditions, whether waves or rapids, since their low sides and tippy hulls make them susceptible to swamping and capsizing. I learned this first-hand on a trip down the broad Colorado River of central Texas with a pirogue and a canoe. The pirogue fell far behind, then swamped when

Canoe and sea kayak are two popular means of exploring state waters.

we got to some easy rapids with standing waves. It was at its best on a trip down the upper Amite River of southwest Mississippi. That time the canoe lagged behind as the pirogue slid through tight spots and over shallow logs that the canoe couldn't negotiate without portaging.

Like pirogues, whitewater kayaks and sit-on-tops are suited mainly for day trips on small creeks. Such boats are extremely responsive, which is a drawback on any but the smallest of streams since they turn with every paddle stroke. But given the abundance of crooked little creeks in Mississippi, there's a place for such boats. I know people whose favorite pastime is taking their kayaks down creeks too small for easy canoeing.

Sea kayaks, meanwhile, don't like to turn at all. They're designed for tracking straight across open water, and equipped with rudders to make turning easier. With their decked hulls, spray skirts and watertight gear compartments, they are extremely seaworthy and can hold gear for long-term camping. They're useful on wide rivers and lakes and along the Gulf Coast. People even paddle sea kayaks to Mississippi's barrier islands. And why not? Eskimos used them in Arctic seas, and they have made open ocean crossings. But it's a real chore getting them down a winding creek. And they cost more than any boats mentioned, with most models priced in the thousands.

Johnboats—also called flat-bottom boats, flatboats, and bateaux—are widely used in Mississippi, especially by fishermen and usually with motors. They're the workhorse of the waterways, the pickup truck of watercraft. But they don't get much respect in paddling circles. No one stands around admiring their lines. Most are mass-produced aluminum with little difference except size. Nevertheless, the johnboat can serve a paddler well under certain conditions. It's versatile, stable, and not too slow as long as you choose a small one, 8 to 12 feet long, the narrower the better.

Johnboats handle differently than other boats. For making progress with two people, the easiest way is one man in the stern and one in the middle, so the bow glides over the water. But for two-man fishing, a popular method is to take the boat down stern-first, with one man in the stern and one in the bow. That allows ample casting room for both men. It's slower, but float-fishing doesn't require speed. For one-man handling, many fishermen like to sit in the bow and go down stern-first. Strange as it seems, the johnboat handles well that way. The reason is that when you're in the bow, the stern rises out of the water and the curve of the bow minimizes resistance. When you're in the stern, on the other hand, though the bow rises, the sharp-cornered rear transom sinks deeply, causing more resistance. On larger rivers, paddlers may opt for a small motor. I'm not a fan of motors, but having, say, a 3.3-horsepower outboard on a johnboat can eliminate the need for a shuttle, since you can ride up a river, then float back down. Johnboats cost several hundred dollars new, but because of their abundance in Mississippi, used ones are often available cheap.

I became an admirer of johnboats when I took a 10-footer down the Tangipahoa River in Louisiana. Though not as fast as a canoe, it was speedier than I expected. Its broad, stable bottom made it safe to stand in, and it handled nimbly in swifts and bends. There's also something indigenous about a johnboat, which evolved from the flatboats of yore and is now universal in the South.

All in all, though, the johnboat can't compare with a canoe. In fact, the only

The Backwoods Drifter, a combination canoe and johnboat, is efficient on twisty creeks.

boat I've found that is equal to or better than a canoe for Deep South streams is a wooden boat built by Mississippi craftsman Scott Williams of Prentiss. It's called the Backwoods Drifter and is designed specifically for Mississippi waters.

The Drifter, which was featured on ETV's *Mississippi Roads* in 1999–2000, is stabler than a canoe or pirogue, faster than a johnboat, and supremely maneuverable without being jerky. What Scott did, in essence, is take a johnboat, do away with the wide stern, and make both ends like the bow, upswooping and tapered but still square. The result incorporates elements of canoe and johnboat. He uses composite construction—mahogany plywood, fiberglass, and epoxy—to create the flat-bottomed vessel, which is a good bit heavier than a canoe. Mine measures 12 feet long, 30 inches across at the bottom midcenter, 40 inches at the gunwales, and weighs probably 100 pounds (canoes average 70–75 pounds). Incidentally, that's not unlike those Indian dugouts found in the Homochitto River area: 12 feet long, square-ended, with platforms on each end. Talk about indigenous!

As I said, every boat has its drawbacks, and the Drifter may feel too responsive to folks accustomed to using only a straight downriver paddle stroke. A correction stroke is needed, but in my opinion every serious paddler needs to know that stroke, which I describe below. The Drifter is slower than a standard canoe, though it easily outpaces a johnboat. It's a great vessel for many Mississippi streams since it handles the twists, swifts, logs and shoals better than a canoe, and is reasonably efficient on flatwater.

That's the high end of the spectrum. The low, in terms of simplicity and cost, is the inner tube. Used by thousands, tubes will certainly get you down a stream, albeit at the stream's pace. A tube is to a canoe what a hot-air balloon is to a jet. Nevertheless, tubes have a certain charm. You sit back in the rubber circle, suspended between cold water and warm air, letting the river carry you along. I'm a paddler, not a tuber, but I admit that even jet pilots need to let go of the throttle once in a while, and a tube is a sure way to do it.

I've floated Mississippi streams in a wide variety of vessels. Each was an adventure in its own right. Currently I've settled on the Backwoods Drifter for creeks and a 17-foot fiberglass canoe for bigger rivers and lakes, but who knows? There may be more boats in my future.

Paddling

A canoe isn't much good without a paddle—and the ability to use it. Paddle designs are nearly as varied as boats, and as adaptable to Mississippi waters. Only the cheapest models are worth avoiding, since frail wooden ones soon break and aluminum-handled plastic ones turn your hands black (from the bare metal). I love the smooth, warm feel of wood, but a simple $20 plastic paddle with sheathed aluminum shaft is perfectly acceptable.

Quality paddles generally start at around $35 and go up—way up. I like the traditional design, the height of my chin with a 6–8-inch nonlaminated beavertail-shaped blade. Wider blades provide more immediate force, which is good for quick maneuvering but can be fatiguing on a long haul as each stroke takes a bit more effort. More expensive paddles tend to be lighter, which means less effort. Bent-shaft paddles are a neat innovation—lightweight, short, and easy to handle. They work best from the bow position since they're a bit clumsy on the steering strokes executed from the stern. Hold the paddle with the blade bent toward the bow. The angle maximizes efficiency since a blade loses power past mid-stroke.

If boat and paddle designs seem a bit excessive, just look at the paddle strokes diagrammed in how-to books, magazines, and videos. There are dozens of basic strokes, plus maneuvers like the inside pivot, outside pivot, eddy turn, peel out, Duffek turn, cross Duffek, ferry, back ferry, side slip, ess, and surf. As usual, the benign waters of Mississippi don't demand all that. A handful of simple strokes will do what needs doing. On the other hand, some technique is needed. For lack of basic skills, many a person has capsized in waters that should have been easily handled.

Yours truly, for instance. Like probably most people, when I started out I assumed paddling was like walking—anybody could do it. On those early trips I pinballed down the rivers, bouncing off every log in sight. I gradually learned some strokes, but my greatest advances came from traveling with experts, like New Guinea tribesman Leslie Minduwa.

I met Leslie on a bush trip in Papua New Guinea in 1985. In 1991 a missionary invited Leslie to the States, and I got to take him canoeing down Black Creek. (Incidentally, Leslie saw the nation from California to Florida and declared Mississippi the finest state by far, due to its abundance of woods and waters.) Leslie grew up handling dugout canoes on the Sepik River, where children learn to paddle about the same time they learn to walk. The first thing he did was banish my J stroke, which I had spent a week in the Atchafalaya Swamp perfecting. The J is a classic method of paddling on one side of the boat without having to switch sides, but it involves rotating the paddle shaft in your hand. Leslie preferred a technique similar to the guide stroke, in which the paddle is braced against the gunwale and flicked out (see below), and he did it with the vigor of an Evinrude. He also told me that, in Sepik River dugouts, men stand and women sit. In the larger dugouts, as many as fifteen men use rhythmic, forceful strokes to move upriver or down, while a man in the stern uses a paddle as a rudder.

Learning his version of the guide stroke revolutionized my floating, giving me a super-efficient means of paddling without switching sides for long, straight stretches. I also became comfortable paddling upstream and, at times, standing when paddling. Most southern canoers, male or female, prefer to sit, finding no need to kneel like whitewater river runners do. Kneeling comes in handy in tight situations, though—such as big waves or tricky currents—since it lowers the boat's center of gravity, stabilizing it.

Likewise, I picked up some tactics on floats down the Coco and Patuca Rivers of Central America, watching the clean, brisk strokes of Miskito Indians, who use maximum efficiency and minimum effort. On the forward stroke (see below) they keep their arms lightly flexed, not bothering to bend them at the elbows between strokes. And they perform a version of the C stroke from the bow, starting the paddle sideways in the water and describing a "C" to keep the boat straight. The Miskitos typically paddle downstream and pole back up, a laborious process but probably the easiest way for a small crew (as opposed to fifteen standing men) to get up a big, strong river without a motor.

Poling isn't a tradition in Mississippi like it is in Central American jungles or in ultra-swampy Cajun Louisiana. Still, it's useful on shallow rivers where the bottom is just inches below the surface. Properly speaking, a pole should be at least 10 feet long and, in muddy areas, equipped with a metal "duck-bill" device that spreads apart to keep the pole tip from getting stuck. But for occasional poling, a regular chin-high paddle will suffice. I have a specially-made 6-footer that will double as paddle or pole when I know I'm going to float a shallow river like the Chunky or Homochitto.

There are plenty of good instructional books on the market, like Bill Mason's *Path of the Paddle*. Here are the basic strokes needed for Mississippi waters:

- Forward stroke. Put one hand over the end of the paddle and the other around the shaft a comfortable distance down. Reach out, dip the blade into the water and push with the top hand, keeping the shaft perpendicular to the boat hull (not angled outward). As you return the paddle forward, slice it sideways through the air to minimize wind resistance; this is known as feathering.
- Draw. Stick the blade in the water parallel to the boat and pull. This yanks the boat sideways. This stroke is especially effective from the bow and can be used to avoid obstacles in a hurry.
- Sweep. To turn the bow away from the paddle side, execute the forward stroke but with the paddle angled way outward, nearly horizontal. This can be done backward (reverse sweep) to turn the other direction.
- Pry. Use the gunwale, or edge of the canoe, as a fulcrum, and lever the boat sideways in the water. This works better from the stern.
- Guide stroke. This one, used only by the stern paddler, is designed to keep the boat going straight without changing sides every few strokes. Near the end of a forward stroke, use the gunwale as a fulcrum and flick the blade outward. This corrects the natural tendency of the boat to turn.
- Rudder. From the stern, stick the paddle in the water behind the boat like a

rudder and use the handle as a tiller. This is great for weaving through rapids when you don't want to increase your speed by paddling. (It's also a good way for the stern paddler to goof off while the bow person does all the work.)

Duties are different in the bow and stern. The bow person provides propulsion and wards off obstacles, applying the draw or sweep or using the paddle like a pole to push away from an object. The bow person is usually in a position to see the best route to take; he or she can even stand up for a better look, but be sure the stern person isn't standing at the same time or somebody could wind up overboard. The stern person also provides propulsion but is in charge of steering, which means using the guide stroke for straight stretches and other strokes to turn. When the way is not certain, the bow person should call out which direction to take.

The point of mastering strokes is to control the boat, just as an athlete learns to control his or her body. But knowing how to execute the basic strokes is just part of it; applying them in current or wind is something else. It's rather like learning a foreign language from a cassette tape, then conversing with a native speaker. Learning to read and negotiate a river comes from experience and is one of the most fun parts of canoeing. Figuring out exactly how and where to put the boat—spotting submerged obstacles, shoals, and crosscurrents—is like chess, and paddlers are forever honing their skills.

The two major types of obstacles in Mississippi are logjams and shoals. Weaving your way down a log-studded creek can test your paddling skills nearly as well as a whitewater river, with about as much chance of capsizing. Hauling a boat over downed trees provides as good a workout as a day at the fitness center. Avoiding shoals is more cerebral, requiring expertise in interpreting the patterns on the surface of a river. The price for failure is getting out and towing.

Techniques differ for lakes and streams. Creek paddling involves a sometimes swift current, sharp turns, and obstacles. In a typical rapid, the bow paddler sits ready to ward off obstacles while the stern person rudders. Ignore the urge to paddle harder in rapids. It's usually better to slow down, even backpaddle for better control. Lake paddling calls for brooking the wind, keeping a straight course and handling waves. It's almost axiomatic that you'll face a headwind; don't ask why. I sometimes suspect I have my own personal headwind, like a reverse guardian angel, waiting to greet me anytime I launch a canoe on open water. Canoes are considerably more seaworthy than they're given credit for—if you know how to control them. For instance, don't swing broadside to big waves or you may roll. If possible, meet them at an angle. If things get dicey, kneel. A heavy load helps, too. Using such methods, I've taken canoes across lakes with whitecapping waves and barely gotten wet.

A significant amount of Mississippi paddling involves a leisurely downstream rhythm, with occasional swifts to keep you alert. I deeply enjoy the Zen-like rhythm of paddling, which I'm convinced is good for mind and body.

Gear

The gear needed for Mississippi river camping is different from that used in many other forms of camping, such as backpacking in the mountains or rafting whitewater rivers. Rubber boots and tennis shoes are better choices than hiking boots; large, airy tents more comfortable than cramped, airless domes. With a bit of experience, the floater learns what to take and what to leave at home. It used to take me an hour to get ready for a day float and a day to get ready for a canoe-camping trip. Now it takes me ten minutes for the day trip and an hour or so for the campout. This evolution did not come easily: It took years of honing equipment choices.

For a day trip, I keep a knapsack packed with these essentials:

- Poncho. It doesn't provide perfect protection in a downpour, but a poncho allows plenty of movement and you don't get too hot. Unlike a rainsuit, it's easy to take on and off without getting out of the boat, a useful trait in those intermittent southern showers.
- Sunscreen.
- Insect repellent.
- Iodine water purification crystals. There's a variety of products to purify water, from Halogen tablets to expensive filters. Polar Pure iodine crystals are effective, easy to use, and inexpensive, and a bottle lasts years.
- Lighters.
- Fire starters. You can buy paraffin-soaked sticks of compressed wood in barbecue-supplies sections of grocery stores. If that seems too fancy, take fat pine sticks you collect in the woods, or any good tinder. Store in a zipper seal storage bag with a lighter. Even frontiersmen wore a watertight metal cylinder containing dry tinder around their necks.

- Eyeglass holders. Wear them no matter how calm the water is. If you capsize without them, you'll probably lose your glasses.
- Compass. I never go into the woods without one.
- Toilet paper, in zipper seal storage bag with lighter. Bury the paper when you're through with it or, better yet, burn it like people do in Central America—taking care not to set the woods on fire.
- Snakebite kit. I take the kind with suction syringes. Keep it close at hand so in the unlikely event you need it, you won't have to search for it.
- Canteen. A 1-quart model is easy to sip from and can be replenished from a larger jug.
- Sunglasses.
- Lunch.
- Wool shirt or sweater in cold weather.

If I'm feeling luxurious, I may take an ice chest.

At home I also keep an old canvas duffel bag full of boat gear, which includes:

- Bailer. Slice an empty bleach bottle in half, leaving the cap screwed on, and use the top part, with the handle, to bail.
- Sponge. Keep a big one in the bottom of the boat for sopping up water.
- Life vests. Cheaper is not better in this department. A life vest should be comfortable and not interfere with paddling. Some designs chafe the neck when you move. I prefer the accordion style even though they cost a bit extra.
- Seat backs: If you spend all day, or several days, in the saddle, a seat back is a treasure. Good models include plastic ones that hook around the seat and cushioned nylon seats which can also be used around camp.
- Small waterproof dry bag. For wallet, keys, watch, film, camera, and lighters.

Of course, every boat needs a spare paddle. Paddles can get lost by capsize or carelessness. An extra one stows easily and can prevent lots of trouble.

Now, just grab a hat, the already-loaded day pack, the boat-gear duffel, extra paddle, optional fishing gear and ice chest, and you're ready for the day.

Camping trips are more complicated, of course. A concise list appears in the appendix. Here's a detailed look at what to take:

- Day pack, with the above-mentioned items already packed.
- Duffel bags. There are many good choices available, including waterproof river bags, Boundary Waters-style portage packs, and canvas or nylon duffel bags. Some waterproof river bags have shoulder straps for portaging. The downside is there's no way to tie gear to the outside of such bags. That's not the case with Boundary Waters packs, large knapsacks made of canvas or nylon. The North Country tradition calls for two people and three such packs per boat: one for food and tent, one pack for each person's clothes and sleeping bags. At a portage, each man dons his own pack, then one man takes the canoe while the other straps the food pack across his chest. Portaging is part of canoeing in the North Country, where trails connect countless lakes. In Mississippi, "portage" generally refers to hauling the boat over or around a logjam, so portage packs aren't necessary. A good inexpensive alternative is a large canvas or nylon duffel bag. When using canvas or nylon, items like clothes and sleeping bags should be wrapped in heavy-duty plastic garbage bags. I use a waterproof river bag for clothes and sleeping bag, a big canvas duffel for tent and other gear, and a third bag, or buckets, for food. Plastic paint or detergent buckets are good ways to carry food.
- Sleeping bag. Ideally, southern outdoorsmen should own two bags, a warm mummy bag (rated to 5–10 degrees) for cold weather, and a lightweight one for warm.
- Sleeping pad. After years of sleeping on hard ground I finally got a self-inflating air mattress and will never go back.
- Pillow. Call me a sissy, but I find that a small, compact pillow far surpasses a heap of clothes or, worse, a lumpy life vest under your head at night.
- Cooking utensils. Coffee pot, cook pot, aluminum skillet, spatula, filter for coffee, can opener. Some people take a small cutting board.
- Eating utensils. Plate, bowl, fork, spoon, cup.
- First-aid kit. All size bandaids, bandage, tape, gauze, tweezers, sewing kit, disinfectant, diarrhea medicine, antacids, pain medication, sunburn lotion, poison ivy lotion, antifungal powder, lip balm, personal medicines, etc.
- Flashlight.
- Candle lantern. It's compact and provides a source of light if you have to make camp in the dark or don't want to bother with a campfire. Butane or gasoline lanterns are too bulky and fragile for canoeing. Besides, they shut out the starlight, which is one of the big attractions in camping.

- Ground cloth. Protects the bottom of the tent. Some people put the ground cloth inside the tent to block leakage through the floor.
- Tent. The tent industry got a boost from the backpacking craze of the 1970s, but designs were geared toward a mountain environment. That was bad news for Deep South campers, who need the very nighttime breezes that expedition tents eliminate. In the 1990s tent makers wised up and realized most of their customers weren't scaling the Himalayas. Now there are plenty of practical designs on the market. A good canoe-camping tent is easily pitched, spacious but not huge, well-ventilated, and sturdy in rain and wind.
- Light tarp. This is a necessity for Mississippi's frequent rains. If a shower strikes at midday, a tarp provides a quick shelter on the nearest sandbar. In a rainy camp, it creates a haven for cooking, sitting, and storing gear.
- Machete or hatchet. Axes or hatchets are standard fare for North Country canoeists, and far be it from me to question such a hallowed tradition, but I prefer a machete. Since there's usually deadwood aplenty along rivers, there's little need to chop firewood. You're more likely to need a blade for cutting a path through swampy woods, and for that a hatchet is inefficient.
- Water jugs. Nothing beats 1-gallon bleach jugs. Unlike many commercial water containers, they're virtually indestructible.
- Canteen. Take a 1-quart bottle so you don't have to swig from a big jug.
- Knife. A Swiss Army knife or its equivalent, with assorted tools ranging from corkscrew to scissors, is perfect for a campout and will also clean fish.
- Lighters. I scatter them liberally throughout all my bags, and keep one in my pocket, so there's a lighter within reach any time.
- Map. Stored in zipper seal plastic, of course.
- Notebook, pen. It's easy to forget some details of river trips if you haven't made notes.
- Toiletry items. Toothbrush, toothpaste, comb, cotton swabs, etc. Store these items in a small bag or shaving kit. I take ear plugs too, since some campsites are close to highways.
- Extra toilet paper.
- Hammock. The hammock rates right up there with canoes when it comes to high points of human inventiveness. A camping model is inexpensive and compact, and oh so nice at the end of a back-straining day of paddling. If you have a layover day, it's irreplaceable. Make sure your partner brings one so he or she won't try to commandeer yours.

- Biodegradable liquid soap and scrub pad: Such soap is good for bathing and washing greasy dishes. Sand is usually sufficient for scrubbing dishes, but a small dish pad is nice when you're in mud country.
- Stove, fuel. For years I did my cooking only on fires, but it's hard to beat a stove for a quick pot of coffee in the morning. Fires are impractical in some environments, such as marsh. There are many good models available. I prefer a simple propane stove with an extra bottle or two—no smell or spilling as with liquid fuel.
- Trash bags. Obviously, canoers should not leave even a speck of litter anywhere.
- Book. Essential for layover days and early stops.
- Duct tape. Keep in a zipper seal storage bag. Duct tape repairs nearly everything, including a leaky boat.
- Fishing tackle. Even people like me who aren't diehard fishermen would do well to take fishing tackle, considering how much time you're spending on or by the water.

Clothes:

- Camp shoes. During the day wear shoes that can get wet, whether river sandals, tennis shoes, or rubber boots. At night a dry pair of shoes will feel wonderful.
- Extra pants. Forget blue jeans. Once wet, they take days to dry. Use khaki-type material, which dries quickly yet is thick enough to thwart mosquitoes.
- Extra long-sleeved shirt. Long sleeves protect against sun, chilly air, and insects. The sleeves can always be rolled up.
- Two pairs of socks.
- Bandannas.
- T-shirt.
- Shorts.
- Hand towel.
- Cold-weather clothes as needed. In autumn conditions I take a wool shirt or sweater and light wool gloves. In winter I'll add long johns for nighttime, insulated vest, wool coat, and wool socks. Wool retains insulating power when wet. Fleece is a popular modern alternative. The key is to have warm, dry clothes for camp.

- Cap or hat. In hot weather, take a wide-brimmed hat for protection from the sun. It can cook you.

Food is a matter of personal taste, of course, but here are some suggestions that work well on a canoe trip:

- Breakfast: Coffee, tea, or hot chocolate. Instant oatmeal sticks to your ribs. Alternatives are powdered milk and cereal, or pancakes if you want to take the time and trouble. Add honey or molasses for sweetening.
- Snacks: When paddling all day, snacks keep you from sagging. Raisins, dates, prunes, nuts, and chocolate all boost energy levels. Fresh fruit like oranges, apples, and bananas will last a few days. Lemons are good for perking up the drinking water or making impromptu lemonade when mixed with honey.
- Lunch: A river lunch is usually a glorified snack. For instance, crackers with cheese, peanut butter or sardines, spiced up with olives, followed by crunchy carrots and granola bar.
- Supper: The formula for keeping the body properly fueled on outdoor trips is plenty of carbohydrates with a dash of protein and vitamins. For instance, rice with onion, dried soup mix and tuna or chicken. Or pasta with tomato paste, olives and cheese. Don't forget salt and spices. If you plan to fish, bring aluminum foil for grilling, corn meal and peanut oil for frying, or just cook the fish whole on the coals. After supper it's time for cookies, herb tea, or hot chocolate.

The above items are for float-camping. If you truck-camp at a campground, you can take pretty much whatever you want, like lawn chairs, lantern, and musical instruments.

Camping

To illustrate Deep South river-camping techniques, let's follow an imaginary pair, Dad and his fifteen-year-old son Billy, through a typical evening and morning.

As they float downriver in a canoe, Dad glances at his watch, then at the sun, which stands roughly an hour above the treetops. "About time to start looking for a place to camp," he declares.

Billy, in the bow, reaches for his fishing rod. "I'll see if I can catch some supper."

While Billy casts, Dad scans sandbars. Forty-five minutes later he's spotted a likely site, and Billy has two yearling bass and a hand-sized bream on a stringer. (He didn't fish earlier in the day because they don't have an ice chest and he didn't want to drag the fish alongside the boat all day.) Approaching the sandbar, Dad swings the canoe around and they paddle upstream to nose against the beach; that way the current won't push the boat around. Billy jumps out, pulls the vessel up a bit, and Dad climbs out. They check the sandbar to make sure there are properly-spaced hammock trees, a place to pitch a tarp in case of rain, plenty of nearby firewood, and shade, also taking note of where the sun will rise. Satisfied, they haul their bags up to a level area.

"You rustle up some firewood. I'll pitch the tent," Dad says.

Billy sprays insect repellent on his legs to ward off redbugs and ticks, and walks into the woods looking for dry sticks, from twigs to logs. Dad picks a spot for the tent—flat, smooth, away from overhanging dead limbs. He unrolls the four-man tent—which in reality is comfortable for two—assembles the poles, attaches the fly, stakes everything down, and tosses in his sleeping bag, pad, and clothes, zipping up the mosquito net.

"You want to build the fire or clean the fish?" Dad asks Billy, who has amassed a supply of wood.

"I'll clean the fish," Billy says with a shrug.

"Just gut them. Don't scale them. We'll cook them in the fire."

As Billy goes to the water's edge, Dad picks a spot for the fire well away from the tent so they won't be pestered by smoke during the night. He lights a paraffin-stick fire starter and assembles a teepee of twigs over it, adding larger and larger sticks. If the wood was wet he would shave off the bark with his pocket knife. Soon the fire is crackling and smoking. Billy returns with the fish in a skillet and sets it on the ground.

With the fire busy making coals, Dad yawns and looks at the late-afternoon sky. There's no sign of rain, so he doesn't bother pitching the tarp. "Hammock time," he says.

"I think I'll fish some more," Billy says. "There's a good spot at the end of this sandbar."

Dad slings his hammock between two medium-sized trees, cutting away the underbrush with his machete, while Billy walks down the sandbar with his rod.

Dad nibbles the tender tips of young sawbriar vines, which have a sweet, nutty flavor. Then he stretches out in the shade for a nap. Half an hour later Billy has another bass and Dad is through napping. Billy describes his battle with the 1-pound bass while Dad lights the campstove and puts on a big pot of river water, which boiling will purify. He dices an onion into it, and adds a pack of vegetable soup mix. Billy mentions the animal tracks he saw at the water's edge: raccoon, mink, otter, plus some freshly peeled beaver sticks. While waiting for the water to heat, Dad changes into clean, dry clothes and camp shoes. Then he adds rice to the fragrant, boiling water.

"Might as well get the fish started," he tells Billy.

He and the boy run a stick through the lower jaw of each fish and lay it directly on the hot coals. After several minutes they turn them over. When the fish are done, Dad and Billy pull them out of the fire and peel back the charred, crusty skin. Dad takes the pot of rice off the stove, spoons it onto plates, then he and Billy scoop steaming chunks of white fillet on top. Billy adds Cajun seasoning while Dad sprinkles red pepper sauce. The sun is behind the trees when they settle back in their portable canoe seats to eat, sipping from cups of cool water.

When they finish, they go together to the water's edge to scrub the dishes with sand. Then they haul the canoe well away from the water and tie it to a root. Dad read that some people turn their canoe upside down, chock it with pieces of wood, and use it as a table, but he's never acquired that habit. With night falling, Billy stokes the fire and Dad boils water for hot chocolate. Then they settle back to sip, chat, gaze at the fire and the stars, and listen to the sound of tinkling water, whippoorwills, and owls, applying insect repellent when mosquitoes sing around their ears. Before going to bed, they make sure food and gear are stowed in the bags so they won't get pilfered by raccoons or drenched with dew.

In the morning, birdsong awakens Dad. Leaving Billy asleep, he washes his face in the river, dries with a hand towel, and scoops his enamel coffee pot three-quarters full of water. He sets it on the campstove to boil, pushes unburned sticks into the smoking ashes to catch fire, and pours the hot water into a bowl of instant oatmeal and raisins as Billy emerges from the tent. Dad shakes coffee into the rest of the hot water in the pot, estimating a tablespoon per cup, and lets it steep while he eats the oatmeal with a squirt of honey. After several minutes he adds a dash of cold water to the coffee pot to settle the grounds, then strains the black liquid through a metal filter into his cup so there are no grounds. Billy peels and eats an orange, then pours dry cereal and raisins into a bowl, sprinkles powdered milk over it, adds cold water from a jug, and stirs.

After breakfast they wash dishes and take turns using the bathroom in the woods well away from the water, burying the waste and burning the paper. After washing up, Dad strikes the tent, shaking the dew off the fly and brushing sand off the bottom as he folds them. Billy packs other gear, carrying bags to the water's edge. The sun is above the trees now. They slide the boat into the water and lower the bags in, tying down only those items that wouldn't float in a capsize. Dad kicks sand over the fire, and Billy tosses the charred pieces in the river. The next rain will smooth the sand, and there will be no sign they've been here. Dad takes five minutes to stretch his limbs while Billy sharpens the hooks on his favorite lure; then they climb into the canoe and set off down the river in the cool morning air.

A few notes on this story: First, Dad is canoeing with his son. I am concerned about the apparent lack of outdoor skills among children. Kids learn early on how to use a computer; how many can paddle a boat, pitch a tent, catch a fish, build a fire, identify animal tracks, and perform routine camp chores? How many know what it's like to sit in a remote spot listening to a campfire crackle and owls calling?

Much of what Dad and Billy do is based on experience. Dad has learned to camp on the high part of a sandbar and pull his canoe well up since rivers can rise unexpectedly overnight. He keeps the fire away from the tent because he knows what it's like to try to sleep with smoke wafting through the tent all night. He makes sure there are no dead limbs overhead, for he's heard the crash of branches before and thanked goodness he wasn't under them. He has also camped in spots with nowhere to sling a hammock, and regretted it. He's failed to bring a tarp and wound up cooking in the rain. He knows how to build a fire from scratch but found paraffin-sticks make the job easier. He can do all his cooking over a fire too but prefers the convenience of a stove. He loves fish fried and grilled but enjoys the simplicity of cooking directly on coals.

Billy has learned how to cast in a pocket of still water beside the current and pull out a bass or perch; in fact, he's a better angler than Dad. He knows how to clean fish at the water's edge, throwing the offal into the current for catfish to eat or on the bank for raccoons. He's adept at identifying tracks of all sorts of animals, which adds zest to a campout—like the morning he saw the sinewy scrawl where a wide-bodied snake had wriggled past the tent in the night. He also knows to watch his step instinctively so he doesn't step on such a snake. Billy's proud of his ability to perform camp duties that aren't all that different from the tasks done by Native Americans and frontiersmen.

Navigation

Mississippi is not the Amazon rainforest, but it contains enough big woods and swamps to require basic navigational skills. But technology is advancing so rapidly that almost anything I write on the topic will soon be outdated. As of this writing, devices like handheld global positioning system (GPS) units and CD-ROM topographic map collections are available at increasingly affordable prices. But just as schoolchildren shouldn't neglect long division just because calculators are available, outdoorsmen should hang onto basic map-and-compass skills.

Actually, even maps and compasses are technological artifices that can blind us to the lay of the land like a flashlight obliterates night vision. If you follow a trail, you're a mental prisoner of that corridor of dirt. If you venture cross-country with map and compass, you gain a much richer understanding of the land. Leave behind the map, and you start to notice the natural drainages and vegetation types that are nature's signposts. Omit the compass and—well, even I don't do that. But I know people who do. My grown son, for instance. I've taken him on cross-country swamp treks—at night, even—in which I consult the compass, then ask him to point out the direction of the truck. He does so unerringly.

If you simply float from one bridge to another, about the only navigating required is driving to the bridges. That's not always as easy as it sounds, though. Some put-ins are tucked away on rural backroads not shown on standard highway maps. Any traveler in Mississippi can benefit from *Mississippi Road Atlas,* a collection of county maps published by the University Press of Mississippi. For details on the lay of the land, *Mississippi Atlas and Gazetteer,* published by DeLorme (P.O. Box 298, Yarmouth, ME 04096, phone 207-846-7000), offers a set of topographical maps for the entire state in a handy format; they're also available on CD-ROM. In swamp country, U.S. Geological Survey quadrangle maps are well worth taking. If there's not a map store handy, call the U.S.G.S. office in Denver (303-202-4200; their information number is 1-888-ASK-USGS) and request a free index map for the state; from the index you can select specific quadrangle maps. These maps typically sell for $4 each plus $5 handling per order.

Some paddlers like to get quad maps for every float, and such maps are inform-ative and fun, but if you canoe a lot of rivers they can add up.

Keep in mind, however, that even good maps can deceive. And too much re-liance on them can pose problems if they fail. A classic example: When Scott Williams and I floated the Patuca River of Honduras, we took highly detailed topo maps of La Mosquitia, a wild region of mountains, jungles, swamps, and marshes. The maps showed a branch of the river leading to Brus Laguna, our destination. What they didn't indicate was that during the dry season that branch dried up. After a week of paddling, we found our route blocked, and we faced the awful prospect of having to head back up the river. Fortunately, a lo-cal Indian told us a back way consisting of tiny channels between lakes—chan-nels that did not appear on our maps. By the grace of God we got out.

On an exploratory day trip in Louisiana's Atchafalaya Swamp, I didn't take a map, figuring a compass and common sense would do. Some friends and I headed west on a large bayou, then turned north onto a narrow slough. When it widened into a cypress lake, I tied a strip of red bandanna to a limb at the en-trance, in case we came back that way. I did the same when we portaged over a piece of high ground onto another channel. We then headed east, hoping we'd eventually hit the levee—but knowing that if we couldn't get through, we could retrace our route with the red markers. As it turned out, we got to the levee with no backtracking, making a complete circuit. Such day trips have an urgency that canoe-camping journeys lack, since you want to get back before dark. When you have camping equipment, including food, water, and shelter, losing your way need not be a crisis.

Though I can do without a map in certain situations, I always keep my old Silva compass handy. You don't have to be an expert in orienteering to use one to keep your general bearings. As a perhaps oversimplified example, if you're in the Atchafalaya Swamp, keep in mind that it runs north and south between two levees. If you have to get out, east or west will get you there.

Perhaps the most important skill in navigation—and the most difficult to ac-quire—is the ability to relax. We humans have a natural tendency to panic when we lose our bearings. I recall getting "lost" on a backpacking trip many years ago, and the woods literally seemed to spin around me. But I remembered the importance of remaining calm, took a few deep breaths, got centered, and soon figured out the solution to my dilemma, which really wasn't that hard to do. The fact is, it's virtually impossible to get truly lost in Mississippi, or in the eastern

United States for that matter. For better or worse, you can scarcely walk a mile in a straight line anywhere in Mississippi without hitting some sort of road. That mile may not be easy—wading a swamp, fighting briars—but a mile is just a mile. The biggest danger in getting lost in Mississippi, in my estimation, is dying of embarrassment if somebody sends out a search party.

Fishing

I've heard claims that northern fishing—whether for trout out west or walleye and northern pike in Canada—is somehow superior to what we have in the Deep South. As one Michigan friend put it, "The colder the water, the better the fish."

Nonsense. I've caught salmon in Alaska, walleye and northern pike in Ontario, smallmouth bass in Minnesota's Boundary Waters, and so on, and none is better than southern largemouth bass, golden-fried catfish, bream, or white perch. Nor is the experience of northern fishing any better than drifting down a blissful southern river casting for bass, bobbing a cane pole for bream or running catfish lines in the bullfrog-thrumming night. On one memorable trip, my then fourteen-year-old son Andy and I took a pirogue loaded with camping gear down a log-choked creek, caught seven bass in an afternoon, grilled them over coals, and slept under the crisp autumn stars and towering oaks to the racket of wood ducks. Next morning Andy caught a rod-bending 6-pounder. Who needs trout?

In bass fishing, the first choice river anglers face is what type of reel to use: spinning, baitcasting, or spincasting. A spinning reel is open-faced with the spool parallel to the rod. It is located on the underside of the rod and is activated by flipping a bail, though some models have a trigger release. It's particularly effective on open water for wide-open casting but lacks pinpoint accuracy, and as a result is probably the poorest choice for river fishing, though it will do the job. A baitcasting reel also is open-faced but with the spool crossways to the rod. It's positioned on top of the rod and activated with a thumb release. When casting, the angler keeps his thumb on the line for peak accuracy, but the reel is notoriously prone to backlash. This is the best type for river fishing—if you can master it, a task not all casual anglers are up to. A spincasting reel is the one everyone starts with and many stay with. It's the standard closed-faced reel. Just push the thumb release and throw. It's prized for its simplicity and low cost but lacks the accuracy of the baitcaster. It's reasonably effective on a river.

Next decision is lure, and the assortment is large but restricted by the river environment. A float fisherman is moving, which excludes slow-working lures like artificial worms. Anglers who wade or who tie up in one spot, of course, can fish as slowly as they want. Also, a river is often gridded with underwater limbs and logs, which argues against using non-weedless deep-running lures like crankbaits since they'll get snagged. However, wade-fishermen can get away with throwing such lures if they're careful. The all-around most popular picks for river bass are topwater lures, spinnerbaits, and beetlespins. Bass fishermen use anything from a 6- to a 20-pound test line. The best way to float fish is for the stern paddler to guide the boat while the bow person casts, swapping places every hour—and a canoe moves at about a mile an hour float fishing on most Mississippi streams. River anglers soon learn to cast underhand and side-arm since overhanging limbs restrict traditional casting. Conditions for bass are best when the water is clear or slightly milky.

Catfish favor muddier water. Some of the stranger substances that have been known to catch the bottom-feeding fish are slivers of Ivory soap, chunks of styrofoam, hunks of cheese, hot dogs plain or spiced with oil of anise, coagulated beef blood, pieces of deer heart, bits of sponge dipped in melted cheese, even naked hooks. Commercial fishermen vary their bait according to season. I consulted a Mississippi River commercial fisherman, and he told me that in late August, the preference is shad, a small, minnow-like fish collected by trawling oxbow lakes. Later in the fall when shad cease to school and can't be caught easily, fishermen use cut bait such as chunks of buffalo fish, carp, and shad. In early spring, it's shad again, then crawfish, which can be raked up from just about any mudhole or ditch. As crawfish age and their shells harden, they become less tempting to Old Whiskers, so it's time to use skipjack, which make good cut bait. In the summer, live bait like small fish and catalpa worms are the trick.

All of that is a tad involved for the casual canoe camper. Those who tight-line—fish by cane pole or rod and reel—will likely go for night crawlers (earthworms) or minnows, available at any bait shop. For running lines at night—whether trotlines, droplines, or yo-yos—catfishermen are more likely to use something simple like stink bait, hot dogs, cheese, or chicken livers. One friend of mine takes shrimp in an ice chest, which is quite effective.

In May and June, some brave souls grab catfish from underwater holes.

That's when the fish whip out dens in cavities such as cypress trees, hollow logs, and bank holes. After the female lays eggs, the male drives her off and stands guard. Such fish may weigh 70 pounds or more. Contrary to popular opinion, snapping turtles, beavers, alligators, and snakes are rarely a danger, since they mostly live above water, not in underwater dens. Grabbers (also known as grabblers and noodlers) reach into bank holes or old cypress trees, feeling for a clean den, which indicates a fish is present. Once a den is found, they locate the fish by touch. A grabber actually wants the fish to bite his or her hand. Catfish have sandpaper teeth which can tear the skin. They also have tremendous power. The sensation can be alarming, especially when accompanied by the sound of the fish against the hollow tree, known as thundering. With the other grabber blocking any exit holes, the lead man prepares to catch the prey. Sometimes the fish will spook and flee to a hard-to-reach pocket, so grabbers carry a stick to prod it back within reach. Then it's grabbing time.

Grabbers compare the catfish's lower jaw to a suitcase handle. Grasp the suitcase handle with thumb outside, fingers inside, pull it up in the hole and hold the fish tight so it can't spin. Run a stringer through the gills or a thirteen-aught hook with a rope through the lower lip to secure the creature (be careful with those big hooks). Then hang on for the ride. After boating the fish, check for a second fish since both male and female stay in the hole early in the season before the eggs are laid.

There are alternative methods. Some enthusiasts use a stick to locate the fish, plug escape holes with gunnysacks, then secure the fish with a grappling hook. Really serious grabbers use scuba tanks or, more convenient, an air compressor with a three-horsepower motor mounted on a floating inner tube with a pair of hoses and regulators, providing an almost unlimited amount of air.

Things are drastically easier for bream fishing. Use cane pole or rod and reel with 4–8-pound test line, a small hook (for example, No. 8) with a split-shot lead sinker placed 6 inches above and a tiny plastic bobber or cork another 6 inches up. Bait with a cricket or bit of worm, or use a $1/64$ or $1/32$ ounce jig. The best action comes in spring and early summer when bream spawn and go on their beds. They nest in colonies on beds of sand or gravel in shallow water. If you find the beds, dangle the bait about 6 inches above it, twitching periodically to get the fish's attention.

Fly-fishing is also effective for bream, and bass too. It can be done from a canoe or wading, though it may be awkward when there are overhanging limbs.

Nevertheless, it can make for some exciting fishing. Fly-fishermen accustomed to trout will find that, while trout tend to run, bass are brawlers, and bream can be feisty too. Many fly-fishermen use barbless hooks to release their catch unharmed, and enjoy tying their own flies. Keep a variety of lures on hand to imitate the hatch present in the waters you're fishing. Nymphs are underwater lures meant to resemble flies before they emerge from the water. Dry flies are topwater baits which represent mature flies. You can tell what kind of flies are present just by looking. For underwater nymphs, stir up the water and dip samples with an aquarium net. To make a typical nymph effective in Mississippi waters, flatten the barb on a No. 10 hook; clamp the curve of the hook in a vise; wrap the stem in black thread, in lead wire to add weight, then in more thread; cement with a drop of nail polish; wax the dangling thread and apply dubbing, or matted fur such as shed cat hair, to give the fly a small gray body; insert a white chicken feather, spinning it around to make the fibers stand out in a spiral; put more thread around the loop of the hook to make a head; tie it off in a half-hitch; add a touch more nail polish; stroke the dubbing with a wire brush (the type used to clean .22-caliber rifles) to give the fly legs. Voilà! With practice, the whole process takes just five minutes.

Rivers offer some white perch (or crappie) fishing, though not with the consistency that lakes do. Find a likely hole and drop a jig or minnow, bouncing lightly from time to time. Serious white perchers use a long, willowy jig pole, especially made for white perch. Slide a plastic jig, which looks like a miniature forked-tail worm, onto the hook so it lies at right angles to the line. Pull out the right amount of line according to how deep you're fishing, drop the lure into the water, and sit back, bouncing the lure now and then. Unlike bass and bream, white perch bite gently, and if you're not paying attention you won't know you've caught one. When you feel a tug, yank the line up quickly or the fish will get off.

If you have an ice chest, you can fish anytime, drifting and casting for bass or tying up at good-looking spots for other fish. Long-distance campers without an ice chest are better off fishing an hour or two before mealtime and trailing the catch beside the boat on a stringer. Boatside stringers are risky for any length of time since the numerous branches and logs in a river will yank fish off the line, if a gar doesn't do so first. Another option is fishing from camp, wading upstream—if you wade downstream the stirred-up silt will precede you and can alert fish—and casting in deep holes beside the current, keeping your catch on a long stringer tied to your belt. Catfishermen should carry catfish pliers and a cord so they can hang the fish from a tree limb for skinning.

To cook your fish, fry in peanut oil with spiced cornmeal; grill over the coals on aluminum foil; or lay it on the coals a few minutes, turn, then peel back the skin and add lemon juice, salt, and spices for perfect fillet.

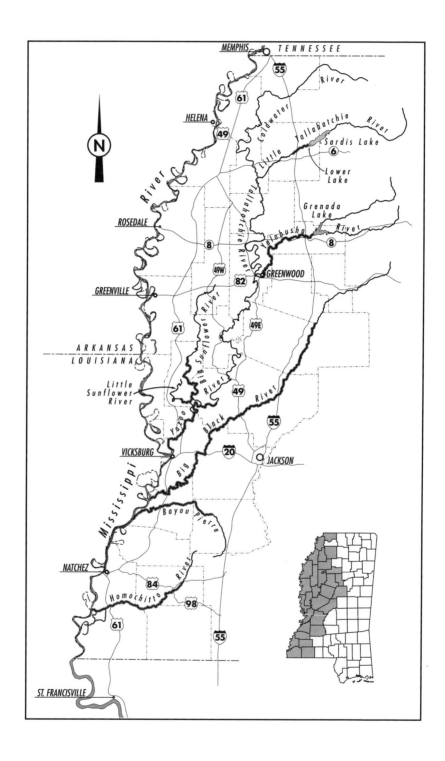

3. The Mississippi and Its Tributaries

Mississippi River

Granted, the Mississippi River is not the sort of place most paddlers go for a Saturday float with family and dog. In fact, some folks advise against canoeing it at all. However, people have paddled the Mississippi River since time immemorial, and they're still doing it. I recall meeting a father and son who were traveling pioneer-style from Idaho to New Orleans. The man had been a California corporate executive whose stressful lifestyle got out of hand, so he quit his job and built a 16-foot cedar canoe. Wearing buckskins and using frontier-style implements, he and his son made their way across the continental divide and floated down the Jefferson, Missouri, and Mississippi Rivers, and ultimately did get to New Orleans. Or consider the case of John Ruskey. The Rocky Mountain native floated the Mississippi on a raft made of plywood and oil drums in 1982 and fell in love with the Deep South. Settling in Clarksdale, he began giving guided canoe tours on the Mississippi in 1992 and opened Quapaw Canoe Company in 1998. While fully attuned to the dangers of the big river, which he compares to "a moving ocean," he takes everybody from schoolchildren to foreign tourists to local chamber of commerce officials on it.

The Mississippi River demands extra caution not only because of its size and power but because of the steady deluge of towboat traffic. I got a taste of that as a teenager when two pals and I paddled a canoe from West Memphis, Arkansas, to Memphis, Tennessee, and back. We got caught between two towboats pushing barges and had to paddle frantically. As a huge wave rocked our relatively tiny craft, I realized vividly that the Mississippi is not to be trifled with. And yet, when we stopped to explore some woods just below Memphis, I glimpsed the attraction of the big river. Even this close to the city we startled a drove of wild turkeys in the dense forest. Later, in my short-lived career as a deckhand, I saw vast herds of deer trotting through the riverbottom woods near Clarksdale. When I finally learned to handle a canoe, I floated and camped on the Mississippi, marveling at its blend of nature (glancing up at a bank to see a beaver in a hole calmly watching the world go by) and commerce (waking up in the middle of the night as towboat searchlights sweep the tent).

The state of Mississippi lays claim to approximately 400 of the river's 2,350 miles. The word *Mississippi* is a northern Native American term meaning, simply, big river. Since many tribes lived along it, it has gone by many names, including Chucaga, Tamalisieu, Nilco, Mico, Okachitto, Olsimochitto, Namosi-sipu, Sassagoula, and Culata. Spanish explorers ignored the native names, calling it Espiritu Santo or Rio Grande. But when French explorers came down the river, they took the label they learned from northern Indians, for whom "mis" meant big and "sipi" was river.

The Mississippi is so strong that my buddy Scott Williams averaged 50 miles a day in a sea kayak when he paddled from Minnesota to Vicksburg. Canoes average 20 to 35 miles a day. Paddlers intent on making time could conceivably cover 75–100 miles a day. The general strategy for floating the Mississippi is to follow the channel and pull aside for barge traffic. The quickest method of travel is to go in as straight a line as possible, crossing the channel as needed. For short trips, paddlers may prefer to stick close to shore to avoid traffic.

Ironically, upstream eddy currents at times can feel nearly as strong as the downstream flow. In a bend, the current circles around, a fact taken advantage of by occasional upstream paddlers. Dangerous whirlpools can occur where an eddy meets the main channel as the two currents collide. They also may occur downstream from bridge pilings and at the mouths of rivers. Buoys create miniature torrents as they bob up and down in the rushing current. Wind poses hazards too, especially when it's out of the south, against the current, and whips the river into whitecaps. Such factors make a sea kayak a good vessel for the Mississippi River. Its spray skirt keeps the boat from swamping, the rudder helps track straight on the big water, and the hull design is wonderfully seaworthy. However, canoes can certainly handle the river if their paddlers are skillful and prudent, knowing not only how to handle waves and currents but when to get off the water.

A greater danger than the river itself is the almost constant stream of tow-boats pushing barges, thirty or forty at a time, day and night. Paddlers should always be ready to get well out of the way, even if that means landing. It's also good to become familiar with basic navigational markers. For instance, the nautical slogan "red on right returning" indicates that a red channel marker should be on your right if you're returning from the sea—or, in this case, coming into a channel from open water. A green marker will be on your right if you're leaving the channel to enter open water. Paddlers, of course, can go where they want, but by understanding channel markers they may anticipate the movements of deeper-draft vessels. Also, red lights mark the port or left side of commercial vessels, green the starboard or right. If you see both lights, the vessel may be bearing down on you. Barges move with deceptive speed. They may appear to be standing still when actually they're clipping rapidly along. Some small boaters carry a VHF radio to communicate with commercial captains.

If you had paddled the river in frontier times, you'd have encountered dugout canoes, plank pirogues, log rafts, flatboats, keelboats, and shantyboats. Later, steamboats came along, littering the bottom with their wrecks, typically from fire from overheated boilers. Nowadays, in addition to towboats pushing barges, you'll encounter flat-bottom fishing boats, tugboats servicing the usually stationary government dredges that keep the channel clear, paddlewheel cruise boats, moored gambling boats, and perhaps an occasional canoe, kayak, or yacht. You'll also encounter abundant birdlife such as white pelicans, hawks, seagulls, terns, ducks, geese, and turkeys; herds of deer and wild hogs; and foxes, which take advantage of the remote riverside environment.

Fishing can be good if you know what to look for. Areas where grain is loaded onto barges—such as Helena, Clarksdale, and Greenville—can provide dramatic catfishing action. Fish lurk near the bottom and will take worms or cut bait. The best action is at night, but daytime yields results too. I know guys who have hauled in 50-pounders with a cheap rod and reel around grain bins. In spots where water spills over rock dikes, use large silver or gray crankbaits to catch white and striped bass. White bass feed in schools and typically weigh from half a pound to 2 pounds. Stripers are bigger, around 5 pounds. When you're cleaning stripers, cut away the red meat on the outside, which is gamey-tasting. For bream, paddle up oxbow lakes such as Lake Ferguson at Greenville and fish in the willow flats. Generally speaking, the best fishing action comes when the river is on a slow fall. When it's rising, the fish spread out and are less likely to bite. Floating is compatible with jug-fishing: Put out empty plastic bottles with hook, line and sinker attached, baited with cut bait at 6 feet deep or so. When a jug bobs, check it out. Trolling for catfish can work if you're just drifting. At night before you make camp, use jugs, yo-yos, trotlines, or droplines to catch breakfast. Jugs may be placed in the still pools below dikes with hooks 20–30 feet deep. Tie a trotline to a dike 20 yards from the end and run it to shore. If you catch a big catfish, incidentally, pull it in from the end of your canoe, not the side, since the weight can unbalance you—no small factor considering the size of Mississippi River catfish.

There is no shortage of camping spots on the river, whether on the numerous islands or shoreside sandbars. These sandbars can easily stretch for more than a mile, providing wondrous beaches but little protection from the elements. Being camped on open sand a mile from the treeline when a raging thunderstorm blasts in can be terrifying; be sure your tent, gear, and boat are well secured. The sandy beaches just downstream from dikes can make secluded campsites as well as prime fishing spots, but beware of the turbulent water around the dikes when you're landing. It's best to float past them in the main channel, then turn in and paddle to shore. Campers must also be conscious of the possibility of rising water. The National Weather Service reports river stages daily, published in various newspapers. They tell the flood stage, daily stage, and how much the river is rising or falling. Look at the upstream stages to anticipate what's coming, and make it a habit to camp well above the water line.

Weather conditions can be extreme on the big river. If you capsize in winter, hypothermia can set in before you can get to shore, so dress with insulated clothing such as wool or fleece beneath your life vest. In hot weather, the wide-open river can feel like the Sahara desert, making wide-brimmed hats, sunscreen, and ample drinking water essential.

William Faulkner once wrote that Mississippi begins in the lobby of a Memphis hotel, and the same principle applies to the Mississippi River: The northern portal to Mississippi's share of river is Mud Island Harbor at the foot of Beale Street in Memphis. Visitors to that city won't want to miss the incredible quarter-mile-long replica of the entire Mississippi River found at the city park on Mud

Island, as well as the museum of river history there. In Memphis, as in most cities located on the river bank, there's a landing in the downtown vicinity.

From Memphis it's 10 river miles to the state line. There are various landings all along the river, but many are remote and seasonal, hard to find, and subject to flooding in high water. As John Ruskey points out, the best way to find many of these landings is to ask directions when you get near. Or get the free maps, "Access Roads Along the Mississippi River," from any U.S. Army Corps of Engineers map sales office (601-631-5042 in Vicksburg). Relevant maps for the state's portion show the stretches from Cairo, Illinois, to White River, Arkansas (across from Rosedale), from White River to Jackson Point just above Mississippi's southern border, and from Jackson Point to the New Orleans area.

The surest stopping points are the cities of Helena, Arkansas; Rosedale; Greenville; Vicksburg; Natchez; and St. Francisville, Louisiana. Memphis, Helena, and Natchez are the only towns actually on the river—good to know if you expect to walk in and stock up on supplies or make a phone call. The others lie back off the river accessible by road or inlet. Stopping at any prearranged destination requires planning, however, for if you don't aim well in advance, the river's powerful current will sweep you past.

From Memphis it's 18 miles to Norfolk-Star Landing, 20 from there to Mhoon Landing, and another 24 to Helena, which lies on the west bank—a total of 62 miles from Memphis to Helena. At Helena you can take out behind the Delta Cultural Center in Helena Harbor downtown. It's 43 miles from there to Island 67 (Quapaw Landing) near Clarksdale. Paralleling the river at Clarksdale is Highway 61, the blues highway. The Mississippi Delta Blues Museum at 114 Delta Avenue features photos, 78-speed records, old guitars, even a life-sized figure of the late bluesman Muddy Waters. A chart lists blues musicians from towns and counties throughout the state. Local juke joints also help keep the blues alive. On a typical Saturday night in such a spot, customers sit at tables with quart bottles of beer, bottles of whisky in brown paper sacks, and cans of Coca-Cola while a band belts out heavy-duty blues interspersed with soul and rock numbers. If you like what you hear, there's a huge selection of albums at Stackhouse/Delta Record Mart, 232 Sunflower Avenue.

From Island 67 it's 28 miles to Terrene Landing just north of Rosedale. Terrene Landing is located 5 miles north of town. An alternate launch site is the Rosedale Harbor Project south of town, but it requires paddling 2 miles out to the river. Between Rosedale and the river, inside the levee, is Great River Road

State Park, which pays tribute to the historic route that parallels the river from its headwaters to the Gulf of Mexico. In Mississippi, it follows Highway 61 in the north, picks up Highway 1 in the middle, then rejoins 61 through Vicksburg, Natchez, and into Louisiana. The park lacks a boat landing but offers great views, including one from a 75-foot observation tower. There are 61 developed campsites, a lake with boat rentals, picnic areas, and nature trails, with paths to river sandbars.

It's 55 miles from Rosedale to Warfield Point at Greenville, punctuated by Mounds Landing 30 miles down. Greenville is home of the renowned Delta Blues Festival, held the third Saturday of each September. Greenville is also known for its barbecue; just follow the smell of hickory smoke. That's assuming you're willing to paddle the 4 miles of slack water up the inlet along which the city sits. If not, stop at Warfield Point Park on the river south of town. The city-owned park has picnicking, showers, and campsites.

It's 40 miles from Greenville to Mayersville and another 60 to Vicksburg, perched on a bluff, which made it nearly impregnable during the Civil War. It took a tremendous amount of force and strategy before General Ulysses S. Grant's troops captured it after a siege. Vicksburg National Military Park and Cemetery, 3201 Clay Street, tells the story and also features a display of the USS *Cairo*, a Union ironclad vessel sunk during the war and later raised and restored. To get to Vicksburg from the river, paddle about a mile up the Yazoo River Diversion Canal and take out at the harbor at the foot of Clay Street. If you're hot and thirsty, make your way over to the Biedenharn Museum of Coca-Cola Memorabilia on Washington Avenue, which parallels the canal a quarter mile away. The museum is in the old building where Coke was first bottled in 1894. In addition to mementoes, there's a fully operating soda fountain. Grand Gulf Military Monument 30 miles downriver near Port Gibson also provides a fascinating history of the area, as well as a campground. There's a public boat ramp a few miles from the park. (See Big Black River section for more.)

Some 73 miles downriver from Vicksburg, Natchez too stands on a towering bluff overlooking the lowlands of Louisiana. There's a public boat ramp at Natchez Under-the-Hill north of the river bridge. From the hill above the bridge it's possible to imagine how far floodwaters extended in pre-levee days (or even in post-levee days when the manmade banks couldn't hold back the waters, such as the great flood of 1927). One of the most gripping accounts I've read of such conditions is in the appendix to Mark Twain's *Life on the Mississippi*, where he presents newspaper accounts of the flood of 1882 when waters extended from Natchez to Catahoula Lake, Louisiana, more than 50 miles away. A look at a map makes this understandable. The Red River flows southeast across Louisiana, absorbing the Black, which in turn has gathered the Ouachita, Tensas, and Little Rivers, among others. When the Mississippi flooded, all these streams did the same, forming a sheet of brown water from the Mississippi bluffs to the edge of the piney hills in central Louisiana. When you read about the human tragedy resulting from such floods, it's easy to understand why society has tried to master the river with levees, dredging, and other projects. But by confining the Mississippi between levees, we have forced its load of silt farther and farther into the Gulf of Mexico. The channeled water flows faster, in turn sucking water out of the tributaries faster, causing bank caving, or headcutting. This problem is particularly noticeable on sandy streams like Bayou Pierre and Homochitto.

Native Americans like the Natchez Indians made far smaller but nonetheless lasting changes to the landscape by building mounds. By the end of the seventeenth century, some four thousand Natchez lived in about ten villages east of the modern-day town, ruled by the Great Sun, who lived in a 45-by-25-foot cabin on a 10-foot high earth mound. The mound still stands, along with a museum and replicas of Indian houses, at the Grand Village of the Natchez off Highway 61 in Natchez. The arrival of Spanish, French, and British settlers sounded the death knell for the Natchez. Overall peace was maintained until an oppressive French governor commandeered the Grand Village of the Natchez in 1729. The Indians attacked the trading post at Natchez, killing two hundred. French vengeance was swift. Aided by Choctaw and other Indian allies, the French drove the Natchez out of their homeland, forcing them to seek refuge with the Chickasaw, Creeks, and Cherokee. Some descendants still reportedly survive, but about the only relics of the once-great Natchez culture are the mounds and untold numbers of stone artifacts. We also have a living link in the form of the popular powwows held at Grand Village every spring. Powwows are based on the customs of the Southern Plains Indians, not Southeastern tribes like the Natchez, but most tribes did gather for various ceremonies, festivals, and dances. Another living relic of frontier times is the Natchez Free Trappers Pre-1840 Rendezvous Camp held each November on the campus of 195-year-old historic Jefferson College off Highway 61 north of Natchez. Men and women dressed in frontier garb pitch canvas tents and for a few days live the lifestyles of their forebears.

Natchez is now a modern city, but the downtown area and Natchez Under-the-Hill maintain a wondrously historic feel with carriage rides, antebellum homes, and other old buildings. The Mississippi River has worked its way a good 400 yards east since 1800, doing away with much of the original under-the-hill district, but there's still a line of rustic buildings, not to mention a paddlewheel gambling boat. On top of the hill, one of the most impressive sites is the recon-structed, brick and wood, three-story King's Tavern at 619 Jefferson Street, built around 1789 as an inn at the southern terminus of the Natchez Trace. The restaurant is in the basement of the original inn, and the smoke-stained bricks seem to whisper dark tales, like the time dueling gamblers Jim Bowie and John Sturdevant sat facing each other at a table, lashed their left arms together, held knives in their right hands, and fought to the death. Bowie won.

South of Natchez lies St. Catherine Creek National Wildlife Refuge, the mouth of the Homochitto River, the flatlands around Lake Mary, then the mouth of the old Buffalo River. The Buffalo used to spread out into a series of lakes just east of Lake Mary, but somewhere along the line it turned north into the Old Homochitto River, which was the channel of the Homochitto River until the U.S. Army Corps of Engineers rerouted it to the Mississippi in 1938. The Old Homo-chitto empties into Lake Mary, itself an old oxbow channel of the Mississippi. Now the old Buffalo is little more than a muddy ditch except in flood. Below it looms the majestic bluff where Fort Adams once stood. The bluff was visited by French explorer Robert de LaSalle, who began his famous expedition down the Mississippi River in February 1682 from what is now Illinois. After forty-four days he reached the mouth of Red River, and on March 29 Father Zenobius Membre held Easter mass on the high bluff on the east side of the Mississippi River—the first definite record of a Christian service in Mississippi. LaSalle pro-ceeded on to the mouth of the river, and in 1698 Jesuit missionaries from Que-bec arrived at Fort Adams to work among the Houma Indians, building a chapel on Blockhouse Hill, as the bluff was later called. The church was abandoned in the early 1700s, but in 1706, Father Antoine Davion, a missionary among the Tunica Indians on the Yazoo River, moved to Fort Adams. He built a new chapel on the same spot as the first church and stayed until 1722 when the Capuchins, a French missionary legion, took over the work in the southern part of the Mis-sissippi Valley. For years the bluff was referred to as La Roche a Davion in honor of Father Davion. The high bluff also served as a military site: Forts Prudhomme and Assumption for the French, Fort Ferdinand for the Spanish, and Fort Adams for the United States. Fort Adams was the site of treaties, negotiations, conspiracies, and battles. In the Civil War, the Union stationed its gunboat Chilicothe on the river to defeat Confederate attempts to take the hill. After the war, the adjacent town thrived until the Mississippi River channel began swinging west. Now the fort is gone, the river is 2 miles away, and the town of Fort Adams, located on Highway 24 about 20 miles west of Woodville, serves mainly as an isolated retreat for hunters and fishermen.

Across the river stands a Corps of Engineers structure at Old River, Louisiana. The Red River, having absorbed all the water north Louisiana has to offer, joins the Atchafalaya River just 7 miles from the Mississippi, linked by Old River. Since the Atchafalaya provides a shorter route to the sea, if left on its own it would become the main Mississippi River channel. So in 1963 the Corps built the Old River structure to control the Mississippi's flow into the Atchafalaya and provide an emergency outlet for floodwaters. During serious floods a spillway at Morganza, Louisiana, can also be used to take pressure off the Mississippi. In 1987 the Corps added another structure near Vidalia, Louisiana. Even with all this, there is no guarantee the Mississippi River won't eventually change course.

Just downriver from Fort Adams, Clark Creek tumbles out of the rugged hills known locally as the Devil's Backbone. The woods around the mouth of the creek are posted by a hunting club, but a short distance inland is Clark Creek Natural Area, including 430 acres donated to the state in 1978 by International Paper Company and 166 adjacent acres later purchased from a landowner. The area features waterfalls up to 20 feet tall, rugged hills and hollows, lush forest, abundant wildlife, clear streams, and bizarre clay formations. The state has built gravel walkways with wooden bridges, benches, and observation posts. State officials estimate the area gets at least 100,000 visitors a year. Visitors have come from thirty-five states and fourteen foreign countries. To get to the park, take Highway 24 west through Woodville, then turn south at the Clark Creek sign. Go several miles to the Pond community, turn right, cross a cattle gap, pass the historic country store; the natural area parking lot is up the hill to the left.

The state of Louisiana has taken advantage of the remote and rugged Tunica Hills to the south as a site for its prison at Angola. Just past it, some 72 miles from Natchez, is a landing on the Mississippi River at the town of Tunica, Louisiana. And 26 miles below that is a ferry that links St. Francisville, Louisiana, on the east and New Roads, Louisiana, on the west. The town of St. Francisville lies a short distance inland from the ferry landing.

Mississippi River routes (major landings in capital letters)

1. MEMPHIS, TENNESSEE, to HELENA, ARKANSAS, 62 miles. In Memphis, launch at the foot of Beale Street. At Helena, launch behind the Delta Cultural Center in Helena Harbor downtown.

    a. Memphis to Norfolk-Star Landing, 18 miles.

    b. Norfolk-Star to Mhoon Landing, 20 miles.

    c. Mhoon Landing to Helena, 24 miles.

2. HELENA to ROSEDALE (Terrene Landing), 71 miles. Terrene Landing is located 5 miles north of town. An alternate launch site is the Rosedale Harbor Project south of town; it requires paddling 2 miles out to the river.

    a. Helena to Island 67 (Quapaw Landing) near Clarksdale, 43 miles.

    b. Island 67 to Rosedale (Terrene Landing), 28 miles.

3. ROSEDALE to GREENVILLE, 55 miles. At Greenville take out at Warfield Point Park east of Highway 82 south of town.

    a. Rosedale to Mounds Landing, 30 miles.

    b. Mounds Landing to Greenville (Warfield Point), 25 miles.

4. GREENVILLE to VICKSBURG, 100 miles. At Vicksburg launch into the harbor at the foot of Clay Street.

    a. Greenville to Mayersville, 40 miles.

    b. Mayersville to Vicksburg, 60 miles.

6. VICKSBURG to NATCHEZ, 73 miles. At Natchez launch at the ramp at Natchez Under-the-Hill north of the river bridge.

    a. Vicksburg to Upper Grand Gulf Landing, 29 miles.

    b. Grand Gulf to Natchez, 44 miles.

7. NATCHEZ to ST. FRANCISVILLE, LOUISIANA, 98 miles. At St. Francisville, take out at the ferry landing on the east bank.

    a. Natchez to Tunica, Louisiana, 72 miles.

    b. Tunica to St. Francisville, 26 miles.

Outfitters

Quapaw Canoe Co., 291 Sunflower Ave., Clarksdale, MS 38614, phone 662-627-4070. Offers guided tours along the Mississippi River and some Delta streams.

Area campgrounds

Great River Road State Park, Rosedale, 662-759-6762.
Bolivar County Lake just east of Rosedale, 662-759-6444.
Warfield Point Park, Greenville, 662-335-7275.
Grand Gulf Military Monument west of Port Gibson, 601-437-5911.

High points

One of the world's greatest rivers, phenomenal woods and wildlife.

Low points

Towboat traffic, headwinds, dangerous currents.

Tips

Don't try it if you're not competent with a paddle.

Homochitto River

My father used to say Homochitto was an Indian word for man-eater. As is often the case with fathers, his pronouncement was truer than mere facts. Homochitto, I later learned, is Choctaw for big red (homo=red, chitto=big). But plenty of people have died in the river's flash floods and shifting sands; I've seen the bodies myself. That's not to say the river is an uncanoeable torrent. If anything, it tends to be too shallow. However, its sands are tricky, its floods rapacious. Yet precaution and common sense can anticipate either.

Starting in Copiah County south of Hazlehurst, the Homochitto meanders west through sparsely populated Franklin, Wilkinson, and south Adams Counties, including the 189,000-acre Homochitto National Forest, en route to the Mississippi River. It used to flow into Lake Mary, an oxbow lake off the Mississippi west of Woodville, but the Corps of Engineers routed the river directly into the Mississippi in 1938 in a project called the Abernathy Channel. That's one of many instances of human tampering that drastically affected the Homochitto. Such tampering dates to the nineteenth century. A 1936 report by the Mississippi Planning Commission said, "Due to the depletion of forest cover in the hill sections of the area, the streams in this area erode large quantities of soil." Before 1915 the river was used by loggers to float logs downstream, "but it is now clogged up and is useless as a waterway," the report said.

From 1899 until 1923, both federal and county governments spent thousands of dollars snagging logs out of the river and straightening bends to curtail flooding and open the channel. Then came the now-infamous Abernathy Channel. Though flooding ceased to be a major problem, others took its place. With a shorter, straighter route, the current moved faster, drawing sand out of the hills and caving in banks in a process known as headcutting. "This cutoff reduced the reach of the river downstream from U.S. Highway 61 at Doloroso (from) about 20 miles of meandering distributaries to a 9-mile, relatively straight outlet," said a 1979 U.S. Geological Survey report by Ken Wilson. The changes in the river are graphically illustrated by U.S. Geological Survey measurements at the Highway 33 bridge at Rosetta. In 1906 the clay-bed channel was 96 feet wide with an average depth of 4.5 feet and a current moving at 0.66 feet per second. In 1976 the bed was sandy, width 328 feet, average depth one foot, speed 1.43 feet per second. Faster, shallower, sandier.

Such "improvements" continued until 1952 at a total cost of $205,000. But these costs were nothing compared to the disasters that ensued. "Damages to highways and bridges between 1945 and 1974 totaled $1,863,115," said Wilson's report. "The cost of replacing the state Highway 33 bridge following the 1974 flood was about $8 million." That doesn't take into account the lives lost in the 1974 bridge collapse and in other, less dramatic instances.

In 1979 I was at my son's Little League baseball practice late one afternoon when a state trooper told me two people had drowned in the river. After arranging a ride home for my son, I took off to the Homochitto National Forest, drove till the road ended, then got out and walked. I followed a muddy track into deep pine woods; when it forked I knew where to go from the footprints. A mile later I met a crowd of hushed spectators exiting wide-eyed in a hurry. When I arrived in the riverbank gloom, where rescuers' headlights bobbed surreally, I saw two boys on their backs, arms out in rigor mortis. The two brothers had been swimming. One dove and didn't come up; his brother went in after him and also didn't surface. Rescuers had dragged the hole until they hooked clothing. Now we had to get the bodies out. There was no way to drive a truck to this spot, which meant the men had to put the bodies in a flat-bottom boat and tow them upstream to the nearest accessible site—tow because the Homochitto is too shallow for a motor, upstream because if you wade downstream the sand can shift underfoot. The Homochitto's unstable sands have claimed the lives of people not even in the river by shifting suddenly and dropping them unexpectedly into water. While some men towed the boat, the rest of us hiked back out and drove around to a remote pasture, in places miring down in mudholes. We finally made it to the bank, a 30-foot bluff overlooking the dark stream where the headlights of the boatmen inched toward us. Though I was there as a reporter, I joined in to haul boat, bodies, and gear up the bank.

The loss of property as a result of Homochitto erosion pales before such incidents but is nevertheless a big problem. Huge amounts of riverside acreage cave into the river each year, to the dismay of landowners. Some have called for the Corps of Engineers to restore the river to its original route. The Corps hasn't ruled that out, but it's a long shot. In the meantime, restoration proceeds piecemeal, such as a clever U.S. Forest Service effort to save an eroding tributary in the Homochitto National Forest. In 1992 the creek was 3 feet wide and 3 feet deep. A year later it was 20 feet wide and 2 feet deep. The speed of the erosion astonished Forest Service officials, but it's symptomatic of the Homochitto River Valley. The creek flows from an 80-acre wetland known as the Johnny Pond, and if the headcutting had been allowed to continue, it would have drained the wetland. However, the Forest Service spent some $45,000 laying concrete mats across the stream to check the destruction. It seemed to work, but that's just one tributary among many. As for the Homochitto itself, what was once a normal river is now wide and shallow, subject to flash floods, gnawed by erosion, rife with unstable sands including quicksand—in short, a man-eater, just like Dad said.

The quicksands are usually just shin-deep, but I interviewed one man who claimed he sank to his armpits before his companions pulled him out. Ken Wilson of the Geological Survey recalled seeing an 8-foot wall of water that came and went in a 2-hour period in the 1950s. I almost got swallowed myself when a flash flood struck as Dan Banks and I were canoe-camping between Highways 98 and 33. It rained a bit on our second day, but seemingly just enough to pick the current up a bit. We happened to camp on a bluff instead of a sandbar, and as I tried to sleep, I heard a roar like a jet readying for take-off. Climbing out of the tent under a moonlit sky, I saw the river had risen perhaps 6 feet, with sheets of foam bearing huge logs. I scrambled down the oozing mud bank to check the canoe. Its rope was already underwater, beyond my reach. I cut it with a knife and tied it to a stump as high as it would go. Ten minutes later the river was up another 3 feet. I slid back down and attached an extra line to the rope, then lashed it to a tree. Finally I fell into a sleep of bad dreams of trying to cross a flooded brown river without success.

In the morning the roar sounded like Armageddon. The canoe was floating 6 feet above the spot where I had tied it. I calculated the river had risen at least 15 feet overnight. The formerly broad sandbar across from us was submerged. The channel churned with rapids. I heard a babylike squall and saw a mother beaver and her kit, separated in the swirling water, trying to find each other as they battled the currents. I wished them luck. We broke camp and paddled out. The force of the current was daunting. To get to the shallow side we passed through 3-foot waves which dumped gallons into the boat. We made it to the remaining rim of sandbar next to a willow thicket and stopped to bail. Surveying our prospects, we decided to stay on the shallow side as much as possible, meaning we would have to cross the river periodically. As we paddled downstream, we could see 5-foot waves in the channel, while downstream a long stretch of bank caved in. Suckholes opened and shut around us with ominous popping noises. We crossed in the bend, just ahead of a tree bobbing along like a charging horse. To our left coiled a whirlpool as wide as a house. My life vest no longer gave me confidence. We decided to take out at Brushy Creek, a tributary with a bridge a short distance up it. To get to its mouth we had to cross. We started well above the creek but overshot and had to claw our way upcurrent, paddling for all we were worth yet barely moving. After moments of suspended tension, the creek's backwash grabbed us and pulled us into quiet safety. The flood, we later learned, washed out the railroad bridge at Rosetta. It taught me a profound respect for the river, which the day before had been just inches deep.

Fortunately the Homochitto is not usually so violent. But it's wild in other ways, home to alligators, bears, deer, snakes, catfish, and gar. In addition to the usual cottonmouths along the river, the national forest is renowned for its massive timber rattlers, which reach 5 to 6 feet in length. A local hunter, Roger U. Lewis of Smithdale, was camping out under the stars one October night when he awoke to feel a rattlesnake in his sleeping bag. His account of the experience, "Rattlesnake in My Sleeping Bag," appeared in the February 1986 *Reader's Digest*.

The river harbors some big fish too, including catfish upwards of 30 pounds. Set trotlines or droplines in still, muddy pools. Worms are unbeatable for bait.

Beware of hooking gar; the river teems with them. I had one snatch a bass off a metal stringer trailed behind my canoe. For bass, cast spinnerbaits into the relatively deep pockets where bass shelter under logs. I know some fellows who caught more than a hundred in a day float, many of them too small to keep, of course.

The Indian tribes who lived along the river used a more primitive method of fishing: weirs. They cut pine saplings with stone tools, trimmed them to poles and sharpened the ends. Using wooden mallets, they drove the posts about 2½ feet apart in the river bed in a V-shaped enclosure, mouth facing upstream. They wove leafy saplings and branches or cane mats among the posts to serve as walls. Fish were channeled to the tip of the V, where they would swim into a small, enclosed area. The Indians would net or club them, no bait needed. In 1975 Thomas Sturdivant of Rosetta found some posts sticking up after a bank collapsed. Archaeologists dated the Sturdivant weir to 1465 A.D. In 1991 Lydell Rand of the Bunkley community found one dating to 1350. The earlier model used saplings instead of cane mats. Archaeologists took sample posts from both weirs to Jackson and chemically preserved them. Indian canoes have also turned up in the Homochitto. One discovered in the early 1970s measured 12–13 feet long and dated to 1465. It had squared-off ends with a platform at each end. A hole was bored into one of the platforms, presumably for mooring pole or rope. Such finds are extremely fragile. They typically come to light after the channel changes or a bank washes away. Once exposed to air, they decompose so swiftly it calls to mind science fiction movies, changing from a fresh appearance to black in fifteen minutes. Weirs dating to the 1800s have also been found. The presence of nails and boards indicates they were used by settlers.

One such settler was Lewis Wetzel. The famous—or infamous—Indian fighter from the Ohio Valley occasionally visited his cousin Phillip Sycks (or Sykes) at Sycks's farm on the Homochitto at Havard's Ferry, now Rosetta. Born in 1763, Wetzel was "by far the greatest Indian fighter this nation has known," said researcher Robert Hand of Newtown Square, Pennsylvania. Wetzel apparently developed his hatred for Native Americans after being captured and brutalized as a boy before making a daring escape. After that he vowed to kill every Indian who crossed his path, and he meant it, whether peacetime or not. He grew his black hair to knee-length, learned to reload a muzzle-loading rifle on the run, and disappeared alone into hostile territory across the Ohio River, returning with strings of scalps. His bravery, strength, and speed were Olympian, and there's a natural tendency to heroize him, which Zane Grey did in novels like *Spirit of the Border* and *The Last Trail*. But Grey and some historians glossed over Wetzel's brutality, such as the cold-blooded murder of peaceful Indians. Wetzel and his brother Martin even reportedly participated in one of the most infamous massacres in the history of the Ohio Valley, the slaughter of unarmed Christian Indians at a Moravian mission. In Mississippi Wetzel ran a horse-stealing ring, rustling horses from settlers and selling them up north, Hand said. For a while Wetzel had a cabin on the lower Big Black River, and a visitor reported seeing him shoot two Choctaw canoers from his front porch for no reason except that they were Native Americans. Wetzel was arrested in Natchez and imprisoned in New Orleans on charges of counterfeiting—charges Hand thinks were trumped-up since Wetzel was said to be illiterate. But imprisonment aged the frontiersman. By the time he was in his forties, observers reported that his hair had turned white. Hand notes that Wetzel's dark deeds should be taken in the context of an astonishingly cruel era. Wetzel indeed saved many lives, rescuing people captured by Indians, warning settlers of impending attacks. His single-handed attacks on bands of Indians in their own territory showed utter fearlessness. His expertise in guerrilla warfare was unsurpassed. He excelled in war—but came up sorely lacking in peace.

Opinions about where and when he died are divided. Hand and some others, including Allan W. Eckert in his book *That Dark and Bloody River* (Bantam, 1995), opine that Wetzel died in the mid-1800s in Texas after many more adventures. Earlier researchers believed he died of yellow fever in 1808 at Havard's Ferry and was buried on the south bank of the Homochitto. Dr. Albert Bowser dug up the supposed remains in 1942 and transported them to West Virginia for a monument. I interviewed a woman who was present as a girl at the exhumation. She recalled a wooden casket containing a rusted gun barrel and the imprints of long hair in the dust. A similar account was written by another eyewitness, the late Marie T. Logan, in a document provided to me by Dr. Bowser's daughter Maria Wetzel Bowser: "Parts of the rifle and the beads of a bullet pouch forming the letter 'W' were beside the bones. Shortly after the air hit it the bones crumpled to dust, but beneath the body were the marks of wavy hair in the hard clay—marks that reached from the head to the knee."

Around the time Wetzel may have been buried on the south bank of the Homochitto, a white settler named John W. Miller gave 10,000 acres across the river to his half-Choctaw daughter, Clorie Miller. Later another white man in the area, John Wilson, married an African-American woman known as "Black Mary," and they produced offspring. The families linked up through marriage, producing progeny that combined three races. The owners of the Miller tract decreed that there would be no enslavement of their offspring. Thus began Free Woods, one of the most unusual communities in the South, an area where slavery was abolished and races intermingled before the Civil War. The community thrived during the 1800s, with church, school, cemetery, and houses. Early in the 1900s the residents began to scatter, both to find better economic opportunities and to prevent the possibility of inbreeding. But the families stayed in touch and meet each July for a reunion, coming from as far off as California and Detroit. Driving into Free Woods is like driving back in time. What's left of the community lies along Forest Service Road 105 south of the community of Knoxville, which is located off Highway 33 north of the river. As you drive along the narrow, winding, deep-woods road, you'll see relics of the past: the old church and cemetery, an ancient unpainted wooden house, a log cabin, a culverted spring, an old barn. Old stories seem to waver in the air like Spanish moss. You may come across a fresh-dug hole, for people in these parts still dig for buried treasure, such as the fortune Clorie Miller's father reportedly left her.

Where there's treasure there are haints, and ghost stories abound in the Homochitto area. Residents have told me about a ghostly red horse that rides the back roads at night, men with no heads, and invisible rattling chains around the old movie theater in Crosby. One of the better-known local legends concerns a ghost at the old Wilson's Landing above Rosetta. Coon hunters report hearing a crashing sound in the woods, like a mule, but when they shine their lights on the spot, there's nothing there. Considering the area's raw history and lonely forests, there's little wonder such tales persist.

There's more to the woods than haints and legends, though. Clear Springs Recreation Area south of Highway 84 between Bude and Roxie has a beautiful campground and picnic area with a 12-acre lake, swimming area, pavilion, developed and primitive campsites, and a nature trail around the lake. The nearby Clear Springs trail, some 20 miles long with various loops, has drawn national attention in mountain biking circles, and it's fun for hikers too. Northeast of Gloster, at 5939 East Homochitto Road, the privately operated Brushy Creek Guest Ranch (601-225-7010) offers horse rides in the national forest as well as cabins, fishing, and other activities. There's a small fishing lake and limited primitive camping at Pipes Lake on Forest Service Road 121-A west of Garden

City, and Nebo Lake Recreation Area along the river between Highways 98 and 33. Scheduled to open in 2005 is a new 1,000-acre lake and 4,000-acre recreation area on Porter Creek, a tributary to the Homochitto. Entrance to the area will be at Bude Tower Road, which intersects Highway 98 three miles south of Bude near the Forest Service work center. For national forest information call 601-384-5876. Fees are charged for the campgrounds, recreation areas, and trails.

For paddlers, the Homochitto River is beautiful but difficult. Except in floods, it's never free of shallows, even as far down as Highway 61. At the community of Eddiceton just south of Highway 84, the river just will float a canoe. The 7-mile stretch from there to Highway 98 at Bude is the prettiest on the river. The water on this segment is so clear at times it's like floating on air. A canoe-wide channel wends beneath river birch, sycamore, water oak, beech, cypress, willow, catalpa, and spruce pine, while the rest of the river spreads over the sandy bottom like a layer of varnish. In every bend the channel unbraids, which means you must get out and tow. Because of the unpredictable nature of Homochitto sands, I recommend wearing a life vest and/or holding onto boat or rope at all times, even when the water's only an inch deep. A mile or so below the bridge, McGehee Creek comes in from the east. Just before Highway 98, Porter Creek enters from the southeast.

At Highway 98, a long erosion-control structure stretches along the southeast bank, evidence of the continuing battle landowners wage. Gloster Road crosses the river 5 miles below 98. These two stretches are the most accessible for day floats. The *Franklin Advocate* newspaper in Meadville sponsors a canoe race each May, usually on one of these segments.

Below Gloster Road, it's a lonely 24-mile float to the next take-out at Highway 33. Woods alternate with pastures, and more tributaries come in, including the Middle Fork of the Homochitto on the north, then Middleton, Caston, and Brushy Creeks on the south (among unnamed smaller ones) and Richardson on the north. As a result, the river widens, and has some deeper holes, but it's still riddled with shoals—so much so that on one trip a group of us, weary with towing, nicknamed ourselves the Shoal Brothers. The white sandbars, huge to start with, become increasingly vast, and corresponding bluffs reach 30 feet. Although the river slices through the middle of the Homochitto National Forest, rarely does it actually touch Forest Service land, the shores usually being privately owned. An exception is Nebo Lake Recreation Area on the south bank 4 miles upstream from

Highway 33. This primitive campground and picnic area borders the river, but access up the steep, wooded bank is difficult—not a good take-out.

On the 21-mile stretch between Highways 33 and 61, sandbars become muddy, but not to an unpleasant degree. The softer soil holds animal tracks longer, and you may see prints of alligator and black bear, big ones at that. Louisiana black bears, a black bear subspecies, roam the rugged blend of swamp and bluff from the Homochitto area south to the Tunica Hills where Mississippi and Louisiana meet. Both bears and gators are shy, and you never know where they'll turn up. A black bear was hit by a car crossing a road south of Liberty in 1998, and an alligator shocked Franklin Elementary School officials in Bude by crawling into the playground during school hours. On the river, you're more likely to see gators at night by shining a light to pick up the red reflection in their eyes.

Below Highway 61 the now-murky river flows 9 miles to the Mississippi. A vestige of the Old Homochitto, which once turned south toward Lake Mary, is visible a few miles below 61. Water still spills over there during flood. (If you're curious, you can drive to Lake Mary and travel up the Old Homochitto—a popular fishing area—until logs block your way.) On the north side of the river stretches the St. Catherine Creek National Wildlife Refuge. Despite the man-made Abernathy Channel, the Homochitto's final miles to the Mississippi have acquired enough curves over the years to lose the appearance of a straight canal. There are no take-outs below Highway 61 unless you choose to continue down the Mississippi. Even then, the nearest landing on the east bank is Tunica, Louisiana, 50 miles below the mouth of the Homochitto. However, I once paddled from the Homochitto 30 miles down the Mississippi to the mouth of Buffalo River and up the Buffalo to the Jackson Road bridge, camping on the way. I had a great time, but I can't say I recommend it. We went during low water, and the Buffalo was so shallow we wound up wallowing in knee-deep mud as we pulled the canoe the 2 miles to the bridge. And since the land around the bridge is private and posted, you must have permission to take out (which we did).

The Homochitto's myriad difficulties render travel daunting, but they also make it feel, at times, like one of the wildest places on the planet.

Homochitto routes

1. Eddiceton to Highway 98 at Bude, 7 miles.
2. Highway 98 to Gloster Road, 5 miles.

3. Gloster Road to Highway 33 at Rosetta, 24 miles.

4. Highway 33 to ramp at Highway 61, 21 miles. It's another 9 miles to the Mississippi River, but there is no take-out.

Area campgrounds

Nebo Lake Recreation Area, Forest Service Road 191-A east of Rosetta, bordering river, though access is difficult. Primitive camping. 601-384-5876.

Clear Springs Recreation Area, south of Highway 84 between Bude and Roxie. Signs mark the way from 84. Full facilities. 601-384-5876.

Pipes Lake Recreation Area, Forest Service Road 121-A west of Garden City. 601-384-5876. Tents only.

Natchez State Park, just east of Highway 61 north of Natchez. 601-442-2658.

High points

Sweeping vistas, wildlife from bears to alligators.

Low points

Endless shallows, broiling sands.

Tips

When wading or towing, wear life vest or hold onto boat or tow rope due to danger of quicksand and unstable bottom.

Bayou Pierre

Bayou Pierre, which rises from the high ground of Lincoln County and tumbles west to the Mississippi River between Vicksburg and Natchez, was named not for some old French trapper but for its rocks. Pierre is French for stone, and bayou comes from a Choctaw term for stream. It's well named. Bayou Pierre contains gravel bars, colorful clays, and rock ledges to an unusual degree for southwest Mississippi. Typically clear and shallow, it runs past Port Gibson into the Mississippi River floodplain, where it becomes muddy and subject to seasonal backwater flooding. Bayou Pierre's shallow, meandering channel is fun though difficult to paddle, and the geology and wildlife are fascinating. But the waterway suffers considerably from erosion due to farming, logging, and gravel mining as well as Mississippi River channelization, which draws the water out faster, causing banks to collapse.

Bayou Pierre's first good floating stretch starts at Carter Hill Road just south of the community of Dentville near Hazlehurst. From there to Highway 18 is a nice day float of 11 river miles, though like most of the river it may require occasional wading.

Next is a 9-mile leg to Carlisle Road just north of the community of Carlisle. White Oak Creek comes in from the northeast, making the river wider if not significantly deeper. In places the river cascades over clay shelves, the roar sounding like whitewater as you approach. If the water's high enough you can slide thrillingly over. Otherwise you'll have to get out and pull.

About 7 miles below Carlisle, the river passes under the Natchez Trace (no access), with the Willows Road bridge 2 miles farther on. From the Trace down, Bayou Pierre is subject to high water from the Mississippi River, which is some 26 river miles distant. In low water the bayou may be just inches deep, but when the Mississippi backs up—which can occur intermittently from February through May—the current slows and depths can reach 20 feet at the Trace. There's a broad beach just southeast of Willows Bridge popular with summer weekend picnickers. Four-wheeler riding is also popular on the broad sand and gravel bars until, several miles below Willows, the river gets a bit wide and deep for it.

About 8 miles below Willows Road the river passes under Highway 61, where access is poor due to lack of parking area and steep, weedy banks. On this stretch the river passes some of those namesake rocky ledges, providing a rather startling contrast with the usual dirt and clay banks. About 3 miles past 61, Bayou Pierre merges with Little Bayou Pierre. It's another half mile to the Anthony Street bridge northwest of Port Gibson, by which point the river has made the transition from sandy hills to muddy floodplain. It's 2.5 more miles to a boat ramp on the north side of the river, the final take-out. Alligators up to 15 feet long are said to proliferate in this area, but they're shy, likely to flee at the sight of a human. The bayou continues for 17 miles to the Mississippi River, but the nearest take-out is 30 miles down the Mississippi to Natchez. During low-water periods, Bayou Pierre, like the Homochitto, remains distressingly shallow all the way to Highway 61. You can expect periodic wading, and paddles are used more for pushing than stroking. But even in times of drought, the bayou just will float a canoe.

The Mississippi River keeps Bayou Pierre well stocked with fish, especially catfish. Local fishermen report bluecats up to 38 pounds and flatheads up to 42 on the lower river. Chicken liver makes a good trotline bait, and deer liver is said to be exceptional. Some anglers find the white perch fishing good in the bayou too. Barfish, a type of bass, make their run in the spring, and largemouth bass fishing is good then as well. During the low water of late summer and fall, fishing is pretty sparse, but you can pull a bass out from deep pockets beside fast water using a white spinnerbait.

While plenty of people hunt and fish, few take advantage of wild fruits, and even fewer gather medicinal plants. It wasn't that way in the old days, though. B. A. Botkin's *A Treasury of Mississippi River Folklore* (American Legacy Press, 1955) describes numerous herbal remedies used by residents along Bayou Pierre. St. John's wort, currently used for depression, in earlier decades was believed to protect people against lightning, ghosts, witches, and nightmares. It was also used to treat wounds, and dew collected from its leaves was thought to improve vision. Other Bayou Pierre folk cures: Sampson snakeroot was boiled as a tonic to enhance virility, ward off cramps, prevent snakes from biting, and improve one's skill at trading. A poultice of castor-oil leaves supposedly counteracted fevers, chills, headaches, and hot flashes. Devil's shoestring, a species of cross vine, was chewed and rubbed on the hands to give a man control over a woman and luck in gambling. The sensitive plant theoretically would make a person more willing to give up wicked behavior. Old-timers would chew heart leaves to soften the heart of the person they loved, or plant blue vervain, a member of the verbena family, to attract a potential sweetheart. Botkin enumerates other Bayou Pierre superstitions of interest to campers. Among them: Don't burn wood that pops, like sassafras, or someone may die. Don't burn wood from a tree struck by lightning. Stay away from trees that rub together in the wind and creak, as they may harbor spirits. And avoid a blooming redbud tree at night; also called a Judas tree, it's supposedly the species Judas used to hang himself.

Back in the world of science, Bayou Pierre's gravel bars contain 300-million-year-old clamlike fossils known as brachiopods, and sea lily fossils called crinoids. They were probably washed into the area by meltwater from the north during an ice age a couple of million years ago. Even more interesting are the clays. Bayou Pierre's clays and clay rocks come in a variety of colors, including blue, green, orange, purple, gray, and brown. It's a delight to drift along under the steep banks and admire the earthen rainbow. The greens and blues are probably fresh exposures of deposits from the Miocene epoch some twenty million years ago. The reds, yellows, and browns are due to iron oxide caused by exposure to the atmosphere and percolating waters. The riffles and ledges result where layers of Miocene materials solidified.

On the upper reaches, you can stroll around the gravel bars and pick up pieces of petrified wood, which feel like rock but show a wood grain. Geologists aren't sure of the age of petrified wood, which could be anywhere from millions to thousands of years old—or maybe a lot less—but Bayou Pierre's specimens are believed to be one to two million years old. Wood petrifies when it gets buried under sand or clay and avoids rotting. Groundwater contains silica, and the mineral—which is found in quartz and much sand—replaces the woody material one cell at a time. Fossilized tree species that have been identified in the area include maple, osage orange, mulberry, hophornbeam, red oak, bald cypress, yew, and black walnut.

Also found are geodes, which result from silica-rich fluids percolating through cavities in igneous rocks, leaving colorful bands of crystals. Bayou Pierre's geodes are pretty but not comparable to the huge, glittering specimens seen in rock shops. They rarely exceed a few inches in diameter and tend to be already cracked open. Rockhounds can best find such tidbits on the gravel bars, where they have been deposited and washed cleaned by river water and rainfall.

It was eons after all this geologic activity that the Natchez Indians established their domain between the Yazoo and Homochitto Rivers, which included Bayou Pierre. In the late 1600s or early 1700s a new tribe, the Grigras, showed up, apparently a refugee group fleeing the influx of Europeans into the Southeast. Many tribes, such as the Tunicas near the Big Sunflower, elected to move rather than fight, and it wasn't uncommon for a settled tribe to adopt the refugees. That's what the Natchez did with the Grigras, who established a village in the Bayou Pierre area. The Grigras later joined some Natchez who rebelled against the French in 1729, and both tribes were driven out.

In the late 1700s an Irish settler, Peter Brian Bruin, established the settlement of Bruinsburg at the mouth of Bayou Pierre. Andrew Jackson ran a store there and raced horses. During the Civil War, General Ulysses S. Grant crossed the Mississippi River from Louisiana and landed at Bruinsburg with twenty thousand troops, who camped at Bayou Pierre. The Bruinsburg area is now privately owned, but Grand Gulf Military State Park northwest of Port Gibson has relics and information about local history. Grant went on to conquer Port Gibson, which he called "too beautiful to burn." It still is. Its old homes and stately trees are eclipsed only by the majestic churches along Highway 61. Union troops also spared the Windsor plantation house, largest antebellum mansion in the state, but a careless smoker caused it to burn down in 1890. The ruins' twenty-three massive columns remain as an exhibit off Highway 552 west of Port Gibson on the south side of the bayou. Ruins of another sort are located along Rodney Road, which loops from 552 back to Port Gibson. In the mid-1800s the then-thriving town of Rodney was located on the Mississippi River. The Civil War and several fires devastated the town, which finally expired when the river swung west, leaving it inland. Now all that remains is a "ghost town" with a few old buildings. Highway 552 used to provide access to the Mississippi River at the mouth of Bayou Pierre, but that access is now closed.

All in all, human settlement has not been kind to Bayou Pierre. Pasture, farm-land, and cutover often extend clear to the banks of the river, prompting severe erosion. As you float down the stream, you can hear the persistent plop-plop of dirt clods dropping off into the water. Unusually high rainfall in recent decades has aggravated the problem, according to findings by University of Southern Mississippi researchers. In the natural state, woods protect a stream from ero-sion, but as they're cleared, banks slough off and channels get wider and shal-lower. Erosion in Bayou Pierre has widened the channel and increased water velocity, gobbling up pasture and timber lands. One indication of the damage is evidenced by the status of a 2-inch-long fish found only in Bayou Pierre: the bayou darter, which lives in shallow swifts over gravel beds. Because of habitat degradation, the darter is listed as a threatened species by the U.S. Fish and Wildlife Service. The USM researchers, in a report for the Mississippi Museum of Natural Science, recommend banning or restricting gravel mining, as well as restoring forests that have been cleared from the riverside.

Despite such problems, wildlife seems to thrive on the river. A friend and I were canoeing an upper stretch one January day when we saw movement un-der the high bank to our right. A big buck deer had been standing invisibly among downed logs and branches, and the canoe spooked it. Realizing it couldn't scale the steep bank, it loped along the water's edge, then plunged in just 20 feet in front of us. It angled downstream, only its head showing above the water. Then it reached the shallows and bounded up, water pouring off its back in a silver cape. It dashed across the sandbar, pausing to glance back at us.

I noticed the rack was smaller on one side, indicating an injury to the opposite side of its body. I've seen plenty of deer swim rivers, but none that close.

Biologists believe deer are at least as abundant now as they were when the first explorers arrived. Whitetail deer played a major role in the exploration of Mississippi—and in the eventual downfall of its Native American tribes. In the 1600s, leather was used in all sorts of items, from shoes to clothes to furniture. The trade in deer skins started with a few bold explorers and adventurers swapping European goods for hides to the Indians. It ended with the Indians dependent on those goods, the deer depleted, the land occupied by settlers. Deer, whose numbers were restored in the twentieth century, again fuel the economy as hunters spend huge amounts of money for everything from guns to four-wheel-drive vehicles to pursue them. Far from being threatened, their population has skyrocketed so much that in the late 1990s state officials encouraged hunters to shoot more does to get the numbers down.

Alligator numbers have not reached their precontact levels, but they may be headed that way, judging by populations reported on streams like Bayou Pierre. Gators aren't as aggressive as their cousins the crocodiles, but they shouldn't be treated cavalierly. Indeed, crocodilians, which include crocs and gators, are among the most accomplished hunters on the planet. They rely on silence, speed, and surprise. The typical hunting strategy consists of spotting prey from a camouflaged position, ducking soundlessly underwater to approach closely, then lunging, biting, dragging the victim into the water, and spinning violently. That final lunge can span three times the reptile's body length. And once those jaws are clamped down, virtually nothing can open them. In Africa and throughout parts of southeast Asia and the South Pacific, humans constitute a regular part of crocodiles' diet. The two largest species, and hence the most aggressive to humans, are the Nile crocodile of Africa, and the Indopacific, or saltwater, crocodile, which ranges from India to Australia and beyond. Both grow to the 20-foot vicinity and can top a ton in weight. In Papua New Guinea I've seen saltwater crocs as big as 15 feet, which looked large enough to swallow not only me but a canoe as well. Even 6-footers are terrifying when they rise up on bandy legs and come running toward you like a hungry cat toward a fresh bowl of chow. But what about our good old nonaggressive alligators? Supposedly if a man, a crocodile, and an alligator were to find themselves together in a room, the man and the gator would be in big trouble. I got a vivid glimpse of gators' relative passivity at an exhibit in Florida. My press pass convinced the manager to let me mingle with the animals. I stepped down by a little creek among three or four gators in the 12–13-foot range. They lay still, ignoring me. Foolishly—I was in my twenties—I knelt and placed my hand on one of the behemoth's backs. It slashed its tail and hissed like a half-ton rattlesnake. I jerked my hand back as if from a hot stove and, prickles running down my spine, tip-toed out of there. The manager later told me he had captured that gator in the swamp a week earlier, so it wasn't domesticated, were such a thing possible. Though gators don't normally attack humans, as the two species come into contact, the odds of violence mounts. I know a bass fisherman whose boat was attacked by a 9-footer at a state park, leaving tooth marks on the hull. The incident occurred in a narrow channel in marsh, which suggests the gator felt hemmed in by the boat. Biologists predict that as the federally protected gators live longer and hence get larger, they'll be more likely to attack. Alligators can reach 19 feet; half that size is common these days. But paddlers should be grateful we don't have any crocodilians like those that reigned eighty million years ago. Deinosuchus, or "Terror Crocodile," grew to 30 feet in length and weighed 10,000 pounds, according to archaeological finds in North Carolina, Texas, and Montana. Deinosuchus had a broad, flat alligator-like snout and dagger-like teeth 5 to 6 inches long, similar to those wielded by Tyrannosaurus rex. In fact, the giant croc was a watery counterpart to the terrestrial T-rex, inhabiting the shallow tropical sea that covered much of North America, dining on dinosaurs like modern crocs do on zebras. Their era ended about sixty-five million years ago—fairly recent compared to some of the rocks along Bayou Pierre.

Bayou Pierre routes

1. Dentville to Highway 18, 11 miles.
2. Highway 18 to Carlisle, 9 miles.
3. Carlisle to Willows Road, 9 miles.
4. Willows Road to Anthony Street Bridge, 11.5 miles. Highway 61 crosses the river 8 miles past Willows Road, but access is poor. Anthony Street runs northwest from downtown Port Gibson, passing a cottonseed mill.
5. Anthony Street to boat ramp on north side of river, 2.5 miles. To get to the boat ramp, turn west on the north side of Anthony Street bridge. It's 17 miles to the Mississippi River and 30 miles down the Mississippi to Natchez.

Area campgrounds

Rocky Springs Campground, Natchez Trace Parkway northeast of Port Gibson, 601-680-4025.

Grand Gulf Military Monument west of Port Gibson, 601-437-5911.

High Points

Interesting rock and clay formations.

Low Points

Unusual amount of erosion.

Tips

Spend time on gravel bars examining rocks.

Big Black River

Big Black River slices diagonally across the state from northeast to southwest, plowing a crooked corridor some 300 miles through the line of low hills along the outskirts of the Mississippi Delta. A short distance to the north and west, all streams flow into the muddy Yazoo River; to the southeast, into the sandy Pearl. The Big Black is something of a dividing line; it can't quite decide if it belongs to Delta or piney hills. It contains elements of both, including sandbars and even a few red clay bluffs, but mud prevails. Even in low water, the river is never clear, and knee-high rubber boots are standard equipment. Still, persistent paddlers will find the Big Black rich with history, woods and wildlife.

The Big Black starts as a wiggly creek in Webster County near Clarkson, remaining prone to logjams as it squirms swampishly southwest past Vaiden and West. Only below West does it become relatively open. From Durant to its Mississippi River outlet just north of Grand Gulf more than 150 miles away, the Big Black remains midsized, usually big enough for motorboats, but low and sometimes log-strewn in dry season such as late summer.

The Big Black is a fine waterway for catfishing enthusiasts—indeed, one of the best in the state. Flathead catfish as big as 59 pounds and bluecats up to 30 pounds come out of the Big Black. Popular bait choices are crawfish in the spring and grass perch in the summer, generally with 3- or 4-aught hooks. Some campers take crawfish in ice chests in the spring, eating the big ones and using the rest for bait. Big Black floaters are not likely to encounter many other paddlers, but they can expect to meet occasional fishermen in johnboats. In my experience, fishermen tend to slow down for paddlers, maybe because they know how irritating it is to be sloshed around in someone else's wake when they're fishing.

Access is poor at the Highway 19 bridge at West, especially after a rain when the narrow stream tends to overflow the banks. Below West two tributaries come in, Jordan Creek from the west and Apookta Creek from the east, and by the time the river reaches Durant 20 miles away, it's big enough for canoe or johnboat.

The 12-mile segment between Durant and Goodman makes a good day trip, with plenty of sandbars. The Highway 12 bridge 1.5 miles east of Durant provides good access. The river is typically sluggish but can rise quickly after a rain. The National Weather Service reports river stages daily, published in various newspapers around the state, and they can tell you how high the river is in comparison with its flood stage. Campers may choose to stay at Holmes County State Park between Durant and Goodman and commute to the river for day floats. The beautifully wooded 444-acre park straddles a range of hills between Interstate 55 and U.S. Highway 51, offering a free primitive campground that is small but secluded, with water faucets, tables, barbecue grills, and trash cans; a developed campground with full facilities; 4 miles of trail; two lakes with bass and bream fishing; and a spacious day-use area that includes a roller skating rink and picnic tables. Unfortunately, neither campground is located beside the lakes.

Two sizeable tributaries enter the Big Black on the Durant-to-Goodman stretch: Seneasha Creek from the east and Tacketts Creek from the west. Plenty of smaller sloughs offer access to the swampy environs flanking the river. Paddle up a quiet, shady channel and you may startle a beaver out of its bank hole—or rather, it may startle you when it hits the water like a cannonball. The tree-bark-gnawing rodents can easily weigh 50 pounds and have a habit of whopping the water with their tails for dramatic effect.

Towering, vine-draped trees hint at the virgin forests that inspired French author François René de Chateaubriand to write a famous novel, *Atala*, in 1833. That in turn inspired the name for Attala County (people didn't pay much attention to spelling in those days) on the river's east bank. The novel is a Romeo-and-Juliet-type love story about two Mississippi Indians, a Muscogee princess named Atala and a brave named Chactas from the enemy Natchez tribe. Chateaubriand waxed extremely eloquent in depicting a realm that sounds like a cross between the Amazon jungle and the Garden of Eden.

The real history of the area's Indians is less romantic. As settlers encroached and craved more land, they gobbled up Choctaw territory: five million acres at the Treaty of Doak's Stand in 1820, and the rest at the Treaty of Dancing Rabbit Creek ten years later. By then the village of Bluff Springs was established

A narrow slough off Big Black River evokes era when the riverside forests were legendary.

near modern-day Durant, complete with ferry, sawmill, general store, distillery, and grist mill. Bluff Springs was named for fresh-flowing water near the Big Black, and the area has other such sites as well. Earthquake Springs 6 miles south of Kosciusko reflects the tradition that many of the flows emerged following the great 1811 earthquake. Red Bud Springs to the east became the town of Kosciusko, incorporated in 1836. Resort hotels grew up around Castalian Springs in Holmes County and Artesian Springs north of Canton in the mid-1800s.

In the latter half of the century the railroad arrived, paralleling the Big Black a mile or so to the west from Vaiden south to Way, where the river swings southwest under the tracks. If you had been camped on the river near Vaughan on April

30, 1900, you might have awakened to the crash that went down in history. J. L. "Casey" Jones was a hot-rodding engineer known for his willingness to take risks. That night, late on his southbound run from Memphis, Tennessee, to Canton, he ran through a stop signal and suddenly saw a freight train crossing up ahead. He ordered his firemen to jump just before his "Cannonball" rammed into the freight, killing Jones. Later a railroad employee, Wallace Saunders, wrote "The Ballad of Casey Jones," which became a nationwide hit and propelled Jones to legendary status. The Casey Jones State Museum (662-673-9864) at Vaughan, located in an antique depot less than a mile from the crash site, tells the story of Jones and the railroad's glory days with artifacts and an authentic steam engine.

The forests along the river are no longer as awesome as they were in Chateaubriand's day—there are depressing stretches of cutover and fields without a buffer of trees—but there are still some impressive water oaks and cypress along the banks. More common species are river birch, notable for its curly bark, and maple, the leaves of which flutter brightly in the wind as their silvery underbellies are exposed. Both species often angle out toward the sunlight. In the spring you'll see native azaleas, pink as strawberry ice cream; cross vines, whose red-throated yellow flowers drape trees and logs; and dewberries, whose red thorny-velvety vines and white blossoms blanket the edges of sandbars before yielding fruit in April and May.

The ground is punctuated with tracks of deer and raccoon—hunters pursue both in the swamps—and the sky rings with the whistles of hawks. Red-tailed hawks have a whitish breast and rust-colored tail, while the slightly smaller red-shouldered hawks have rusty underparts, reddish shoulders, and a narrow banded tail. A quick way to tell them apart when they're soaring is the chest: white on red-tails, rusty on red-shoulders.

The river continues essentially the same on the 12-mile stretch between Highway 14 at Goodman and Highway 51 at Pickens. On the 22-mile portion from Pickens to a boat ramp at Highway 16, the river turns southwest under I-55. Distances between bridges grow even greater below Highway 16. It's 30 miles to a boat ramp at Highway 49 south of Bentonia. Plenty of sloughs and oxbow lakes provide detours, with views of wildlife, including abundant waterfowl. The presence of alligators, some reportedly as long as 16 feet, adds to the wildness of the river. The wet forest also breeds mosquitoes and biting gnats, which are active even in cool weather, so bring plenty of insect repellent. Visitors who want a glimpse of the area's truly ancient forests can go to the Mississippi Petrified Forest in nearby Flora. The privately owned park is a national landmark whose outdoor exhibit features fossilized logs 7 feet thick. There is also a museum, gift shop, picnic area, and campground.

From Highway 49 to Highway 27 west of Utica are 62 long and lonely miles. It's broken by rural Cox Ferry Road, I-20 at Edwards, and Old Highway 80 near Bovina, but none of those, unfortunately, offers good access even for canoes. Farm fields continue past Highway 49, along with hardwood forests, sandbars, and bluffs. Woods along this stretch have been logged in recent decades and don't reach the size found in some areas along the river. Bogue Chitto Creek (not to be confused with Bogue Chitto River in southwest Mississippi) enters the Big Black from the south about 5 miles below Highway 49. Paddlers can go up it a bit during higher water levels, but it's generally blocked by logs. Cox Ferry bridge crosses about halfway on the 49-mile stretch from Highway 49 to Old 80. The winding course of the Big Black continues to give it a natural, almost pristine feel. The feeling diminishes a bit as the river crosses I-20 and swings west to parallel Old Highway 80.

That feeling will shrink even more if a proposed casino ever gets built on the river near Old Highway 80, a controversy exacerbated by the proximity of a Civil War site. When General Ulysses S. Grant tried to topple the seemingly impregnable citadel of Vicksburg in 1863, he fought battles at Port Gibson, Raymond, Jackson, Champion's Hill, and Big Black River before laying siege. A battle of a different sort took place in the 1990s when developers wanted to put a casino on the Big Black. Opposition arose from several corners, and the state gaming commission rejected the application. A Hinds County Circuit Court judge overturned that decision, and the case went to the Mississippi Supreme Court. Meanwhile the developers and a landowner filed a $200 million-plus lawsuit against Vicksburg casinos, claiming they masterminded the opposition to keep out the competition. A jury awarded them $4 million. That too was expected to go to the Supreme Court. A similar lawsuit was subsequently filed by others claiming to have been wronged by the Vicksburg casinos. While bright lights may someday glitter over Big Black near Old 80, for now there's not even a place to launch a canoe. There used to be a take-out, but it was done away with when the bridge was reconstructed, which means paddlers must go an additional 13 miles, to Highway 27.

From Highway 27 to Fisher Ferry Road is another 13 miles. Campbell Swamp extends to the right several miles below Fisher Ferry Road, with impressive stands of cypress and tupelo gum. A rustic fallen-in bridge at the old Hankinson Road crossing gives this stretch a breath of antiquity. Rocky Springs on the Natchez Trace Parkway a few miles to the southeast provides a base-camp area for day trips both here and on nearby Bayou Pierre.

Some 26 miles below Fisher Ferry Road, the Big Black passes under Highway 61, where there is a good take-out on the southwest side of the four-lane. The river winds on toward Allen, where an abandoned railroad trestle crosses, and straightens out as it enters the Mississippi River floodplain. Forests give way to large farm fields, with camps along the river. A road runs along the north bank for a few miles, large enough for eighteen-wheelers carrying logs or soybeans. A boat ramp at Karnac Ferry on the southeast bank about 9 miles below Highway 61 is the last public take-out before the Mississippi.

Five miles below Karnac Ferry, the river empties into the Mississippi about a mile above the Upper Grand Gulf Landing, which is a good take-out. According to one story, Grand Gulf's original English name was Grand Gulp because of a notorious boat-eating whirlpool where the Big Black enters the Mississippi. There's still an eddy there, and though not as dangerous as it once was, it demands caution, especially during high water. A couple miles inland by road from the landing is Grand Gulf Military Monument, which provides a fascinating historical account of the settlement, which started as a French village on the Mississippi River in the early 1700s. It grew into a major port city during the cotton heyday in the 1800s but returned to village status after a yellow fever outbreak in 1843, a tornado in 1853, and a shift in the Mississippi River channel which washed away much of the town. Then came the Civil War, and Union troops torched what was left. The 400-acre park opened in 1962. In addition to historical exhibits, it has a beautiful hiking trail with views of the Mississippi River and a fee campground. The huge cooling towers of the Grand Gulf nuclear power plant a few miles away provide a stark contrast to the rustic setting.

Because of the mud, the sluggish current, and the presence of motorboats, Big Black is not a big draw to paddlers. Increasingly, however, farmland is being converted to timber and recreational uses, spelling hope for backcountry enthusiasts. In the meantime, for those willing to overlook the difficulties, the Big Black has charms that can still conjure up the frontier romance of old.

Big Black routes

1. Highway 19 at West to ramp at Highway 12 at Durant, 20 miles, narrow at first, gradually widening to become free of logjams.
2. Highway 12 to ramp at Highway 14 at Goodman, 12 miles.
3. Highway 14 to Highway 51 at Pickens, 12 miles.
4. Pickens to ramp at Highway 16, 22 miles.
5. Highway 16 to Highway 49 south of Bentonia, 30 miles.
6. Highway 49 to Highway 27, 62 miles. Neither Cox Ferry Road, Interstate 20 or Old Highway 80 are recommended put-ins.
7. Highway 27 to Fisher Ferry Road, 13 miles. Fisher Ferry Road joins the communities of Reganton east of the river and Big Black west of it.
8. Fisher Ferry Road to Highway 61, 26 miles.
9. Highway 61 to Karnac Ferry boat ramp on Old Grand Gulf Road on the southeast bank, 9 miles. Karnac Ferry is at the end of Old Grand Gulf Road off Shiloh Road, which leads west a mile south of the Highway 61 bridge.
10. Karnac Ferry to the Mississippi River, 5 miles. Upper Grand Gulf Landing is located on the east bank of the Mississippi a mile below the mouth of Big Black.

Area campgrounds

Holmes County State Park, Highway 424 off Interstate 55 between Goodman and Durant, 662-653-3351.

Mississippi Petrified Forest at Flora, 601-879-8189.

Rocky Springs Campground, Natchez Trace Parkway northeast of Port Gibson, 601-680-4025.

Grand Gulf Military Park west of Port Gibson, 601-437-5911.

High points

Lush forest in places, plenty of sloughs for exploring, great catfishing.

Low points

Mud, slow current, motorboats.

Tips

Wear knee-high rubber boots.

Yazoo River

The Yazoo River is Mississippi's Congo: a large, muddy river draining a vast area once covered with forests of equatorial proportion, with some still-formidable remnants. The Yazoo begins at Greenwood at the confluence of the Tallahatchie and Yalobusha rivers and snakes southwest to the Mississippi River at Vicksburg. For the first 140 miles or so, the Yazoo flows mainly through farmland, posing little interest to paddlers. Below Satartia, however, portions of Delta National Forest appear, offering a hint of the once-mighty forests that used to dominate this quintessential Delta waterway.

In its long and colorful history, the 189-mile Yazoo has accommodated everything from cypress dugouts to steamboats to Civil War gunboats to modern barges, which journey the length of the river when water levels are sufficient. Yazoo tributaries are navigable for great distances as well: 171.4 on the Big Sunflower, 62.9 on the Yalobusha, 40.1 on the Tallahatchie and its tributary the Coldwater, plus 28.3 on the Little Tallahatchie, according to the Corps of Engineers. That doesn't take into account the upper reaches of those rivers or lesser streams such as the Yocona and Skuna. Most of these waterways are a far cry from their original condition, having been channelized and otherwise refashioned to curtail floods, accommodate agriculture, and drain once-malarial swamps. Several have been dammed to form reservoirs, whose spillways release their streams onto the flat floodplain of the Delta. On the way to the Yazoo, the rivers are thickened with silt and seasoned with chemicals from farm fields and industries. Given such factors, the Yazoo seems to offer little enticement for paddlers. Yet this is a river rich in history and lore—launching the careers of author Willie Morris and humorist Jerry Clower, for instance—and with many attractions even yet.

The Yazoo once had an international reputation as something of a Shangri-la. French explorers had scarcely arrived in the South before they began to realize the potential of the incredibly lush Delta soil. Speculators like John Law of France enticed settlers with claims of an agricultural paradise. Companies and government officials competed to get their hands on tracts of Yazoo farmland. Settlers discovered the land to be fabulously rich, sure enough, but also fraught with fevers and swamps. Considering the Native American meaning of Yazoo— river of death—that's not surprising.

No one is quite sure how the river got that name, but one plausible theory is malaria. Since the parasite leaves no fossil record, researchers can't be sure whether the disease existed in North America before Columbus, but the consensus is that it didn't. Regardless, by the time the first European farmers cut trees and plowed ground, the malady was entrenched. Malaria, which at one time spread across the United States, has since been relegated to the tropics thanks to public health campaigns against its carrier, the anopheles mosquito. But as recently as the 1940s, catching malaria, once known as ague, was the risk taken for canoeing a river like the Yazoo. "Malaria" means "bad air" due to the long-held theory that it was caused by humid nocturnal "miasmas." It wasn't the night air that caused it but the mosquitoes that rode that air, as researchers finally determined in the late 1800s. Mosquitoes inject their victims with malaria parasites, which cause chills and fever. The parasites stay in the liver and can recur for years, and some strains are hard if not impossible to cure. Even prevention is problematic, as the parasites become resistant to medicines after a time. African American slaves used a concoction made from soaking red-oak bark in water to combat it. In 1988 I interviewed a one-hundred-year-old African American in Amite County who recalled his mother making a tea from "yellow-top weeds" to treat malaria. Peruvian Indians used a medicine from the bark of the tropical cinchona tree, and for centuries the essential ingredient, quinine, proved to be the most effective treatment, long before scientists knew what caused the disease. Mississippi physician Henry Perrine was a pioneer in using this wonder drug. Numerous patent medicines contained it as well, and you'll still hear old-timers talk about remedies like 666 and Grove's Chill Tonic. Quinine is a harsh drug, however, with a host of bad side effects, including tinnitus, or ringing in the ears. Fortunately, safer versions like chloroquine were devised in the twentieth century. In addition to treating the disease, health officials mounted a huge campaign to eradicate it: draining standing water, promoting the use of screen windows and doors, and spraying the pesticide DDT to wipe out anopheles mosquitoes. As it turned out, DDT too had bad side effects, especially when used in quantities by farmers to kill other insect pests. As it got into the food chain, DDT caused the eggshells of predatory birds such as bald eagles to break before hatching. The eagles dwindled from tens of thousands in the 1700s to fewer than 450 nesting pairs in the lower 48 states by the 1960s, due to DDT along with habitat loss and illegal shooting. Banning the chemical played a major role in the eagle's rebound. By the end of the twentieth century eagles numbered more than 4,500 nesting pairs in the lower 48 states. The ban also ended hopes—unrealistic anyway—of eradicating malaria worldwide, but not before it disappeared from the United States.

The Yazoo was a hotbed of another sort of battle in the 1800s, as the Civil War raged across the South. Generals Ulysses S. Grant and William Tecumseh Sherman tried to use the Yazoo as a back-door entrance to Vicksburg since it was impregnable from its Mississippi River bluff perch. Union troops blasted the Mississippi River levee at Montezuma Bend 60 miles south of Memphis and rode the water across Moon Lake, Yazoo Pass, and Cassidy's Bayou to the Coldwater River, a high-water route used in the days before levees were built. Confederate troops had felled hundreds of trees across the path, but Union soldiers painstakingly cleared them out and continued down the Coldwater and Tallahatchie toward the Confederates' Fort Pemberton near Greenwood. There they found the Rebels had sunk a huge steamboat across the river as a barricade, and that, along with heavy fire, turned the Yankees back. Meanwhile another Union contingent tried to take gunboats on a 200-mile bayou passage to the Yazoo via Steele Bayou, Deer Creek, and Rolling Fork, but they were turned back by impenetrable willow thickets and sniper fire. The Yazoo campaign failed, and Grant had to use another strategy to win Vicksburg.

In 1876, the Mississippi River swung away from Vicksburg, leaving the waterfront stranded. The cutoff lake left in the old river channel was named Centennial since it was one hundred years after the nation's founding. With the Vicksburg waterfront silting in, Congress authorized the Corps of Engineers to close off the natural mouth of the Yazoo and divert it through the city. The Yazoo Diversion Canal was completed in 1903. That was one of many man-made changes to the Yazoo and its tributaries. From earliest settlements, landowners built countless drainage canals and levees to ward off floods, thus accounting for the tatterdemalion landscape we see today. But it took the flood of 1927 to convert haphazard skirmishes into all-out war. In that disaster, the Mississippi River broke the levees and turned the Delta into a swirling brown sea, claiming an estimated one thousand lives in the Delta alone and costing the nation a billion dollars. I talked to one man who said his grandfather rode a motorboat straight across from Satartia to Monroe, Louisiana—a distance of more than 75 miles—in that flood. Rather than bowing to the river's dominance, the government responded with ever grander schemes to thwart it. Since part of the problem was the tendency of Delta streams to flood, between 1937 and 1954 the Corps of Engineers dammed Coldwater River to form Arkabutla Lake, Little Tallahatchie and its tributaries for Sardis Lake, the Yocona for Enid Lake, and the Skuna and Yalobusha for Grenada Lake, among other flood-control projects. In the late 1970s, the Corps completed the Yazoo backwater levee, which roughly parallels the north bank of the river, to protect the lower Delta from Mississippi River flooding. Big and Little Sunflower Rivers and Deer Creek, which once emptied into the Yazoo, were blocked off from their natural outlets and steered into a long auxiliary channel that parallels the Yazoo to the north. The Corps installed flood control structures at Little Sunflower and Steele Bayou. The Corps intends to build a huge flood-control pumping plant at Steele Bayou, despite opposition from the U.S. Fish and Wildlife Service and conservation groups. The $150 million Yazoo Backwater Pumping Plant, designed to reduce flooding on farmland behind the levee, will be the world's largest facility of its kind.

In spite of all this, there is adventurous paddling to be had on the 53-mile segment from Satartia to Vicksburg, where the river passes some good Delta woodlands. It's possible to shorten the trip by taking out at Highway 61, 36 miles below Satartia, and a few other spots between there and Vicksburg. Access is difficult at most places because of steep mud banks and long carries. At Satartia, launch at the Highway 433 bridge. Wear knee-high rubber boots and expect to keep them on for most of the trip. The river sports a clipping current, more than you might expect from a Delta stream. Take care should barges approach; if the river is narrow, don't hesitate to land and pull the canoe well above the waterline. Otherwise, stay close to shore and angle the bow into the swells. National forest appears on the right bank just under 8 miles below Satartia. There's rarely any doubt about the presence of national forest since private land usually takes the form of farm fields. Fortunately a border of trees often lines the river between the levee and the fields.

The old mouth of the Big Sunflower River enters from the north about 8.5 miles below Satartia. The backwater levee has cut off its flow, leaving just a shallow remnant of old river fed by other drainage canals. Across the Yazoo from the mouth of the Big Sunflower stand some wooded Indian mounds, one of which has a brick cistern in top, apparently from an old house site. The old mouth of the Little Sunflower appears another 11 miles downriver on the right. The shallow stretch of water is blocked off by steel gates. You can walk to the levee and see the auxiliary channel paralleling the Yazoo to the north. Haynes Bluff, once the site of the main Tunica Indian village, stands to the south some 33 miles below Satartia. In 1706, as tensions mounted among French, English, Chickasaws,

A towboat dwarfs a canoe on Yazoo Diversion Canal at the Vicksburg waterfront.

and other tribes, the Tunicas abandoned their homes and moved to Houma In-dian country in southwest Mississippi and adjoining Louisiana. The Houmas took them in, and the Tunicas responded by massacring many and driving the rest farther south, taking over their homeland. Now that area is known as the Tunica Hills. A decade later, the French built a fort at Haynes Bluff. The town of Red-wood grew up a couple miles south. Nowadays heavy industries are the main feature, sucking river water out from huge pipes, pumping foul-smelling efflu-ent back in. Evidence of industrialization persists from here to Vicksburg.

It's possible to take out at Highway 61, but access is long and muddy from the northwest side. There's a better spot on the north bank at a railroad bridge half a mile to the west. Or continue to Steele Bayou 7 miles below Highway 61, paddle north into the bayou and take out at the landing on County Road 465. Despite the industry and occasional towboat, there's an appeal to going on to Vicksburg. A mile and a half past Steele Bayou, a channel to the right shows the old route of the Yazoo before it was diverted to Vicksburg. Now it's silted in to a narrow creek connecting with a wider river bed. At King's Point Ferry, 5 miles past Steele Bayou, ancient rusted barges litter the banks, reminiscent of the wrecked steamboats on the Congo River in Joseph Conrad's great river novel

Heart of Darkness. The Yazoo is wide and slow by this point. As it approaches Vicksburg you see the high bluff that almost thwarted Union forces. At the base, the river intersects a canal that leads from an industrial harbor on the left to the Mississippi River on the right, past rows of moored barges and a casino beside the landing at the foot of Clay Street. It's another mile out to the Mississippi.

On the Yazoo, bank fishermen use redworms and cut shad to catch flathead catfish ranging from a couple pounds to 50 or 60. Commercial fishermen also catch buffalo in hoopnets. Wildlife abounds on the river, with beavers swimming about openly and coyotes yodeling at night. You may surprise mink or otter on a moonlit walk, and muddy shores usually reveal the prints of deer, beaver, great blue heron, and occasionally alligator and wild turkey.

Yazoo routes

1. Satartia to Highway 61, 36 miles. Launching is difficult at both locations because of long carries and steep mud banks. Best access at Highway 61 is on the northwest side. There's also access on the north side of a railroad bridge half a mile west of Highway 61.

2. Highway 61 to Steele Bayou, 7 miles. From the river, turn north onto the bayou and paddle a short distance to a landing at County Road 465.

3. Steele Bayou to King's Point Ferry Road, 5 miles.

4. King's Point Ferry Road to Vicksburg, 5 miles. Take out at the foot of Clay Street on the waterfront.

Area outfitters

Quapaw Canoe Co., 291 Sunflower Ave., Clarksdale, MS 38614, phone 662-627-4070. Offers guided tours.

Area campgrounds

Designated campsites scattered throughout Delta National Forest (permit and fee required during hunting season), 662-873-6256.

High points

Sense of remoteness and adventure due to few access sites and portions of Delta National Forest.

Low points

Steep mud banks, difficult put-ins, industrial discharge on lower stretches.

Tips

Brush up on Civil War activities in the area to get a feel for the river's profound history.

Sunflower River

Although the Big Sunflower, like all Delta rivers, is a tributary of the Yazoo, in other ways it's an exception. For one thing, it was never impounded into a reservoir, though parts have been dredged and confined within levees. It starts in the Delta itself, not in the hills, originating at Long Lake between Friars Point and Coahoma—ironically, just a few miles from the Mississippi River into which its waters eventually flow some 200 river miles away. The Big Sunflower slides south through Clarksdale and meets Hushpuckena River, a juncture that the Corps of Engineers considers the head of navigation, or highest navigable point. The river swells a bit as it absorbs more waterways, such as Black, Burrell, Jones, and Porter Bayous, Quiver River, and Bogue Phalia. By Highway 14 east of Anguilla, it's a wide, muddy, currentless stream, seemingly of no interest to paddlers. But things change just south of there when the Sunflower enters the 60,000-acre Delta National Forest. From there to its confluence with the Little Sunflower River, the Big Sunflower fascinates. It doesn't gain a significant current or become free of mud, but it winds beneath awesome forest rich with wildlife.

When you drive along Highway 61 between Vicksburg and Greenville, it's hard to imagine any forest at all. That's not surprising considering only 5 percent of the Delta's original bottomland hardwoods remain. Then, out on the horizon, rising like an island in an ocean of cotton fields, stands the national forest. In places it's a jungle of giant, vine-draped trees rising out of black muck—one of the few hardwood forests remaining in the Delta and the only bottomland hardwood national forest in the nation. Some trees are more than three hundred years old in the 60-acre Green Ash Research Natural Area on Forest Service Road 717, the 40-acre overcup oak area on F.S. Road 706-I, and the 40-acre sweetgum area on F.S. 706. Green ash is pretty enough to be used as an ornamental, its leaves growing in ranks down the stem to an end leaf. Overcup oak, which has long, relatively narrow leaves with the distinctive oak pattern, gets its name from the fact that the acorn's cap almost completely encases the nut. Sweetgum is one of the most prolific trees in Mississippi, to the point that many people consider it a "trash tree"—rather unfairly, considering its colorful fall foliage. In the depression, children would cut the bark and let the sap ooze out, using it as a crude chewing gum when it became sticky. It's amazing to see this taken-for-granted tree grow to 5 feet in diameter and 150 feet tall in the natural area. There are also impressive trees in the 320-acre Cypress Bayou Botanical Area in the southeastern part of the forest, and a half-mile trail at Clark Lake leads to the largest tree in the forest, a cypress with a 13–14-foot diameter. Cypress, properly called bald cypress, is the quintessential swamp tree, quite at home in standing water with its flared buttresses and protruding "knees."

Miles of dirt-road trails, closed to all traffic except foot, horseback, and all-terrain vehicles, provide access throughout the national forest, much of which is subject to seasonal flooding. There are several greentree reservoirs, areas deliberately flooded in the winter and drained in the spring to provide waterfowl habitat. Designated primitive campsites are scattered across the national forest instead of at a central campground; permits and fees are required during hunting seasons. The national forest boasts two wildlife management areas (WMAs) managed for hunting by the state Department of Wildlife, Fisheries, and Parks. Other WMAs and national wildlife refuges (NWRs) lie scattered across the vicinity, including Panther Swamp NWR a few miles east of the national forest.

Delta National Forest's fine woods provide excellent hunting for squirrel, wild hog, deer, and raccoon, all of which thrive in hardwood forest. Don't be surprised at night to hear the bay of coon dogs. I like their music, but they can throw a start into you when they crank up in the middle of the night when you're asleep. However, there aren't enough hunters to keep up with the exploding coon population. Fur trappers once helped keep them in check, but the flagging market made most hang up their traps. Even hunters often let their prey go to run another day, though raccoon meat is as good as dark turkey meat when the glands, or "kernels," are removed from the joints and the meat is parboiled, then baked with sweet potatoes, onions, and red pepper. Raccoons are adorable animals, mind you, and far be it from me to advocate their consumption. They have hands almost like humans, a bearlike playfulness, and the curiosity of a cat. They like to follow streams, grab at shiny objects, explore crossing logs, and poke their noses into holes in the bank. Once, as an experiment, I put a can of apple wine at a raccoon watering hole. Next morning the wine was gone and the coon tracks looked suspiciously erratic. Coons eat everything from muscadines to minnows. In their wanderings they're prone to chance upon the ground nests of wild turkeys and dine on eggs or poults. That's fine when the wildlife is in a natural state of balance, but there are no longer big predators like red wolves and Florida panthers keeping raccoon numbers down, though non-native coyotes help. When humans fail to fill the big-predator niche, the coons gobble too many eggs, and the turkey population suffers, which happened dramatically across the state in the 1980s and 1990s. Coon hunting can be dangerous for the dogs in this area, what with poisonous snakes, alligators, and wild hogs.

By day you may see men on horseback pursuing Russian boar. Many hunters chase them with hounds, and when the hog is bayed, a "catch dog" like a bulldog holds it until the hunters either shoot it or tie it up for transport and release elsewhere. The boar is an impressive animal. Its head is long and narrow, adorned with inches-long tusks. Its bristles stand thick and tough. Though it may weigh several hundred pounds, it's surprisingly fast and nimble. Wild hogs have a tremendous sense of smell, making them hard to sneak up on. I was standing in the woods by the Big Sunflower when I heard a scuffling noise and saw a trio on a morning trot. The lead sow froze, sensing me, but I didn't move so they wandered on. The hogs may look fierce, but their reputation for aggressiveness is reportedly overrated. Hunters tell me that if a hog races at a person, it's usually just trying to flee, not attack; step aside and the hog will barrel past. One old-timer told me, with a straight face, to leap straight up with your legs spread wide and let the hog run underneath. Fortunately, hogs usually run the other direction.

Black bears sometimes wander through the national forest; maybe they're descendants of the ones Theodore Roosevelt hunted near here in 1902. Roosevelt's zealous guide captured a bear and tied it to a tree for the president to shoot, but being a sportsman he declined. The story, illustrated by a cartoonist, appeared in national newspapers, and a canny toy maker created the first Teddy bears. The Onward Store at the town of Onward on Highway 61 south of Rolling Fork tells the story of the hunt with photos and memorabilia.

About the same time Roosevelt was chasing bears, archaeologists were inventorying the numerous Indian mounds in the area, including one at Spanish Fort near the west bank of the Big Sunflower inside the national forest and others around the towns of Panther Burn, Anguilla, Holly Bluff, Cary, and Rolling Fork. One mound known as Mount Helena, topped by a handsome old mansion a couple miles northeast of Rolling Fork, is visible from Highway 61. The Native American mound-building culture dates back thousands of years. When European explorers arrived, the area was home to Yazoo, Koroa, Tioux, and Tunica tribes, who raised impressively tall stands of corn and sunflowers in the rich Delta soil—hence the name Sunflower River.

It's about 7 river miles from the boat ramp at Highway 14 east of Anguilla to the boundaries of the national forest. With a road running along the west bank, only a thin border of trees, if any, and no current, this stretch is not exactly charming. However, pay attention and you may spot alligators. I saw an 8-footer here, and specimens as long as 14 feet have been spotted on the river. When the river reaches the national forest, it appears to fork. The channel to the left is actually Holly Bluff Cutoff, a 6.5-mile-long man-made canal that rejoins the river just west of the town of Holly Bluff. The main river veers right at the fork and meanders along the western side of the national forest. At last, with looming trees and no traffic or camps, the peaceful solace of the Big Sunflower begins to emerge. There's even a hint of a current. Along the banks you'll see huge trees, such as a double-trunked sycamore 6 feet thick at the base.

The Little Sunflower gets its start by branching off the Big Sunflower to the right about 14 miles below Highway 14. In high water, it conceivably could provide an alternate route, since it leads past Highway 16 half a mile away and a boat ramp at Dummy Line Road 16 miles away. However, in lower water the upper Little Sunflower has ankle-deep water and knee-deep mud, plus its bed is so narrow that a fallen tree would pose problems. The Big Sunflower, meanwhile, swings southeast and curves back into the national forest. Highway 16 runs along the west bank—with a boat ramp about 5 miles west of Holly Bluff—as the river winds through 5 miles of national forest and emerges into farmland.

For the next 12 miles the river is flanked by fields. In October that can almost be pleasant as trucks pulling cotton wagons bump past on streamside roads and across the Highway 16 bridge, leaving stray cotton puffs to drift down like snow.

The river skirts the town of Holly Bluff and makes a sharp turn to the southwest, with narrow Lake George branching off to the east to form the southern boundary of Panther Swamp National Wildlife Refuge. About 4 miles downriver, national forest resumes on the right bank for 2.5 miles, then more private land for 4 miles until the river forks again. Six-Mile Cutoff leads off to the right, running straight for 2 miles until the Little Sunflower comes in on the right. As you pass under a bridge near the start of the cutoff, you may see local kids shooting turtles and gar with .22-caliber rifles. It's a 5.5-mile paddle up the Little Sunflower to the boat ramp at Dummy Line Road. The lower Little Sunflower is a quiet, curving, currentless passage through oak bluffs, joined on the right by narrow Six-Mile Bayou, which allows some exploration.

In all, the Big and Little Sunflower offer 45 miles of paddling from Highway 14 around to Dummy Line Road. The 16 miles between boat ramps on Highways 14 and 16 provide a long day trip. To avoid shuttling, paddlers can launch at put-ins like Dummy Line Road or Highway 16 and explore in either direction, returning to the starting point. Since there's normally little current, the rivers can be paddled up almost as easily as down.

The Delta can make for tricky navigation at times. The landscape is stitched with a bewildering embroidery of cutoffs, drainage ditches, auxiliary channels, creeks, and bayous. Navigation isn't as big an issue in summer and fall when many of the side bayous are too low to paddle. Winter high water is prime-time for exploring the bayous and lakes off the main river or even paddling into flooded forest. Visibility is better then too since undergrowth has died back. The U.S. Forest Service map of Delta National Forest is sufficient for river floating, while U.S. Geological Survey quadrangle maps give more details for backcountry peregrinations. Relevant maps are Rolling Fork East, Red Rock, and Valley Park.

Except in coldest weather, campers should bring not only insect repellent but mosquito coils or citronella candles since mosquitoes can get fierce at night. Also pack plenty of drinking water since there's no fresh water to be found along the river. A sturdy groundcloth will protect the tent floor against clinging mud. The mud along the Big Sunflower is memorable, a boot-sucking sludge whose official name is alligator dowling but that is locally known as blue gumbo since it turns a bluish gray when wet. Knee-high rubber boots are a must; hip boots wouldn't be a bad idea. A stray board in the canoe can serve as a walkway across the deepest muck at the water's edge. Lacking that, use logs, and be careful where you step since some areas are deeper than others.

Greg Bond of Memphis hoists a bluecat from the Big Sunflower River.

The water is too muddy for bass fishing, but it's fine for catfish and even white perch at times. Some trotline fishermen cut chunks of buffalo fish for bait and soak them in commercial catfish lure. We used yo-yos baited with shrimp to catch 5-pound bluecats, perfect when filleted, battered in stone-ground yellow cornmeal, deep-fried in peanut oil, and eaten with Louisiana hot sauce and slices of fresh sweet onion.

The Big Sunflower provides the best glimpse we have into the type of woods described in William Faulkner's "The Bear." Among Delta rivers, it has probably been the least affected by humans. But that is changing now that the Corps of Engineers is conducting a long-planned flood-control project that calls for massive dredging along the river and its tributaries, a drainage area encompassing 4,200 square miles. The affected area includes the lower 75.6 miles of the Big Sunflower, Holly Bluff Cutoff, the entire Little Sunflower, and 33 miles of tributaries. A host of conservation groups and the U.S. Fish and Wildlife Service opposed the project, scheduled for completion in 2018. In addition to the fact that many believe the Delta landscape has been scarred enough, biologists discovered that the Big Sunflower is one of the richest mussel beds in the world. One of the larger beds lies at the upper end of Holly Bluff Cutoff. The presence of mussels in the muddy river came as a pleasant surprise to biologists since the crustaceans generally prefer clear, running water. Indeed, they are considered an index of the health of an ecosystem.

Mussels are fascinating creatures. Like the running joke, "Clams got feet!" in the *B.C.* comic strip, mussels really do have feet, and they use them, leaving trails in the muck where they "walk." When danger approaches, the strip of grayish white flesh quickly slides up out of sight, like a turtle withdrawing into its shell. You can follow a trail in the silt, plunge your hand in and pull out a live mussel. And you can tell a mussel's age by the number of ridges on the shell, like rings in a tree. Typical mussels may be four or five years old, but they can live to be sixty. Females can be identified by their broad posteriors. After breeding, they give birth to a sackful of baby mussels which clings to mama's shell until a fish scoops it up. The tiny shells then lodge in the fish's gills until they reach a certain size, when they drop off and continue to grow. Certain species of mussel require certain species of host fish to mature. To entice those fish, the sacks of baby mussels sometimes resemble baitfish. Mussels' names are nearly as wondrous as the creatures themselves: elephant ear, southern fatmucket, southern pocket-book, little spectaclecase, Gulf pigtoe, Mississippi pigtoe, pistolgrip, purple pimpleback, southern rainbow, rayed creekshell, hickorynut, to name a few. At a glance, mussels look alike—brownish, chunky things. Up close, they are jewels. The shells, which are mainly calcium carbonate, are darkly lustrous. Mussel flesh was once eaten by Native Americans, and still feeds creatures like raccoons, otters, and ducks. Alas, mussels aren't doing well in North America, because of dams, pollution, and competing alien species. The tiny Asiatic clam—not a true mussel—is an import that apparently migrated from ship's hulls up American rivers. Far worse are zebra mussels. They have spread from the Great Lakes down the Mississippi River, where they are clogging up municipal water pipes and smothering native mussels. Some 43 percent of North America's three hundred freshwater mussel species are extinct or on the way. The Corps plans to avoid some of the beds and create new ones as mitigation.

Big Sunflower routes

1. Boat ramp at Highway 14 east of Anguilla to ramp on Highway 16 west of Holly Bluff, 16 miles.
2. Highway 16 boat ramp to ramp at Dummy Line Road on Little

Sunflower River (via Six-Mile Cutoff), 29 miles.

Outfitters

Quapaw Canoe Co., 291 Sunflower Ave., Clarksdale, MS 38614, phone 662-627-4070. Offers guided tours.

Area campgrounds

Designated campsites scattered throughout Delta National Forest (permit and fee required during hunting season), 662-873-6256.

High points

Massive trees, wild hogs, a landscape right out of Faulkner's "The Bear."

The Yalobusha River borders Malmaison Wildlife Management Area.

Low points

Mud, mosquitoes, little or no current.

Tips

Wear knee-high rubber boots, bring mosquito coils or citronella candles and plenty of drinking water.

Yalobusha River

Despite its history of channelizing and damming rivers and replacing forests with farm fields, the Mississippi Delta offers some pleasant surprises, in places anyway. The Yalobusha River is a case in point. In 1953 the river was channelized from the dam at Grenada Lake to the mouth at Greenwood, a distance of 63 miles. Over several decades the river regained its meanders, so it was dredged again, but this time only from Avalon down. That left nearly 40 miles of good paddling from the dam to Avalon, including a stretch that runs through Malmaison Wildlife Management Area west of Grenada.

The highest launch point is the boat ramp below the dam; there's another ramp 2 miles downstream south of Highway 332 in Grenada. The river passes under I-55 some 3 miles later on the 16-mile segment from Grenada to a ramp at Highway 8 northwest of Holcomb—a town whose Miss Teen U.S.A. winner said her favorite hobby was hand-grabbling for catfish. Holcomb also has a convenience store that is a popular spot to grab biscuits and sausage, honey buns, and coffee in the morning. About 3 miles below Highway 8 the river enters 9,483-acre Malmaison WMA.

Mississippi State University fisheries professor Don Jackson calls the Yalobusha "one of Mississippi's treasures." He should know. He has done research on all the Delta rivers as well as other state waterways. Indeed, Dr. Jackson has worked in wild places the world over, and he claims the Delta tops them all—if we'll only give it a chance. If you float the Yalobusha, particularly through Malmaison, it's easy to understand his enthusiasm. The banks are lined with forests of sycamore, birch, maple, and willow. Beavers den in the banks and swim past carrying bright peeled sticks like kids sucking on candy canes. Overhead, red-tailed hawks, vultures, Mississippi kites, and great blue herons soar on thermal currents. In late winter, migratory waterfowl arrive like feather tornadoes. The Yalobusha has a good current, and during low water passes some fine sandbars. Periodic releases from the reservoir partially submerge them but without muddying the water excessively. During late winter and spring the river may get out of its banks, yet it's canoeable at virtually any level. Even in flood the river is fairly docile after it tops the banks and spreads out. Crappie school in those backwaters, while the river itself provides prime catfish habitat. Yalobusha is a Native American word for "tadpole place," suggesting an abundance of prey for game fish. Flathead catfish eat only live prey, so trotline fishermen use bait such as minnows or sunfish. Cut bait will suffice for bluecats and channel cats, which eat nearly anything. Use heavy tackle, such as 4-aught or better hooks and stout line, since you may haul in a 30–50-pounder.

Malmaison WMA has a boat ramp on the left bank 10 miles below Highway 8. Located in cotton country off Highway 7 southwest of Holcomb, the refuge has big woods, primitive campsites, a 3-mile trail, greentree reservoirs, and wildlife galore. The campsites are mere clearings among tall hardwood trees, just right for roughing it; a free permit is required from headquarters just off Highway 7. The hiking trail, created by the Greenwood Civic Club, goes uphill from the headquarters parking lot, where hills meet Delta flatland. The trail winds through land once owned by nineteenth-century mixed-blood Choctaw chief Greenwood LeFlore. Hunting is best for waterfowl, thanks to the green-tree reservoirs flooded in winter. But there are also raccoons, squirrels, wild turkeys, deer, rabbits—and coyotes, whose eerie howls echo through the woods at night.

It's 7 miles from the Malmaison ramp to County Road 112 west of Highway 7—about half that distance lies within the WMA—and 2.5 miles from there to County Road 136. Below there the river has been channelized by the Corps of Engineers, and the banks form a straight levee topped by young willows. Channelization straightens out natural curves where water slows and fish thrive, cuts back on flooding that enhances crop production, and removes logs and brush where aquatic insects shelter and feed fish. Yet Delta rivers are resilient. Dr. Jackson has found that, even when channelized, they cut new bends and regain fish populations within twenty-five years. Unfortunately, they don't often get that chance.

The Yalobusha continues about 8 miles to its juncture with the Tallahatchie, where the Yazoo is born, and another couple of miles to a ramp at Grand Boulevard in Greenwood.

Yalobusha routes

1. Boat ramp below Grenada Lake dam to ramp in town, 2 miles.
2. Town boat ramp to ramp at Highway 8, 16 miles.
3. Highway 8 to Malmaison Wildlife Management Area ramp, 10 miles. The WMA ramp is located at the end of Malmaison Road west of Highway 7 south of Holcomb.
4. Malmaison to County Road 112 west of Highway 7, 7 miles.
5. County Road 112 to County Road 136 west of Highway 7, 2.5 miles. Below C.R. 136 the river has been channelized by the Corps of Engineers.
6. C.R. 136 to ramp at Grand Boulevard in Greenwood, 10 miles. The Yalobusha joins the Tallahatchie 8 miles below C.R. 136 to form the Yazoo.

Area campgrounds

Malmaison Wildlife Management Area, 662-453-5409, free primitive camping west of Highway 7, permit required.
Hugh White State Park, Grenada, 662-226-5911.

High points

Lots of woods, thanks largely to Malmaison Wildlife Management Area.

Low points

Reservoir upstream and dredged channel downstream belie the sense of wildness.

Tips

Spend some time exploring Malmaison WMA.

Little Tallahatchie River

While the Little Tallahatchie River offers some attractions to paddlers, it also illustrates problems common to Delta rivers. Starting in northeast Mississippi between New Albany and Ripley, Little Tallahatchie runs in straight, channelized segments all the way to Sardis Lake. Below Sardis it enjoys a measure of meandering freedom before channelization resumes with long ditches like the Panola Quitman Floodway and McIvor Canal.

Discussions are under way about restoring flow to the discarded old river channel for some 20 miles above the reservoir, which could be a good place to paddle. For now, though, the main canoeing stretch is from Sardis to Highway 51, starting at beautiful Lower Sardis Lake near Sleepy Bend campground. This scenic campground borders the small lake, where fishing is good for just about everything, and makes a good base camp for exploring the Little Tallahatchie. A low-head dam blocks boat traffic just below the river outlet, so paddlers should launch at a ramp at the end of the gravel road just west of the Sleepy Bend campground. Low-water dams may look easily runnable, but they're hazardous, due to powerful hydraulics. More than one experienced paddler has lost his life in such places. From the put-in it's 6 miles to Belmont Road and 5.5 more to

Highway 51. With a good current, the 11.5-mile stretch makes an easy day float. But there's little shade on this wide river, so bring protection such as a wide-brimmed hat and sunscreen.

Unlike most Delta rivers, the Little Tallahatchie sports some gravel bars; Tallahatchie is a Native American word for "river of rocks." It also has some sandbars, so the water tends to be dingy rather than muddy. It would be clearer if landowners left more buffer zones of woods to prevent siltation. Unfortunately, there are miles of farm fields and cutovers clear to the bank, and the destructive effects are obvious to anybody on the river. Pull up under a bank and listen. You may soon hear the sound of dirt clods with no tree roots to hold them intact. Even when there are trees, they're rarely more than a thin line, though there is a pine plantation or two. The Tallahatchie illustrates why conservation organizations nationwide are begging for restoration of wetlands. The rate of wetland loss in the Southeast is among the highest in the nation. Wetlands serve as natural sponges that store floodwater and release it slowly, filtering pollutants such as farm chemicals in the process. Bottomland woods also slow runoff and curtail erosion. Considering how much the Tallahatchie has suffered from farming, logging, and Corps of Engineers projects, it's a wonder there's any wildlife at all. But, happily, its shores are typically packed with tracks. On one thin strip of mud and sand, backed by a willow thicket, I saw the parallel marks of deer, Valentine-shaped hoofs of wild hogs along with their rootings, handlike prints of raccoons, webbed hind paws of beaver, and coyote pugs and droppings. In the river, fish slap the water. The deep, cloudy water is prime catfish habitat, while the gravel bars provide spawning grounds for bass. This is a good still-fishing river; tie up in a bend or near a shady bank and bounce a plastic worm on the bottom for bass or a live worm for catfish.

Below Highway 51, the river is crisscrossed by canals en route to its junction with Coldwater River just above Highway 332 near Marks. There the Little Tallahatchie becomes the Tallahatchie, which goes on to join the Yalobusha River just above Greenwood to form the Yazoo.

Little Tallahatchie routes

1. Lower Lake to Belmont Road, 6 miles. Launch at the boat ramp at the end of the gravel road just west of Sleepy Bend campground. Belmont Road intersects River Road on the north side of the river east of I-55.

2. Belmont Road to Highway 51, 5.5 miles. At Highway 51 you can pull under the bridge on the northwest side, or if water levels are sufficient, paddle up a canal on the southeast side of the bridge, taking care to avoid submerged iron posts at the mouth of the canal.

Area campgrounds

John W. Kyle State Park, Sardis, 662-487-1345. The park's Sleepy Bend campground is located at Lower Lake just east of the put-in.

High points

Gravel bed and current below Sardis dam.

Low points

Long stretches of farm fields with no woodland buffer; sounds of traffic, farm machinery, construction equipment, and trains.

Tips

Camp at Sleepy Bend campground; you can float the river and also explore placid Lower Lake.

Others

There are several other rivers in the Mississippi River drainage that aren't particularly canoeable, at least in the state, but bear mentioning: the Hatchie, Wolf, Coldwater, Amite, and Tangipahoa. The Hatchie and Wolf flow north into Tennessee, where they become excellent canoeing rivers. The Coldwater is a typical problem-plagued Delta stream that nevertheless has some paddling possibilities. The Amite and Tangipahoa, located in southwest Mississippi, aren't truly tributaries of the Mississippi; rather, they empty into Louisiana lakes that apparently were once part of the Mississippi's channel: Maurepas and Ponchartrain, respectively. For the sake of convenience we'll include them here. Like the Wolf and the Hatchie, they don't reach their paddling potential until they leave the state.

Wolf

The Wolf heads up in Holly Springs National Forest northwest of Ripley, Mississippi. It runs west and then north into Tennessee near Michigan City, turning west toward Memphis. In Mississippi it's possible to float the 10 miles from Highway 72 to Highway 7 at Michigan City and another 10 miles from Michigan City to Yeager Road at LaGrange, Tennessee, provided you're prepared for numerous logjams and the prospects of getting lost in the cypress swamp. U.S.G.S. quad maps Lamar and Canaan will help. On the 14-mile stretch between LaGrange and Bateman Road 2 miles east of Moscow, Tennessee, the Wolf passes through the 4,000-acre Ghost River State Natural Area, a cypress swamp where the river spreads out and markers on trees show the way through. On the 16-mile stretch from Moscow to Rossville, which is subject to logjams, I encountered more snakes than I've ever seen in one area, mostly nonpoisonous water snakes. Obstructions thin out on the 8 miles from Highway 194 just north of Rossville to Highway 196 at Piperton, an excellent day float. The Wolf flows surprisingly fast, its speed in part the result of a 1960s Corps of Engineer channelization project farther downstream that shortened the river a good 15 miles. As an effect of the increased current, erosion is siphoning off the banks. Still, the Wolf is one of the few west Tennessee streams running naturally for most of its length, and it provides a refreshing corridor of forest sandwiched between the ever-expanding subdivisions of Memphis and environs. Outfitters include Ghost River Canoe Rentals (901-877-9954), Wolf River Canoe Rentals (901-465-2975), and A.J.'s Canoe Rentals (901-753-6426).

Hatchie

The Hatchie is born between New Albany and Booneville, crossing into Tennessee at the Hardeman-McNairy county line. It wobbles northwest toward Brownsville, then swings west to the Mississippi River near Covington. The Hatchie is even less tampered-with than the Wolf, remarkable compared with the straight-line channelized routes of so many west Tennessee streams. One of the best floats on the Hatchie is the 12 miles from Highway 76 to Highway 70 near Brownsville. It passes through the 11,556-acre Hatchie National Wildlife Refuge (901-772-0501), which lines the river for 24 miles. In its final miles the Hatchie also goes through the 7,394-acre Lower Hatchie River National Wildlife Refuge (901-287-0650), which borders both the Hatchie and the Mississippi.

Coldwater

The Coldwater faces the usual Delta problems of channelization and agriculture. One possible float is a 12-mile stretch above Arkabutla Reservoir from Holly Springs Road between Cockrum and Hernando to Highway 51. The first couple miles are a wide, channelized ditch; the river narrows as it twists and turns, then enters flooded dead forest before crossing under I-55 a couple miles above Highway 51, where there's a ramp on the northwest side. Logjams are likely on this stretch. Below the reservoir, an easily accessible stretch is the 6 miles from Highways 3 and 4, which run together just west of Savage, to the bridge at Sarah just west of Highway 3. Characteristically for the lower Coldwater, this portion has muddy water and steep mud banks lined with thin woods and levee roads and backed by farm fields. Water levels vary greatly according to the amount released from the reservoir. The Coldwater is a good channel cat river, and soap works well as bait. Get into the logjammed sections to avoid competition from motorboat fishermen.

Amite

The Amite (a corruption of the French word for "friend," describing the native inhabitants) River of southwest Mississippi is a classic "local creek." I've floated it countless times but wouldn't recommend it to anyone since there's probably one logjam per 50 yards. The river's two forks run south through Amite County, converging at the Louisiana line, after which the river meanders south to Lake Maurepas. There are a number of possible trips if you can stand the toil. On the east fork, float 5 miles from rural Mary Wall Road (north of Bean Road, which runs west from Mississippi 568 to Louisiana 1044) to Lindsey Bridge Road (at the south end of Greensburg Road, which runs south from Highway 584 in Liberty); this stretch is fairly open since local residents with camps on the banks keep the worst logjams cleared out. Below Lindsey Bridge it's 4 miles to the state line, another mile or so to the juncture of the forks, and 5.5 more to Louisiana 432 near Felixville. Unfortunately, access to the bridge at 432 is now fenced off, a shame since the best Amite River float used to be the 9 miles from Louisiana 432 to Louisiana 10 east of Clinton. That leaves a 15-mile stretch between

Louisiana Highways 10 and 37, a less-than-perfect float since gravel mines are plentiful and the river is wide and shallow. Meanwhile, on the west fork you can float 5 miles from Highway 24 west of Liberty to Highway 48 south of town, with roughly half that distance bordering the beautiful Ethel Stratton Vance Natural Area on the east bank, which has a campground (601-657-8078). Continue 10 miles to Lower Centreville Road and 4 more to Powell Road; both roads run east from Highway 569. From there it's 3 miles to the state line.

Tangipahoa

The Tangipahoa (Native American for "cornstalk gatherers") starts northwest of McComb and is impounded at 700-acre Lake Tangipahoa in Percy Quin State Park. From there it crosses I-55 and Highway 51 as it journeys southeast to Chatawa, then roughly parallels Highway 51 en route to Louisiana's Lake Pontchartrain. At this writing, Louisiana state advisories are posted against swimming due to bacterial pollution from dairy farms, camps, and municipal lagoons. Nevertheless, the river offers fine vistas and good paddling once the obstructions clear out. Mississippi's portion of the Tangipahoa is every bit as rugged as the Amite when it comes to logjams. Even so, local fishermen tackle the 5 miles from Chatawa to Osyka-Progress Road east of Osyka, preferably when the water is high enough to slide their boats over the logs. To launch at Chatawa, go east from Highway 51 to the railroad crossing just west of the river, then follow the railroad's gravel access road south to a launching site. Below Osyka it's 3.5 miles to Louisiana 1054 at Greenlaw, 5 more to Louisiana 38 east of Kentwood, and another 6.5 to Louisiana 440 east of Tangipahoa, Louisiana, where logjams finally disappear. The 13-mile stretch from Tangipahoa to Louisiana 16 east of Amite makes a delightful day trip, and since it's split two-thirds of the way down by Highway 10, it can be broken into shorter segments.

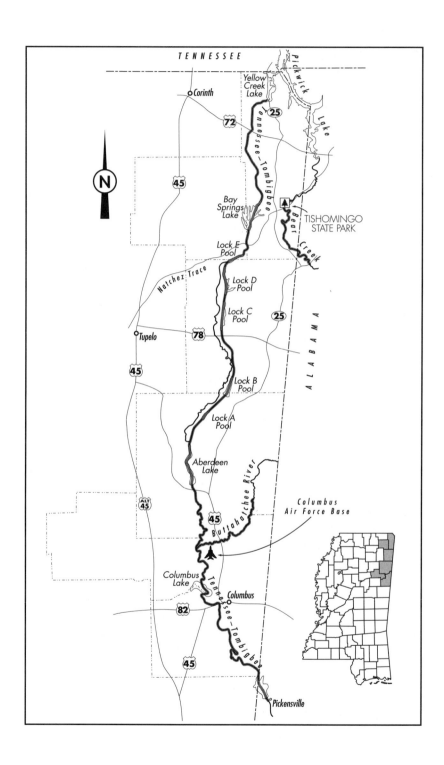

TENNESSEE

Corinth

Yellow
Creek
Lake

Pickwick Lake

72

25

Tennessee-Tombigbee

Bay
Springs
Lake

TISHOMINGO
STATE PARK

Bear Creek

Lock E
Pool

N

45

Natchez Trace

Lock D
Pool

Lock C
Pool

25

ALABAMA

Tupelo

78

45

Lock B
Pool

Lock A
Pool

Aberdeen
Lake

Buttahatchee River

Columbus
Air Force Base

ALT
45

45

Columbus
Lake

Tennessee-Tombigbee

Columbus

82

45

Pickensville

4. Northeast Mississippi

Tennessee-Tombigbee Waterway

The Tennessee-Tombigbee Waterway, which links the Tennessee and Tombigbee Rivers in northeast Mississippi, has no current, is frequented by barges and motorboats, and often presents nothing more than a rock-lined canal. But it's one of the major waterways in the South, if not the nation, and it passes through some superb wildlife areas. All in all, it's definitely worth considering for paddlers willing to set aside their usual criteria and try something different.

Mississippi can claim half of the Tenn-Tom, which extends from Pickwick Lake to Demopolis, Alabama. The 234-mile series of canals, lakes, and river is home to bald eagles and loons, to walleye and smallmouth bass, all of which are more typically associated with the Far North than the Deep South. It's chockful of hunting, fishing, camping, and other recreation areas. Yet it's plagued by erosion, and the projected barge traffic for which it was largely built never met expectations.

The idea of connecting the Tennessee and Tombigbee Rivers was first studied during the administration of President Ulysses S. Grant. A look at a map shows why. The westbound Tennessee River swings down into Alabama and Mississippi before swooping north toward the Ohio River. It comes temptingly close to the Tombigbee River, which heads up in northeast Mississippi and winds southeast to the Gulf of Mexico at Mobile, Alabama. Joining them would cut off up to 800 miles for boat traffic accustomed to following the Tennessee, Ohio, and Mississippi Rivers to get to the Gulf.

Congress authorized the project in 1946, and after numerous studies and hearings, work began in 1972. Completed in 1984, the waterway cost $1.8 billion in tax dollars to build. Neither the Suez nor the Panama Canal can match the Tenn-Tom when it comes to earthwork. Builders moved more than 307 million cubic yards of dirt, nearly a third more than for the Panama Canal. The 150 million cubic yards of earth from the Divide Cut alone—the canal across the topographic divide between the two river valleys—exceeded Suez Canal excavations. Ten locks drop the water level 341 feet between Pickwick and Demopolis.

This feat of engineering is based on centuries-old principles. Man-made canals date to ancient times and flourished during the 1700s and 1800s, though most have since closed as roads and railroads sprang up. Locks were in use at least as early as the 1400s, when artist and inventor Leonardo da Vinci built six in the canals of Milan, Italy. The Tenn-Tom locks are based on the same hydraulic principles that George Washington used in the C&O Canal. A standard 110-by-600-foot chamber is drained from the bottom, rather like pulling the plug out of a bathtub. It takes about ten minutes for millions of gallons of water to refill it from the upper end via gravity feed. At 84 feet, Bay Springs Lake has the highest of the Tenn-Tom's locks and the third highest east of the Mississippi River. Others on the waterway range from 25 to 30 feet. The locking process is safe and easy for paddlers, though sometimes intimidating to the uninitiated.

All this hasn't proved enough to lure major barge traffic. Three or four towboats a day are a typical sight. But barges are the most common lock-users and remain cost-efficient for products like logs, wood chips, and coal. A barge can carry freight twice as far as a train and six times as far as a truck on the same amount of fuel. A typical eight-barge tow transports as much freight as 120 rail cars or 480 eighteen-wheelers.

If barges aren't taking full advantage of the waterway, recreational craft are. Commonly seen vessels include personal watercraft, bass boats, small sailboats, houseboats, and yachts. Even cruise ships and Mississippi River passenger boats have traveled the waterway. Fall is snowbird season, when yachters bring their vessels down the waterway bound for Florida or beyond. Then flat-bottom boats come out as hunters take advantage of miles of wildlife management area, much of it accessible only by boat. In early spring come the fishermen; then the snowbirds return. Recreation season hits full swing from Memorial Day to Labor Day weekends. The hordes of motorboats can be mildly irritating to a canoer, but they become obnoxious or dangerous when their operators don't bother to

Yachts file out of a lock on Tennessee-Tombigbee Waterway.

learn the rules of the road—like the houseboat that pulled out of a cove right in front of us as we canoed down the main channel, forcing us to brake, or the speedboater who hydroplaned past while we were on the bank, sloshing water into the canoe. Fortunately such folks are rare.

Though the waterway is a boon for motorboaters, those same vessels aggravate erosion when their wakes eat away at sandy-loam banks. Officials have had to install bulkheads or riprap at several areas to keep banks from caving in. A 77-page report issued in 1996 by the U.S. Fish and Wildlife Service cites significant erosion problems. In particular, the report details headcutting—erosion eating its way upstream on the Tombigbee River and its tributaries. "The conditions seen on these streams included: caving banks, fallen or leaning vegetation, vegetation-clogged channels, waterfalls and rapids, scoured bridge pilings, channel deepening, and a general straightening of channels by cutting off of meanders," the report said. Gravel mining on tributaries like Buttahatchee worsens the situation.

To compensate for such problems, the Corps of Engineers set aside 80,000 acres along the waterway and another 88,000 acres elsewhere in Mississippi and Alabama. The Corps built some $50 million in first-class recreational facilities and campgrounds. There are boat ramps galore. With the exception of the Divide

Cut, access is never a problem on the Tenn-Tom, which makes options unlimited for exploring the waterway.

Within a few years after construction was completed, *Sports Afield* magazine rated the Tenn-Tom one of the top ten bass fishing spots in the nation. Crappie and bream fishing are also excellent. Jugfishing and tightlining for catfish are common. Even smallmouth bass and walleye, relatively scarce in Mississippi, can be found. Walleye fishing is restricted to certain areas, and smallmouth have minimum legal size limits, so check current state regulations before trying. The state record walleye tops 9 pounds, but 2-pounders are more common. Smallmouth bass rarely get farther south than Bay Springs. They'll exceed 7 pounds but typically go 2 or 3. Standard bass lures such as spinners and crankbaits work for both species.

Wildlife abounds along the waterway. Deer splash across shallow inlets. Geese raise a ruckus like a dog kennel with a loose cat. Bald eagles soar in silent majesty. The Tishomingo County Tourism Council even sponsors an eagle-watching boat tour. Rabbit hunting is popular in brushy areas along the levees, and squirrels are plentiful in the massive hardwood forests. The Tenn-Tom draws abundant waterfowl, and the Mississippi Department of Wildlife, Fisheries, and Parks has stocked wildlife management areas with deer and turkeys. Special Corps regulations apply for hunting along the waterway. For details call 662-327-2142.

The Tenn-Tom can be paddled straight through, in segments, or explored piecemeal from base camps. Unfortunately, most Tenn-Tom campgrounds are designed for drive-in visitors, not long-distance paddlers. Technically you're only supposed to camp in designated camping areas, but that's not always feasible since it's up to 40 miles between campgrounds, which are sometimes a mile off the main channel. Then you must land at a ramp, hike to the office to check in and pay, and haul your gear to a campsite. Compare that with finding a secluded spot and camping in the woods overlooking the water, which is technically illegal. If paddling picks up on the waterway, hopefully the Corps will make some sort of accommodations.

The waterway starts in the north at Yellow Creek, an arm of Pickwick Lake. From there to Columbus is 115 miles, and another 25 miles to the Alabama line. Goat Island Recreation Area, a privately owned park off Highway 25, provides a camping area and launch spot on Yellow Creek. For base camps not on the waterway, J. P. Coleman State Park lies a few miles to the east on Indian Creek, while Pickwick Landing State Park is just over the line in Tennessee, off Highway 57. Or just launch at Scruggs Bridge Boat Ramp where Highway 25 crosses the waterway.

Yellow Creek, which is actually a lake, is worth exploring. Its rocky bluffs are draped with forest that shows gorgeous colors in the fall. But the wind can be stiff on the open water. Weight such as camping gear helps stabilize the boat, and paddlers should try to angle into the waves. If you meet them head-on, water tends to slosh in. Broadside is the most precarious position since a big, wind-driven wave can swamp or even roll a canoe. It's helpful to stay on the lee side of the lake as much as possible, paddling from one headland to the next.

At the south end of the lake, the waterway narrows into the Divide Cut, a 280-foot-wide, 12-foot-deep, 23-mile-long canal through the divide between the two river valleys. With high levees lined with rock—the gray rocks known as riprap or revetment, used to prevent erosion—the cut offers nowhere to take a boat out of the water. And the long, straight channel funnels the wind, usually out of the south. All of this makes the Divide Cut the least enjoyable portion for paddlers. On the plus side, the Corps has built fishing areas along the cut in the form of concrete spillways where tributaries entered the canal. Fish, including smallmouth bass, tend to gather beneath the cascading water.

Posts mark each mile along the waterway, which is convenient for monitoring your pace but can be irritating if you get obsessed with it. Still, I was pleasantly surprised to note that my Old Town Canadienne made 3 miles per hour against a fierce headwind. I had been warned (by nonpaddlers) that barge wakes would blast a canoe out of the water. Not so. Barges on the waterway throw only a gently rolling swell, unlike on the Mississippi River where they confront a rushing current to produce dangerous turbulence. Since the Tenn-Tom is free of current, there is little water resistance against the giant steel hulls. Its narrower channel and locks also limit the number of barges towboats can push. While I understand how barges can seem troublesome to paddlers, I confess to a fondness for the big riverboats. My father worked for years as a radio operator on Mississippi River dredgeboats, and he used to take me out on them when I was a boy. The smell of grease and iron, the grumble of engines, all conjure a sense of tradition stretching back to the days of Mark Twain.

There are some interesting sites along the Divide Cut, but they're inaccessible from the steep-banked, rock-lined waterway. Rather, they can be checked out from the road later. Holcut Memorial Overlook on the east side marks the site of a community that was displaced by waterway construction. A short distance away, Divide Overlook Area stands at the crest between the two drainage systems. Both places, located off Highway 364, provide sweeping views of the countryside.

At mile marker 421, the Divide Cut opens out onto Bay Springs Lake, one of the most beautiful spots on the waterway. The beach-rimmed, piney-woods lake sprawls 9 miles long and less than a mile wide, with countless coves big and small. While heavily used on summer weekends, at off times such as an autumn weekday the lake may be virtually deserted. This is the kind of place to make a base camp and spend days boating, fishing, hunting, or swaying in a hammock with a good book. Piney Grove Campground on the west bank even offers primitive campsites on an island close to shore, by far the most canoe-friendly campground on the waterway. There are also three boat ramps on the east side of Bay Springs, four on the west, six recreation areas, two picnic areas, a marina, beach, and visitor's center. At the north end of the lake, the Crow's Neck Environmental Education Center—funded by Itawamba and Northeast Community Colleges, University of Mississippi, and Mississippi State University—provides environmental courses for kindergarten through high school students, ranging from a day to a week.

The Bay Springs lock looks imposing but is simple even for a canoe. Just wait in the designated area outside the lock until the signal light turns green. Yachters communicate via radio with the lock operator, who also has a loudspeaker through which he can instruct you. When you've got the go-ahead, paddle into the big concrete chamber and loop a loose piece of rope around one of the floating buoys in the wall, holding one end in each hand. Don't tie it; you should be able to release it immediately if needed. Your partner can use a paddle to keep the hull from scraping the concrete. Massive yachts may join you, but they pose no threat. The lock operator may stop to chat and explain safety procedures. Then he'll retire to his office and do his job. The chamber begins to clank, grind, and gurgle. Slowly the water level—and the boats—begin to drop. And drop. And drop. By the time you reach the bottom of the 84-footer, you'll think you're in a canyon. The operator opens the exit gates and a new vista awaits: a 300-foot-wide channel leading to G. V. "Sonny" Montgomery Lock Pool 3 miles away.

On paper, the "lock-and-pool" section of the Tenn-Tom looks scarcely worth seeing. In reality, it's lonely and wild. The section consists of five narrow lakes, or

Riprap, locks, and dams are part of the trip on Tenn-Tom.

pools, linked by canal, with the levee along the west side. The Sonny Montgomery pool is just 2.5 miles long, and its 30-foot lock is small potatoes after Bay Springs' 84-footer. A 2-mile canal leads to 6.5-mile-long John Rankin Lock Pool, bordered on the west by the John Bell Williams Wildlife Management Area. Also to the west is the old Tombigbee River, a wiggly channel of mostly dead water. Old Beaver Lake Recreation Area (no camping at it and most other recreation areas) is to the east.

It was on the John Rankin pool that I saw my first Mississippi bald eagle. Perched in a dead pine, the bird's size grabbed our attention. The head didn't look like a vulture. The chest didn't look like an osprey. The body was too big for either. Had to be an eagle! Inspection through binoculars confirmed the sighting, and when the bird lifted off the branch with wings that may have been 7½ feet across, my heart soared as well. I'd seen eagles in Alaska and northern Minnesota, and it did me proud to see one in Mississippi. This turned out to be the first of many sightings on our journey. We later saw up to four at a time wheeling overhead, an unforgettable sight.

Fulton Lock Pool, just a mile below John Rankin Lock, stretches 6 miles, with the Jamie L. Whitten Historical Center and Fulton Campground on the east. The canal between Fulton and Glover Wilkins Lock Pool stretches 6 miles, with Bean's Ferry Recreation Area on the east bank. Glover Wilkins Lock Pool is 9 miles long and skinny, in places no wider than the canal. Smithville Recreation Area and fishing dock are located at the dam. It's 3 miles to Amory Lock Pool, the smallest at 2 miles long, bordered on the southeast by the town of Amory and Amory Recreation Area.

Five miles below Amory Lock, the canal joins the Tombigbee River and quickly changes character, becoming muddy with big, vine-draped woods—gator and cottonmouth country. As the river expands into 8-mile-long Aberdeen Lake, numerous swampy channels branch off, providing opportunities for exploring. Then the lake widens, and handsome residences outside the town of Aberdeen come into view on the west. Blue Bluff Recreation Area also extends along the west bank with campsites.

After the lock at Aberdeen, paddlers encounter alternating stretches of canal and river for 16 miles en route to Columbus Lake. The river is wide and lonely, with forest brooding on each side like the Congo. There's a just-noticeable current at last. Tree-shaded channels branch off as canals slice through bends on the old Tombigbee. Buttahatchee River enters from the east and is worth exploring. By this point, however, the woodland quiet is shattered by frequent flights from Columbus Air Force Base. Town Creek Campground is located on the west a few miles past Buttahatchee. There's also a campground at DeWayne Hayes Recreation Area on the east bank a couple of miles from Town Creek.

Columbus Lake also features another recreation area, a marina, a waterway management center, and a nature and cultural study center. Because of its numerous islands, Columbus doesn't really feel like a lake until its final 2.5 miles, when it opens up. With several creeks coming in from the west, it too offers exploring potential, though the presence of houses along the shore diminishes the sense of wildness. Luxapalila Creek enters from the east about 2.5 miles below the John C. Stennis Lock and Dam at Columbus. The Lux provides a 9-mile day float from Caledonia Steens Road just north of Steens to Highway 50 in Columbus, with a few logjams in the first mile or so. The Tenn-Tom continues 25 miles downstream from Columbus before crossing the state line into Alabama. The waterway proper ends at Demopolis, Alabama, and boat traffic follows the Tombigbee River on to Mobile, Alabama, 300 miles from the Mississippi line.

South of Columbus, Mississippi produces a host of tributaries that flow east across the state line into the Tombigbee. The Noxubee River gathers creeks like Woodward, Jordan, Wet Water, Shotbag, Yellow, Hashuqua, Plum, Dry, Macedonia, Running Water, Shuqualak, Wahalak, Shy Hammock, Big Scooba, Little Scooba, Flat Scooba, Bodka, and Qudby en route to the Tombigbee. South of that, the 110-mile Sucarnoochee River absorbs Sucarnoochee Creek, Pawticfaw, Blackwater, Ponta, and Alamuchee, among others. This east-central farm country may not offer much canoeing, due to the smallness of its streams and the Delta-like topography, but it's got some interesting country. The 165-mile long Noxubee River, for instance, is narrow enough to be plagued by logjams in low water, and is plenty muddy—Noxubee is a Native American word for "stinking river"—yet in places it stretches beneath towering white limestone cliffs. One such spot is Mahorner Road east of Shuqualak. This is the last bridge crossing in Mississippi, used primarily by catfishermen running trotlines and limb hooks in high water. Intrepid floaters could launch just southwest of Highway 14 in Macon and float 3 miles to Highway 45 (access is difficult at both places) and another 17 miles to the boat ramp at Mahorner Road. Or check out the pair of good canoeing lakes at 47,000-acre Noxubee National Wildlife Refuge northeast of Louisville. The wildness doesn't end at the refuge's borders, as a Noxubee swamp monster legend indicates. One former resident told me about coon hunting at night and seeing his baying dogs stop suddenly, put their tails between their legs, and retreat. A neighbor of his had a large German shepherd "ripped to shreds." My friend knew of only one man who had seen the beast, which reportedly walked on two legs. This old man vanished in the swamp and didn't turn up until my friend was coon hunting and saw in the glow of his flashlight a human skull beneath a hat, then a whole skeleton. Apparently the man had wandered off and died. Not even my friend attributed his death to the monster, however.

Tennessee-Tombigbee routes

With so many boat ramps and access points, Tenn-Tom paddling options seem limitless. Here is a sample route from north to south:

1. Scruggs Bridge boat ramp on Highway 25 at the south end of Yellow Creek Lake to Crow's Neck boat ramp at the north end of Bay Springs Lake, 24.5 miles. This rock-lined, man-made ditch is only for the masochistic. However, Yellow Creek Lake north of Scruggs Bridge is well worth exploring.

2. Crow's Neck to Bay Springs Lock (boat ramps on either side), 8 miles. Bay Springs Lake has numerous boat ramps and other take-outs as well, including Piney Grove Campground.

3. Bay Springs Lock to Saucer Creek boat ramp in G. V. "Sonny" Montgomery Lock Pool, 5 miles.

4. Saucer Creek to Beaver Lake Access Area in John Rankin Lock Pool, 7 miles.

5. Beaver Lake to Fulton boat ramp in Fulton Lock Pool, 7 miles. There's a campground at Fulton.

6. Fulton to Bean's Ferry Recreation Area, 6 miles.

7. Bean's Ferry to Smithville Rec Area in Glover Wilkins Lock Pool, 10.5 miles.

8. Smithville to Amory Rec Area in Amory Lock Pool, 11 miles.

9. Amory to Becker Bottoms Access Area, 8.5 miles.

10. Becker Bottoms to Blue Bluff Rec Area on Aberdeen Lake, 5 miles. Blue Bluff has a campground.

11. Blue Bluff to Devil's Elbow Access Area just below Aberdeen Lock, 2 miles. Morgan Landing, which is operated by the city of Aberdeen 1.5 miles below Devil's Elbow, has camping facilities.

12. Devil's Elbow to Barton Ferry Access Area, 14 miles.

13. Barton Ferry to Town Creek Campground, 1.5 miles.

14. Town Creek to DeWayne Hayes Rec Area, 2 miles. DeWayne Hayes has a campground.

15. DeWayne Hayes to Waverly Ferry Rec Area, 2 miles.

16. Waverly Ferry to Luxapalila Creek Rec Area, 10 miles.

17. Luxapalila Creek to Pickensville, Ala., Rec Area, 21 miles. Pickensville has a campground.

Area campgrounds

Goat Island Recreation Area, Yellow Creek, 662-423-1104.
Piney Grove Campground, Bay Springs Lake, 662-728-1134.
Fulton Campground, Fulton Lock Pool, 662-862-7070.
Blue Bluff Rec Area, Aberdeen Lake, 662-369-2832.
Town Creek Campground, Columbus Lake, 662-494-4885.

DeWayne Hayes Rec Area, Columbus Lake, 662-434-6939.

Pickensville, Ala., Rec Area, 205-373-6328.

Some 60 percent of the campsites along the Tenn-Tom are available for reservations. Campers may make reservations up to 240 days in advance. Call 1-877-444-6777. The hearing-impaired may call 1-877-833-6777. The Tenn-Tom Tourism Association also has stacks of maps, brochures, and booklets on the waterway. Contact it at P.O. Box 671, Columbus, MS 39703, phone 662-328-0812.

High points

Wildlife galore, including bald eagles.

Low points

No current; plenty of motorboats.

Tips

Put aside images of rushing rivers and think of this as southern flatwater extraordinaire.

Buttahatchee River

Buttahatchee River, a tributary of the Tombigbee, was one of the streams included in the pilot program for the state Scenic Waterway Act in 1999, both for its beauty and its problems. The river provides excellent canoeing and fishing but has been heavily affected by gravel mining on the lower end, between Highway 45 and the Tennessee-Tombigbee Waterway.

The 125-mile long stream starts near Sulligent, Alabama, and crosses into Mississippi near Greenwood Springs. There it joins Sipsey Creek, another Alabama stream that comes in from the north. The Buttahatchee's first floatable stretch is the 10.5 miles from a boat ramp at Bartahatchie Road east of Aberdeen to a ramp at Caledonia Road just northwest of Caledonia. Paddlers can expect to encounter some logjams and shoals on this segment, especially in low water.

The 11.5-mile stretch from Caledonia to U.S. 45 north of Columbus is locally considered the best float on the river, though gravel shoals require occasional portages. The Buttahatchee is characterized by its variety. It features long, wide, straight stretches with no current, almost like lake paddling. Then it swerves and shoots among cypress knees into a green tunnel between parklike woods. Next it widens and slows as it passes a gravel bar. The streambed alternates between gravel and mud, so even when clear, the water is slightly dingy. Several miles below Caledonia is a trailer park on the south bank with a private take-out. Farther down, access is possible but difficult on the north side of the four-lane Highway 45 bridge.

Paddlers can also float the 3 miles from Highway 45 to Highway 373, but gravel mining has scarred the lower river and left numerous shoals. Because of gravel mining the river has shifted course dramatically over the years, moving as far as three-quarters of a mile. U.S. Fish and Wildlife Service research shows that gravel mining causes erosion to move upstream in a process called headcutting. The mines continue for much of the 5-mile segment from Highway 373 to the Tenn-Tom, where big woods resume. Columbus Air Force Base, built during World War II, lies just south of the lower Buttahatchee, and the air traffic can be distracting if not intrusive as planes touch down and take off frequently. I just try to tune it out as background noise; if children are along, the silver jets might even make the trip more interesting. From the mouth of the Buttahatchee it's 5 miles south to DeWayne Hayes Recreation Area on the east shore of Columbus Lake.

The area around Caledonia is quickly turning into a countrified suburb of Columbus, with attractive brick houses springing up among shade trees next to cotton and hay fields. This used to be prime quail-hunting country, but as in so much of the state, that has changed. Modern farms are big and clean, no longer containing the little pea patches where quail once cooed and dusted back in the days when a pair of hunters could flush 25 coveys in a day. Modern timber operations consist of even-age pine forests, with fewer legumes and hardwood trees to provide food for birds. What quail there are now inhabit cutovers and briar patches so thick they're nearly impenetrable. The bird population is down drastically, and so are the numbers of hunters, who typically travel to other states or shoot pen-raised birds on special preserves. Between 1980 and 1990, the state's quail harvest dropped from 1.5 million to 429,000. And things haven't improved since then. Deer, on the other hand, thrive in the newer habitats, to the joy of hunters—and the dismay of residents who find their ornamental plants nipped.

Fishing is good in the Buttahatchee, which provides good habitat for catfish, crappie, bream, and bass alike. During high water, catfishermen set trotlines and limb hooks in deep, shady stretches below swifts. Unfortunately, they don't always remove the lines when water levels drop; you may see hooks dangling at head level as you float along. In lower water, bass fishermen use topwater lures and crankbaits. Largemouth bass are found the length of the river, while spotted bass inhabit the lower section, usually near swift water. Try dragging a crankbait across the lower side of shoals. In early morning and late evening switch to a buzzbait in still pockets for surface action. Buttahatchee bass typically weigh 3 to 4 pounds but may go 9.

As of this writing there is no canoe rental on the Buttahatchee, but that could easily change if some entrepreneur recognizes the apparent potential. This is a beautiful, canoeable stream in an area with a booming population. While increasing use tends to pressure a stream, more residents may mean more fans eager to protect the Buttahatchee.

Buttahatchee routes

1. Ramp at Bartahatchie Road east of Aberdeen to ramp at Caledonia Road just northwest of Caledonia, 10.5 miles.
2. Caledonia to Highway 45, 11.5 miles.
3. Highway 45 to Highway 373, 3 miles.
4. Highway 373 to Tenn-Tom Waterway, 5 miles, and 5 more miles to DeWayne Hayes Recreation Area on the east bank of Columbus Lake.

Area campgrounds

Town Creek Campground, Columbus Lake, 662-494-4885.
DeWayne Hayes Rec Area, Columbus Lake, 662-434-6939.

High points

Lots of variety, from long, still stretches to tree-canopied swifts.

Low points

Air traffic, gravel mines on lower river.

Tips

Paddle close to the bank to watch squirrels playing in overhanging trees.

Bear Creek

Bear Creek is not only beautiful in its own right, it runs through the heart of one of the state's loveliest state parks. Tishomingo is the only Mississippi state park with a canoe rental and shuttle service, among many other attractions. Bear Creek starts in Alabama, where it and its tributaries are dammed to form several reservoirs. It enters Mississippi near Red Bay, Alabama, and swings north, which can be confusing to those of us accustomed to south-, west-, or east-flowing streams, as is the case in most of Mississippi. It passes through Tishomingo State Park, which straddles the Natchez Trace Parkway, before crossing back into Alabama into an arm of Pickwick Lake on the Tennessee River. The landscape is rocky and hilly, and portions of Bear Creek scoot over rocks for some exciting swifts. Other stretches, however, are long, straight, and currentless. Outside the park's borders, paddlers encounter fields and thin stands of forest, but inside the park they're enclosed in a canyon of towering trees, lush green in the summer and stunningly colorful in the fall, as the aquamarine water courses below golden hickories splashed with reds, oranges, purples, greens, and browns.

In addition to its scenic qualities, Bear Creek is a prime float-fishing stream. The best way to fish such a stream, in my opinion, is for the stern paddler to handle the boat and the bow person to fish, rotating every hour. The paddler keeps up a leisurely pace while the angler casts. For bass, use colors like white, green, and chartreuse. A white spinnerbait is hard to beat, catching largemouths handily. Smaller lures take smaller fish, and little ones like beetlespins will also catch bream. Catfishing is trickier for canoers, because you need to tie up at bends and pools and stop a while. Chicken livers, blood bait, and worms are all good bait choices on Bear Creek. A local fisherman recommended shad intestines, for what it's worth.

In Mississippi the creek offers several floats, from Golden to Highway 30, but by far the most popular is from Dennis to the park. Upper stretches have been channelized in places and can be prohibitively shallow in low water. The popular section is serviced by the park's canoe rental. Incidentally, the length of this float illustrates the difficulty in pinning down river mileages. The Bear Creek Development Authority, based in Russellville, Alabama (205-332-4392), claims this stretch is 6 miles long. Park literature puts it at 8. The book *Canoe Trails of the Deep South* says 6.5. Take your pick. Similarly, the Bear Creek Development Authority estimates the next leg, from the park to Highway 30, at 8 miles, while *Canoe Trails of the Deep South* puts it at 5.5. I would call it 6. If you're paddling a canoe you could handle both stretches in a day, but for float-fishing, allow a day for either.

Cypress trees and boulders stand side by side at Bear Creek.

Below Dennis the creek makes a huge loop northwest and back southeast, then angles northeast under a rural road (poor access), entering the park 1.5 miles later. Remains of an old Confederate bridge stand just inside the park boundary. Rock and gravel shoals make for fun paddling when the water's normal but may require some towing during low water such as in the fall. The take-out is at the swinging foot bridge at the southeast end of the park.

Below the foot bridge the river remains within the park for several miles. It's also wider and deeper, a good choice for low-water periods. For a long piece below the swinging bridge there is almost no current, which is not what you might expect in this rocky hill country. Shortly before you get to the Natchez Trace Parkway bridge (no access) the water quickens at a row of rocks that looks like a crude attempt to block the river. And that's exactly what it is—an old Indian fish trap. It still works. Just below the swifts my son Andy pulled out a 3-pound largemouth on a white Redneck spinner. Boulders and rocky outcrops keep the river interesting, though never particularly challenging. When the creek leaves the park, you can tell: Farm fields back a thin line of trees as the stream continues to Highway 30.

Tishomingo State Park is a natural place to camp. The 1,530-acre park has 62 campsites around 45-acre Haynes Lake, including a separate wooded area for tents. There are also cabins, group camping in old Civilian Conservation Corps houses, 13 miles of nature trails, an 1840s log cabin and CCC pond, paddleboat and fishing boat rentals at the lake, rock climbing (permit required), disc golf, and dulcimer festivals, among other attractions.

Bear Creek routes

1. Highway 24 at Red Bay, Ala., to Highway 11 in Alabama, 5 miles.
2. Highway 11 to County Road 68 east of Golden, Miss., 6 miles.
3. Golden to county road east of Belmont, 3 miles.
4. Belmont to County Road 86 east of Dennis, 6 miles.
5. Dennis to Tishomingo State Park, 6 miles. Take-out is located beside swinging foot bridge at southeast end of park.
6. Tishomingo to Highway 30, 8 miles.

Outfitters

Tishomingo State Park offers canoe rental and shuttle service from mid-April through mid-October. 662-438-6914.

Area campgrounds

Tishomingo State Park, Natchez Trace Parkway. 45-acre lake, tent and RV sites, cabins and group camp. 662-438-6914.

High points

The section through Tishomingo State Park is simply magnificent.

Low points

Long stretches with no current.

Tips

Take your fishing tackle: This is a great stream for float-fishing.

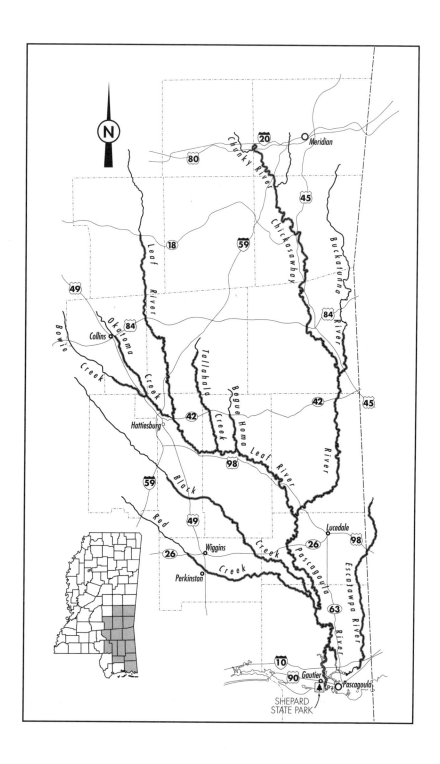

N

20 Meridian

80

45

Chunky River

Chickasawhay

Buckatunna River

18 59

49

Okatoma Creek

84

Collins

Bowie Creek

Leaf River

Tallahala Creek

Bogue Homa Creek

Leaf River

84

42 45

Hattiesburg

42

98

River

59

Black Creek

Red

49

26

Lucedale

98

Wiggins

26

Creek

Pascagoula River

Escatawpa River

Perkinston

Creek

63

10

90 Gautier

Pascagoula

SHEPARD
STATE PARK

5. The Pascagoula River System

Chunky River

Originating north of Interstate 20, Chunky River is the northernmost canoeable tributary in the vast Pascagoula River system. It feeds Chickasawhay River, which joins Leaf River to form the Pascagoula. The Chunky is characterized by long, still stretches alternating with gentle, rocky rapids. The area lies at the fringe of the Appalachians, and it looks it. The rocks, cliffs, ferns, and hardwoods seem more Tennessee than Mississippi.

The Chunky—named not for a portly pioneer but for a Choctaw ball game— rises in the hills northwest of Meridian, crosses I-20 west of the town of Chunky, then swings east toward town, crisscrossing Highway 80. East of Chunky it turns southeast to weave a crooked course past I-59 south of Meridian and Highway 11 to join its smaller sister stream, Okatibbee Creek, and become the Chicka- sawhay near Enterprise. In all, the Chunky River and its main tributary, Chunky Creek, flow 55 miles, of which some 21 miles provide great canoeing—at least when water levels aren't too low. While the rocky ledges provide exciting chutes to pilot a boat through, in low water, which includes much of summer and fall, they can scratch up a boat hull and mandate frequent towing.

Few people canoe east of the town of Chunky since the river there is so small, but some wade-fish or fish from the bank. The biggest bass often come from such narrow stretches. The upper stream was the site of the Chunky River Railroad Disaster of 1863 when a bridge collapsed, dropping a troop train into the river and killing nearly a hundred Confederate soldiers. The Doolittle Cemetery on Highway 80 west near Newton commemorates the dead with stone markers.

The first place to launch a boat is at Highway 80 just east of the town of Chunky. The river swings north and back south to 80 again to make a loop known locally as the 7-mile bend, though in fact it covers 3 river miles and just half a mile on the highway. For many years this stretch was the site of the raucous Chunky River Raft Race in which people competed with all sorts of homemade vessels. The annual event has been abandoned. From a paddling perspective, this segment is the most trouble-free on the river, slower and deeper than farther downstream. Even so, there are a few pullovers due to rock ledges. Because of this, spring is the easiest time to float the Chunky, not during floods but afterward when the water is leveling out. Some holes on this stretch are 10–12 feet deep. Such spots harbor big catfish. I heard about one grabber who hauled in a 57-pounder. Bank-line fishermen use live bait like pond perch to catch spotted cats up to 28 pounds. Cane-pole fishermen hook bluegill and redbellied bream with worms. Bass fishermen drag small lures like black and yellow H&H spinnerbaits and dark green or black-with-white-stripes Tiny Torpedo topwater plugs across rapids or over logs to catch Kentucky redeye and largemouth.

From the second Highway 80 put-in, it's 2.5 miles to the Point Wanita Lake Road bridge at the community of Point, then another 6.5 miles to Stucky Bridge Road. The Point-to-Stucky float is particularly scenic, with rocky cliffs and lush vegetation. It's a good bass-fishing area too. Some people tie boat to waist and wade-fish. The creaky iron Stucky bridge was named after a nineteenth-century member of the Dalton Gang who ambushed travelers at the crossing and left their bodies in the river. The old bridge, first built in 1847, is a Mississippi landmark.

After Stucky, the next take-out is at Highway 513 on Chicksawhay River just below the convergence with Okatibbee Creek east of Enterprise. This shallow, rocky stretch flows past Dunn's Falls Water Park, one of the state's outdoor gems. The park is located 5.5 miles below Stucky Bridge on the river; by road it's 5 miles south of Meridian east of I-59 off the Savoy exit. The park is notable for a 65-foot waterfall that pours from a millpond dam down a rocky cliff into the Chunky. In 1854, Irish immigrant John Dunn diverted a stream down the bluff to create a waterfall to power a mill. He built a three-story cotton factory, and the operation grew to include a gristmill, distillery, blacksmith shop, and hat and clothing plant. The Confederate government commandeered the business during the Civil War to make goods for the war effort. John B. Stetson reportedly learned his hatmaking skills at Dunn's mill. After the war, the business eventually faded, and now the spot is a 69-acre park administered by the Pat Harrison Waterway District. A reconstructed mill wheel and mill house stand by the pond and the waterfall. The pond is full of catfish, and fishing is permitted. Nearby is a picnic area and primitive campground in a beautiful grove of hardwood trees. The water park also has a few

Dunn's Falls Water Park south of Meridian streams down a rock face into Chunky River.

short nature trails for meandering up and down the river. On the rugged slopes you may see low-growing heart plants, the valentine-shaped leaves of which when broken smell like a blend of sassafras and licorice. Large winter huckleberry bushes grow along the banks in abundance, loaded with small black berries in December. They taste faintly of molasses, with a pasty texture. Chuckling water, fresh air, ample exercise, and big woods combine for a bracing tonic. Unfortunately there's nowhere to launch a boat at the park since it's a steep drop to the river.

I canoed the Chunky in late fall when misty, rainy conditions enhanced its mysterious beauty. We paddled into a hard rain, which gave way to thick fog. Cypress knees rose like shrouds from dark water and raindrops fluted down rock cliffs beneath mammoth trees. In one spot a tree arched horizontally over the river and a log curved up beneath it to form the shape of an eye. In the midst of that eye swirled white fog, and into that fog we paddled. We seemed to enter another dimension, another era—the era, perhaps, of frontiersman Sam Dale, who once roamed these woods.

A renowned trailblazer and Indian-fighter, the 6-foot 2-inch Dale was a formidable adversary known as Big Sam to his Native American enemies. His career in the Old Southwest, as Alabama and Mississippi were then known, was full of adventures, none more thrilling than the famous canoe fight in 1813 on the Alabama River. After a skirmish, Dale and three companions paddled their boat toward a vessel containing six Creek Indians. Here's Dale's account of the incident as recorded in *Life and Times of General Sam Dale, the Mississippi Partisan*, compiled by J. F. H. Claiborne and published in 1860:

As the two boats approached, one of them hurled his scalping-knife at me. It pierced the boat through and through, just grazing my thigh as it passed. The next moment the canoes came in contact. I leaped up, placing one of my feet in each boat. At the same instant the foremost warrior leveled his rifle at my breast. It flashed in the pan. As quick as lightning, he clubbed it, and aimed at me a furious blow, which I partially parried, and, before he could repeat it, I shivered his skull with my gun. In the mean time an Indian had struck down Jerry, and was about to dispatch him, when I broke my rifle over his head. It parted in two places. The barrel Jerry seized, and renewed the fight. The stock I hurled at one of the savages. Being then disarmed, Caesar handed me his musket and bayonet.

Finding myself unable to keep the two canoes in juxtaposition, I resolved to bring matters to an issue, and leaped into the Indian boat. My pirogue, with Jerry, Jim, and Caesar, floated off. Jim fired, and slightly wounded the Indian next to me. I now stood in the centre of their canoe—two dead at my feet—a wounded savage in the stern, who had been snapping his piece at me during the fight, and four powerful warriors in front. The first one directed a furious blow at me with his rifle; it glanced upon the barrel of my musket, and I staved the bayonet through his body. As he fell the next one repeated the attack. A shot from Jerry Austill pierced his heart. Striding over them, the next sprung at me with his tomahawk. I killed him with the bayonet, and his corpse lay between me and the last of the party. I knew him well—Tar-cha-chee, a noted wrestler, and the most famous ball-player of his clan. He paused a moment in expectation of my attack, but, finding me motionless, he stepped backward to the bow of the canoe, shook himself, gave the war-whoop of his tribe, and cried out, "Sam tholocco lana dahmaska, ia-lanestha—lipso—lipso—lanestha. Big Sam! I am a man—I am coming—come on!" As he said this, with a terrific yell he bounded over the dead body of his comrade, and directed a blow at my head with his rifle, which dislocated my left shoulder. I dashed the bayonet into him. It glanced around his ribs, and the point hitching to his back-bone, I pressed him down. As I pulled the weapon out, he put his hands upon the sides of the canoe and endeavored to rise, crying out, "Tar-cha-chee is a man. He is not afraid to die!" I drove my bayonet through his heart. I then turned to the wounded villain in the stern, who snapped his rifle at me as I advanced, and had been snapping during the whole conflict.

He gave the war-whoop, and, in tones of hatred and defiance, exclaimed, "I am a warrior—I am not afraid to die." As he uttered the words I pinned him down with my bayonet, and he followed his eleven comrades to the land of spirits.

Dale eventually settled in Lauderdale County 15 miles north of Meridian. The community that grew up around him was known as Daleville. He served as a delegate in the 1816 convention that divided the Mississippi Territory into Mississippi and Alabama, and later in the Mississippi Legislature. He died in 1841 in his late sixties. The residents of Daleville moved their community 2 miles north to locate nearer a school. A statue of Dale now stands at Daleville.

Dale lived through the passing of an era. Another local resident, Jimmie Rodgers, born fifty-six years later in Meridian, ushered in a new one. Rodgers—called the Father of Country Music, the Singing Brakeman, and America's Blue Yodeler, among other nicknames—went to work for the railroad in his teens until tuberculosis forced him to retire in his twenties. By then he'd been informally schooled in banjo, guitar, and vocals, and he pursued a musical career. After a few false starts, his career took off when he recorded "T for Texas." For the next six years he was a national phenomenon; it's said that depression-era Americans bought a Jimmie Rodgers record along with their flour, sugar, and coffee, his music considered as essential as groceries. He died of TB in 1933, and his legacy affected generations of musicians, evidenced by the top country acts who still perform at the Jimmie Rodgers Festival in Meridian every May. The Jimmie Rodgers Museum (601-485-1808) at 41st Avenue and 19th Street in Meridian's Highland Park is open 10 A.M. to 4 P.M. Mondays through Saturdays and 1–5 P.M. Sundays; admission is $2. Rodgers' songs like "T for Texas," "Away Out on the Mountain," and "Never No Mo' Blues" capture a blend of freedom, wanderlust, and melancholy that paddlers can relate to. I imagine him fishing and rambling along Okatibbee and Chunky Creeks, later riding trains across them as he absorbed the rich southern culture he celebrated in song.

Chunky routes

1. Highway 80 just east of Chunky to Highway 80 further east, 3 miles. There's a boat ramp just south of the second bridge crossing.

2. Second Highway 80 bridge to Point Wanita Lake Road bridge at the Point community, 2.5 miles. Point Wanita Lake Road intersects Highway 80 about 3 miles east of Chunky.

3. Point to a boat ramp off Stucky Bridge Road, 6.5 miles. Stucky Bridge Road connects Point Wanita Lake Road to Meehan-Savoy Road on the west side of the river.

4. Stucky Bridge Road to Highway 513 on Chickasawhay River east of Enterprise, 10 miles.

Area campgrounds

1. Dunn's Falls Water Park, Ward Road east of Interstate 59 south of Meridian. Primitive camping only. 601-655-9511.

2. Lake Okatibbee, off Highway 19 north of Meridian. There are full facilities at this 3,800-acre lake on upper Okatibbee Creek. 601-626-8431.

High points

Stone cliffs; swift, clear water; gorgeous foliage in the fall.

Low points

Rocky bottom can scratch up a boat hull during low water.

Tips

Check out Dunn's Falls Water Park, which has a 65-foot waterfall flowing into Chunky River.

Chickasawhay River

The Chickasawhay (pronounced Chick-a-sa-HAY) River begins near the east Mississippi town of Enterprise where Chunky River and Okatibbee Creek come together. From there it flows 159 miles to its confluence with the Leaf River where the Pascagoula is born. At the fringe of the Appalachian Mountain chain, the upper Chickasawhay slices through a seamline of Alabama stone and Mississippi muck, an intriguing region of waterfalls and alligators, cliffs and swamp. Boat ramps have been placed along the river since it's generally inaccessible otherwise because of its steep banks. But the prevalence of rocky shoals along the waterway renders motorboating difficult, and that's good news for paddlers. Except for the lower reaches where it becomes wide and deep, the Chickasawhay provides pleasant floating, with good fishing and relatively little human contact.

Fall is the best time for bass and bream on the upper river. Use topwater lures for bass, and crickets or minnows for bream. Catfishing provides the main action on Chickasawhay, however. Flatheads top 82 pounds, though average catches are far smaller, closer to a couple of pounds, which is prime eating size. Popular baits on the rocky upper river are minnows and catalpa worms. On the muddier lower reaches, fishermen prefer chicken liver and crawfish. Set trotlines or drop hooks at night and check them in the morning. Eat your catch fresh for breakfast or put it in an ice chest for later.

With so little human contact, wild animals are bolder than usual along the Chickasawhay. We saw three alligators in one day, each 6 to 8 feet long, soaking up some sun in brisk spring weather. They slid reluctantly into the river when our canoe approached. Beavers plop from bank dens into the water as a boat glides by. Imperturbable muskrats watch passersby like furry couch potatoes. Deer pause with ears up, then scamper into machete-thick woods, where huge, vine-draped hardwood trees shade tropical-looking palmettoes. As the rock country yields to mud, tributaries change from gorges to bayous, which are great for exploring. Young wild pigs grunt and root in dark swamp like musical musketeers. Adult hogs are more wary and will hightail it for the woods, panicking a whole herd of fellow porkers. Sandbars record the passages of bobcats, otters, raccoons, and opossums. At night, a coyote chorus provides soprano to bullfrog bass.

On this river, things don't seem much different than the days when Hernando de Soto and his army of gold-seeking Spaniards came through the region around 1540. The town of De Soto on the upper Chickasawhay was named for the conquistador, as was the national forest to the south, though whether he actually crossed the Chickasawhay is questionable. Soto and his gang of 650 landed near Tampa, Florida, but from there their route is vague. Apparently they hacked their way north to Tallahassee, Florida, veered northeast into the Appalachians as far north as Knoxville, Tennessee, then back south into Alabama near Montgomery. They crossed into Mississippi over a swift, wide river, which most scholars believe was the Tombigbee but local residents prefer to think was the Chickasawhay. From there they went on across northeast Mississippi to the Mississippi River. Contrary to popular opinion, Soto did not discover the Mississippi; earlier Spaniards entered it from the coast. He crossed it somewhere around Walls, just south of Memphis, Tennessee, looped into Arkansas and back to the Mississippi, apparently near Arkansas City, Arkansas, where he died of fever.

Most of us modern-day paddlers fantasize now and then about being explorers, but we tend to think of buckskinned long hunters like Daniel Boone or Sam Dale, not armored killers like Soto, even if the Spaniards were here earlier. There's good reason for this preference. Guys like Boone loved to ramble through boundless forest, hunting, fishing, and trapping. They fought only when they had to, and were likely to count Indians among their friends. Soto and his ilk, on the other hand, cared nothing for rambling, hunting, or exploring. They wanted one thing: gold. And they didn't hesitate to kill, enslave, and torture Native American inhabitants, even hunting them with war dogs for sport. Soto's general strategy when meeting Indians was to seize the chief and enslave the people. If they resisted, which they naturally did, he was swift to attack. The Spaniards had one major advantage over the Indians: armor. True, they had guns, clumsy things known as arquebuses, but they were so unreliable and inaccurate that they were mainly useful for making a loud noise. Horses, too, gave them an advantage, though not a tremendous one in the forest environment. But their steel and padded armor made them virtually impervious to arrows. In one battle, Soto was hit by twenty-one arrows. But since he was wearing padded armor, they merely stuck out like a pincushion while he continued to fight. Despite the depressing nature of Soto's tactics, it's fascinating to contemplate the wilderness he encountered—and still possible to get a glimpse of it in the big woods along the Chickasawhay.

The highest launch point is at Highway 513 in the town of Enterprise, less than a mile below the confluence of Chunky and Okatibbee. There's also access at a state boat ramp a mile south of town off 513. From there to a boat ramp and small town park in Stonewall is 2.5 miles.

Highway 512 west of Quitman crosses the river 16.5 miles below Stonewall. Just below Highway 512 at Quitman, Souinlovey Creek comes in from the west, a sizeable tributary. Just past Highway 45, Archusa Creek flows in from the north through Archusa Creek Water Park, which has a campground. In 1998 spring rains opened a 60-yard hole in the emergency spillway on 450-acre Archusa Lake. Reconstruction began in August 1999. Clarkco State Park is also located near Quitman. In all there are 10.5 river miles between Highway 512 and a boat ramp on a county road east of De Soto.

The town of De Soto was named for the conquistador, of course, but it has a colorful history apart from the explorer. The area was settled in the 1830s and incorporated as a village in 1896. It remained thus until the legislature did away with village status in the state since most such hamlets lacked sufficient tax base to provide services. De Soto retains its village feel, with a historic old barber shop that operated from 1924 to 1964 and was restored in 1999. Also restored was an old artesian well where trains used to stop for passengers to drink. The town has a weekend flea market in an old-fashioned 32-stall pole barn. On County Road 690 near the river, Gappy's Fish Camp restaurant specializes in catfish dinners, located just across from Chicksawhay River Canoe Rental and Bait Shop.

Sandbars increase on the 13.5-mile stretch from Dc Soto to a boat ramp on Eacutta Street east of Highway 45 in Shubuta. There are about 10 small sets of easy rapids on this segment, including a 2–3-foot dropoff and a roaring 200-yard-long stretch at the mouth of Shubuta Creek called the Old Shubuta Races, 3 miles north of the Shubuta boat ramp.

These upper stretches of the Chickasawhay are particularly scenic, with high clay-rock walls and deep woods ranging from pine plantations to tropical-seeming jungle. The sheer bluffs are natural sources of spring water. In the springtime rainy season, water pours from the mossy clay walls like faucets, making it easy to keep canteens filled. Such springs often disappear during dry season, however.

Tributaries lead to Appalachian-style wonderlands with small, gushing waterfalls, caves, and dripping ferns. Even the sandbars are steep on the upper river, big enough to camp but small enough that a tent may wind up blocking a deer trail. The deer won't hesitate to snort their complaints in the middle of the night if they find something across their path.

The river grows gradually wider and slower below Shubuta, with many large sandbars. It's 21 miles to a boat ramp off Highway 84 two miles west of Waynesboro, and another 5.5 miles to a boat ramp on Highway 63 south of Waynesboro. The river widens even more on the 13.5-mile stretch from Highway 63 to a boat ramp on Chicora River Road east of Chicora. Buckatunna Creek, a canoeable tributary, enters from the east a few miles below Chicora. From Chicora it's 15 miles to Highway 42, where access is extremely difficult due to steep banks. Five miles below Highway 42 is a boat ramp at the county road between the communities of Knobtown and Old Avera. It's 23.5 wonderfully remote miles from there to a boat ramp off Highway 63 in Leakesville. Though there are fewer shoals, the long, lonely stretches of woods are blissful to paddlers. But with the river deeper and wider, motorboats become more common near Leakesville. The banks grow muddy, and trotlining for catfish is popular. From Leakesville, 29.5 sluggish miles remain before a boat ramp at Merrill on the east side of Pascagoula River. Halfway between Leakesville and the Pascagoula, Big Creek comes in from the northwest. It's reportedly canoeable in high water but in low is better for wading. The four-lane Highway 98 crosses the Chickasawhay 24 miles below Leakesville, but there is no access.

It may seem a long way from the Chickasawhay to the Holy Land, but in a sense it's just a few miles: The deep woods east of the lower river north of Highway 98 provide a lush setting for Palestine Gardens, a haunting replica of the Holy Land created in the 1950s by the late Reverend Harvell and Pellerree Jackson and later purchased by Don and Cindy Bradley, both of whom are canoeing enthusiasts. At the gardens, a wide path winds through a shady landscape of miniature rivers, lakes, and ancient towns. But the gardens provide more than a lesson in geography. They're also soothing to the spirit, something any paddler would welcome. The wind moves through pines and bamboo, and sweet olive bushes send forth faint perfume as if the bleak desert environment of the Holy Land has been somehow transported into the Garden of Eden. To get there, take Highway 98 east of Hattiesburg. A sign directs the way about midway between McLain and Lucedale. Take the first left past the Chickasawhay River and follow additional signs. The gardens, which provide a good way to wind down from a river trip, include restrooms, gift shop, a large outdoor theater—even an outdoor wedding chapel—and benches along the trail. The gardens are open 9 A.M. to 4 P.M. Mondays through Fridays, 9 A.M. to 6 P.M. Saturdays and 1–5 P.M. Sundays, March through December. Admission is free; donations are accepted. Reservations are not necessary but are recommended for large groups. Call 601-947-8422.

Chickasawhay routes

1. Highway 513 at Enterprise to state boat ramp off Highway 513 south, 1 mile.

2. Highway 513 ramp to ramp at town park in Stonewall west of 513, 2.5 miles.

3. Stonewall to ramp at Highway 512 west of Quitman, 16.5 miles.

4. Quitman to ramp on County Road 690 east of De Soto, 10.5 miles.

5. De Soto to ramp off Eacutta Street east of Highway 45 in Shubuta, 13.5 miles. Ramp is off street running east from stop light in Shubuta to Highway 510.

6. Shubuta to ramp off Highway 84, 2 miles west of Waynesboro, 21 miles. Ramp is located just north of Old Highway 84 and south of the new four-lane 84.

7. Highway 84 to ramp off Highway 63, 3 miles south of Waynesboro, 5.5 miles. Turn at airport sign just past National Guard Armory, follow to dead end and turn right at boat ramp entrance.

8. Highway 63 to ramp east of Chicora, 13.5 miles.

9. Chicora to ramp at county road between the communities of Knobtown and Old Avera, 20 miles. Highway 42 crosses 15 miles below Chicora, but access is extremely difficult.   .

10. County road to ramp off Highway 63 in Leakesville, 23.5 miles.

11. Leakesville to ramp at Merrill on east side of Pascagoula River, 29.5 miles. Highway 98 crosses 24 miles below Leakesville but there is no access.

Outfitters

Chickasawhay River Canoe Rental and Bait Shop, 565 County Road 690, Shubuta, 601-776-0126 or 776-5594.

Area campgrounds

1. Archusa Creek Water Park off Highway 18 east of Quitman, 601-776-6956.

2. Clarkco State Park, 386 Clarkco Road north of Quitman, 601-776-6651.

3. Maynor Creek Water Park, 1 mile west of Waynesboro on Highway 84, 601-735-4365.

4. Turkey Fork Recreation Area, in De Soto National Forest off Highway 42 between Richton and State Line, 601-428-0594.

High points

Long, lonely stretches of scenic river.

Low points

Motorboat traffic picks up on lower reaches.

Tips

Paddle quietly and keep your eyes peeled for views of wildlife.

Buckatunna Creek

With 13 floatable miles, Buckatunna Creek (also spelled Bucatunna) is some-thing of a Chickasawhay River in miniature. Like the big river into which it flows, Buckatunna occupies a curious verge between rock and mud, with fern-cloaked stone walls next to Spanish-moss-cloaked cypress trees. The water is stained by natural tannic acids common to southeast Mississippi streams, as well as choco-late-colored mud. Often still and slightly murky with some deep pockets, Buck-atunna is good habitat for catfish and bream.

The stream heads up just east of Meridian and runs south parallel to the Al-abama line. It doesn't become navigable until the boat ramp at Denham Progress Road near the community of Denham east of Waynesboro. It's 10 miles from there to Buckatunna-Millry Road and another 3 to Highway 45. From there to the Chickasawhay is 2.5 miles. Occasional logjams and shoals are always pos-sible on this size creek, but it usually holds enough water to float a boat even in dry season.

Even though Denham is the highest put-in, you can paddle upriver from there since there is little to no current for a good ways. This stretch is lovely and intimate, lying shaded beneath rocky cliffs. Solo paddlers who don't want to bother with a shuttle can launch at Denham and paddle both upriver and down for an afternoon's play. Just below Denham the stream is wider and shallower as it wraps around large sandbars. Big Red Creek flows in from Alabama a couple miles above Buckatunna-Millry Road.

At Buckatunna-Millry Road, there is a gravel lane to the creek on the south-west side and a dirt road on the southeast, with 20-foot banks on both sides. But that's easy compared to Highway 45, where options are to risk getting stuck on a dirt road under the bridge (unless you have four-wheel drive) or tote the boat 200 yards.

Buckatunna routes

1. Boat ramp at Denham Progress Road to Buckatunna-Millry Road, 10 miles. Denham Progress Road is just east of the community of Denham, which is about 8 miles east of Waynesboro on County Lake-Denham Road.

2. Buckatunna-Millry Road to Highway 45. Access is poor at Highway 45. From there to Chickasawhay River is 2.5 miles.

Area campgrounds

1. Maynor Creek Water Park, 1 mile west of Waynesboro on Highway 84, 601-735-4365.

2. Turkey Fork Recreation Area, in De Soto National Forest off Highway 42 between Richton and State Line, 601-428-0594.

High points

Neat contrast between rock cliffs and swamp mud.

Low points

Few access points.

Tips

Launch at Denham Progress Road and paddle upriver, then drift back down.

Leaf River

The Leaf River is the western twin to the Chickasawhay, fraternal if not identical. Each flows more than 150 miles (185 for Leaf, 159 for Chickasawhay) through southeast Mississippi before merging to form the Pascagoula. For most of their lengths, both rivers tend to be a bit small for many motorboaters and a bit big for many canoers, making them ideal for someone wanting to get away from it all.

The Leaf starts just south of Interstate 20 near the town of Forest. It meets West Tallahala Creek a few miles south of Highway 18 and grows to a sizeable river as it continues south and east past Hattiesburg en route to its appointment with the Chickasawhay west of Lucedale. Despite its size, the Leaf remains subject to shoals and some logjams during low-water periods as far south as New Augusta.

A 1970s booklet by biologists David Robinson and Kenneth Rich of the Mississippi Department of Wildlife, Fisheries, and Parks said, "According to data contained in an extensive study of the Leaf River system, most if not all of its streams are under-utilized. Repeating: under-utilized, especially from a fishing viewpoint." The same can be said of the paddling viewpoint. Crowds may have picked up a tad since the booklet was published, but then as now you need a lightweight boat to get onto the upper Leaf and its tributaries, which include the Okatoma and Bowie Rivers. As with the Chickasawhay, sheer bluffs on the Leaf mean steep landing sites, and occasional shoals and swifts make the river rough on flat-bottom boats with motors. For paddlers, the Leaf is hard to beat.

Even big rivers start small, and the 9.5-mile stretch from Highway 18 to a boat ramp at a county road between Highways 37 and 531 is hard going. The logjams thin out but shoals persist on the ensuing 8.5-mile stretch to Highway 28 east of Taylorsville and on part of the 11.5-mile segment from Highway 28 to Highway 84. However, a significant tributary, Oakohay Creek, enters from the west 2 miles below Highway 28, leaving the route pretty much wide open for paddling. It's possible to launch into the Oakohay from Highway 37 a couple miles upcreek from the Leaf near Hot Coffee. This crossroads town, located on Highway 532 just east of its intersection with Highway 37 south of Taylorsville, was named for the bracing beverage dispensed by an innkeeper's wife in the 1800s. A tradition of hospitality is carried on at two old-timey general stores: McDonald's Store and J&H Harper Grocery, both on Highway 532. Stop at either or both before your trip to stock up on snacks and let your pace throttle back as you prepare to enter river time.

Big woods and occasional high, powdery sandbars line the Leaf as it continues 13 miles from Highway 84 to Highway 588. Springs pour through moss from undercut clay banks like open faucets. For a delightful restorative drink, squeeze fresh lemon juice and honey into a jug of this spring water and shake well. The wildlife department booklet reported a 3-foot waterfall on the 7-mile segment between Highway 588 and Highway 590, but when I floated there was no evidence of it, either because the water was up and smoothed it out or because the falls had eroded away over the years, as they are prone to do in clay soils. The woods along the river range from swampy cypress to dense canebrakes to tall pines. It's good habitat for snakes, like the pair of copperheads I spied, one in front of the other, while walking barefoot. They stayed perfectly still except for one's wiggling, forked tongue. I admired them for a while—each a couple of feet long, mottled gold and black—before departing respectfully. Being venomous, copperheads have a bad reputation, but I have found them to be passive. My dog once stepped on one unwittingly, and the snake did nothing. Of course, copperheads may bite if threatened, and I keep a safe distance, but I also acknowledge that the deep woods are their territory. According to one old legend, copperheads are "rattlesnake pilots" who travel well in advance of the larger rattler, perhaps laying down a scent trail. According to the legend, if you see a copperhead, it's a dead certainty a rattlesnake will be along on the same route many hours later. I've never waited to see, though it's an intriguing idea.

Towering, 70-foot bluffs and dense forest create a secure, closed-in feeling on the 13-mile segment from Highway 590 to Monroe Road a mile west of Eastabuchie. The riverbottom swamps resemble tropical jungles, while high piney bluffs suggest the Rocky Mountains, as if this part of Mississippi contains the continent's geography in microcosm. This stretch contains numerous swifts, not exactly whitewater but enough to give you a good tossing. The largest is Gordon's Rock, a 3–4-foot runnable waterfall. All these rapids help keep motorboats off the upstream reaches. They also make for good fishing. For bass use beetle-spins and small minnow lures below swift spots. Live minnows are a top choice for catfish, which inhabit the still, deep holes. Below Gordon's Rock, we spotted a dead cypress slough entering the Leaf on the right and turned up it. Only when we had paddled as far as we could did we hear the perplexing sound of falling water. Peering up a narrow ravine to our left, we spotted a waterfall taller than I. We beached our canoe in shallow mud and made our way over slippery clay to the clear fall. I waded into the pool and ducked under, and the coldness sucked my breath away. Where was all this water going? The slough it entered was still as a pond. Back at the canoe, I stuck my bare foot into the water and discovered the answer. The spring water formed a fast, cold current along the bottom of the slough, leaving the upper, warmer level undisturbed. Such are the wonders of the Leaf.

The river widens considerably and sandbars become vast on the 10.5-mile stretch from Eastabuchie to Highway 42 at Hattiesburg. These sandbars are favorite haunts of great blue herons, one of the most common yet most interesting birds encountered by paddlers. These 4-foot-tall water-masters inhabit wetlands from Mexico to southeastern Alaska. Smoky-blue, black-capped, white-faced, orange-beaked, they were once hunted for plumage but are now federally protected. They're incredibly wary—just try to sneak up on one—and are excellent fishermen, studying the water without motion, then stabbing their prey with sharp beaks. When they catch a fish they flip it so it goes down head first, sharp fins safely flattened. Their skill is not appreciated by catfish farmers, who regularly lose part of their crop to herons and their kin. With their S-shaped neck and jerky stride, herons seem awkward, but when they spread their huge wings they rise off the ground like helium balloons, and in flight they're Boeings with 6-foot spans. Adult herons have few natural predators because of their size, though alligators take a few. They like to build gigantic platform nests high in swamp trees such as cypress. In the summer you may see half-grown birds peering over the edge onto their green domain. At dusk, you'll hear them returning home with beating wings. Throughout the night they grunt, snort, bicker, and sometimes squawk raucously—a cantankerous, alarmist village. Since herons are related to Oriental cranes, on which some martial arts techniques are based, I've always hoped to see a pair sparring but never have. But I have followed their big, three-toed footprints, stepping in the tracks, and discovered that for all its height the heron takes baby steps. On the river you'll frequently see great blue herons flying ahead of you in slow, swooping rhythm. I am always comforted by their presence. They seem content to live their lives deep in the forest, disturbing no one, disturbed by none.

At Highway 42, Bowie River enters from the west, carrying water from two significant canoeing streams: Bowie Creek and Okatoma Creek. Motorboats are common on the Leaf from now on, but there is still much river and forest to see for those willing to do a lot of paddling and endure occasional engine noise and headwinds. From Highway 42 the river continues 9 miles to Sims Road and 10 more to a ramp at Farlow Landing near Memorial Church Road. Tallahala Creek, a fine canoeing stream, enters from the north half a mile below Farlow. Then it's 4.5 miles to a ramp off Highway 29 at Old Augusta.

The 14 miles from Highway 29 to the ramp at Highway 15 north of Beaumont is punctuated on the north by another good paddling stream, Bogue Homa Creek, 5 miles below Highway 29. Wingate Road crosses the river about a mile below the mouth of Bogue Homa, but hauling a boat out there feels like crawling out of the Grand Canyon. There remain 15.5 miles from Highway 15 to a ramp at Highway 198 near McLain, and 14.5 miles from Highway 198 to the

Pascagoula River, where there's a landing a half mile farther at Merrill. These stretches are characterized by a wide channel, high clay banks, numerous large sandbars, and little sign of people except for occasional clusters of fishing camps. The route is usually wide open, though in places the river narrows and you must weave among fallen logs. The current is fairly strong but lacks shoals or rapids.

A particularly heinous murder occurred on the Mahned Bridge near Farlow Landing. This book is certainly not the place to catalog crimes connected to rivers, but I include this one as a cautionary note. In 1995 a Hattiesburg couple, twenty-one-year-old Robbie Lee Bond and twenty-seven-year-old William Hatcher, stopped at the bridge after work to look at the stars. They had unwittingly stepped into a nest of human vipers. Hatcher was stabbed to death, and Bond was raped and killed. The perpetrators were caught and convicted. I relate this not to single out Mahned Bridge—such crimes can happen anywhere, anytime—but as a reminder that paddlers, like everyone, should always retain a watchful attitude. That held true in frontier days and it holds true today.

The reputation of the lower river was also tainted by claims of pollution in the 1990s, when thousands of south Mississippi residents filed lawsuits against Georgia-Pacific Corporation and its subsidiary Leaf River Forest Products of New Augusta, claiming its pulp mill released dangerous levels of dioxins into the river. Dioxin is a by-product of paper bleaching that causes cancer in laboratory animals. Starting in 1990, some 5,500 plaintiffs filed dozens of lawsuits in various circuit courts, saying they were exposed to dioxins from eating Leaf River fish. In one case, a woman said the contamination gave her Hodgkin's disease. Plaintiffs presented photographs and videotapes of color changes in the water and stains on sandbars, and relied on test results from American Laboratories and Research Services indicating the mill dumped dioxins in the river, as well as on scientists' testimony about the dangers of dioxin. The paper company, in turn, presented an affidavit from a Swedish dioxin researcher who said that, though tests showed dioxins in the river, they didn't come from the mill. He noted that dioxins can come from natural sources such as forest fires and normal decomposition as well as man-made sources like waste incineration, sewage sludge, chlorine, and various industries. He also said dioxin levels in humans are easily proven with blood samples, which the plaintiffs had failed to do. In 1996 the cases were thrown out for lack of evidence. The courts said there was no scientific proof that dangerous levels of dioxin were in the river, that people were exposed to it, that it caused medical problems, or that Leaf River Forest Products was involved.

Several hundred people appealed to the Mississippi Supreme Court, which affirmed the lower courts' decisions in 1999.

Paper mills aren't the only source of environmental concern. In December 1999 an oil pipeline broke south of Highway 28 near Hot Coffee. The 8-inch pipe, used to transport oil from Mississippi wells to refineries in Baton Rouge, Louisiana, spilled more than 300,000 gallons of crude into the river, requiring some 240 workers to clean up the mess. The company, Genesis Crude Oil L.P. of Houston, Texas, had to pay for cleanup costs and long-term monitoring.

None of this does any good for paddlers' peace of mind. I routinely purify any water I get from a stream, but on a river like the Leaf I don't use river water at all, either carrying all I need or relying on springs. As for fish, the amount a paddler is likely to consume for the relatively short duration of a trip shouldn't be cause for alarm. For what it's worth, plenty of local fishermen continue to run lines in the Leaf.

On a less depressing note, the lower Leaf River floodplain lays claim to one of the state's two wilderness areas: the 940-acre Leaf Wilderness Area in the De Soto National Forest. The wilderness designation precludes any mechanical activity, such as chain saws and four-wheelers. The Leaf Wilderness is considerably smaller than the nearby 5,050-acre Black Creek Wilderness. Its only trail is just 1.5 miles long and subject to seasonal flooding since the area consists mainly of hardwood bottomland near the river. When I visited by road one February, I hiked half a mile before the route disappeared underwater. However, the area's swampiness is its virtue, for it contains such wonders as a water oak 5 feet across at chest height. Unfortunately the designated wilderness area does not border the river, coming only within about a quarter of a mile, a few miles above the juncture with the Chickasawhay. The best way to see it is on foot in the dry season, such as late summer or early fall. It lies east of Highway 57 south of McLain.

A couple of campgrounds are located close to Leaf River, to use as bases for day-floating. Big Creek Water Park off Highway 84 between Collins and Laurel has a 150-acre lake with developed camping and rental cabins. It's administered by the Pat Harrison Waterway District. Lake Perry south of Highway 98 near Beaumont has primitive camping and a 124-acre state fishing lake. It's administered by the Mississippi Department of Wildlife, Fisheries, and Parks and makes a good base from which to explore the Leaf Wilderness as well.

Leaf routes

1. Highway 18 to boat ramp at county road off River Road between Highways 37 and 531, 9.5 miles.
2. County road to ramp at Highway 28 east of Taylorsville, 8.5 miles.
3. Highway 28 to ramp at Highway 84, 11.5 miles.
4. Highway 84 to ramp at Highway 588, 13 miles.
5. Highway 588 to ramp at Highway 590, 7 miles.
6. Highway 590 to ramp at Monroe Road a mile west of Eastabuchie, 13 miles. (There's also a dirt landing 6 miles below Highway 590 near the power plant at Moselle on the river's east side.)
7. Eastabuchie to ramp at Highway 42, 10.5 miles.
8. Highway 42 to Sims Road between Old U.S. Highway 49 West and Old River Road, 9 miles.
9. Sims Road to ramp at Farlow Landing near Memorial Church Road between Mahned on Highway 98 and Old River Road, 10 miles.
10. Farlow Landing to ramp off Highway 29 at Old Augusta, 5 miles.
11. Highway 29 to ramp at Highway 15 north of Beaumont, 14 miles. Wingate Road north of New Augusta crosses 5 miles below Highway 29, but access is extremely steep.
12. Highway 15 to ramp at Highway 198 at McLain, 15.5 miles.
13. Highway 198 to ramp at Merrill on east bank of Pascagoula River, 15 miles.

Outfitters

Leaf River Canoe, 5627 Highway 42 By-pass, Hattiesburg, 601-584-9070.

Area campgrounds

1. Big Creek Water Park off Highway 84 between Collins and Laurel. 150-acre lake with developed camping. Call 1-800-748-9618 toll-free or 601-763-8555 locally.
2. Lake Perry south of Highway 98 near Beaumont. RV and tent camping and a 124-acre state fishing lake. 601-784-6119.

High points

Long stretches rarely visited by either paddlers or motorboaters.

Low points

Oil spill and claims of dioxin pollution taint the river's reputation.

Tips

Master the correction stroke for ease in paddling long, straight stretches (see chapter 1).

Bowie Creek

Bowie and Okatoma Creeks start around Magee and swoop southeast like the V in a flock of geese. They converge northwest of Hattiesburg to form Bowie River, which enters the Leaf just above Highway 42 at Petal. Bowie and Okatoma are both excellent for canoeing, though markedly different—Okatoma a heavily used quasi-whitewater stream, Bowie less traveled but strikingly beautiful. Bowie Creek is smooth, clear, tree-shaded, and as gorgeous as any river any-where on this planet that I have seen—and I include tumbling tropical streams, clean northern waters, and everything in between.

The 55-mile-long Bowie—also spelled Bouie—heads up southwest of Magee and runs south. It doesn't become navigable until the Seminary-Sum-rall Road, and even then there are some logjams and shoals. On the 4-mile stretch from there to Highway 589, jungly woods, high banks, and murmuring springs combine to create a sense of eerie isolation. When my paddling buddy Scott Williams was growing up in Prentiss, the area was known locally as "the Big Woods." Scott's father, Frank, told him about the time he rounded a bend in the creek and saw a shirtless man with a long, matted, gray beard who turned and ran like a deer. And there was the fellow driving in the area at night who collided with something big. He was too terrified to get out, and only a passing motorist discovered he had hit a black bear. This stretch is fairly slow until a low, runnable waterfall about half a mile above 589; then the current quickens.

By Highway 589 the creek is easily floatable, and the 10.5 miles to Highway 49 make a perfect day trip: small enough to savor the deep-woods experience, big enough to avoid logjams, far removed from downstream development. Yet not many people float it. When I paddled this segment, I saw just two other boats, both johnboats with fishermen. The first, just below the Highway 589 put-in, contained a couple angling for catfish or bream, their vessel outfitted with a six-horsepower outboard. The second, under the bridge at Highway 49, held a father and son paddling and casting for bass. Big woods line most of this segment, with oaks, cypress, beech, and magnolias tall enough for Tarzan to swing on. There is evidence of logging—sun-bleached stretches where locust and sweetgum riot like boisterous youngsters. But fortunately those rude tangles give way to the quiet, thoughtful shelter of old, big woods. In such an environment, paddlers are likely to encounter wildlife: a wild turkey exploding off a branch overhead; a swimming snake submerging at the sight of humans; a big owl rising off a leaning birch to the safe heights of the treetops, where it watches with wise, wary eyes.

A half mile above Highway 49, the creek takes a 1–2-foot plunge over a clay shelf. When Scott and I floated it, the tricky part came in the least likely spot. As we approached the rapid in mirror-calm water, I stood up in the bow for a better view of the rapids. Unfortunately, Scott stood up in the stern, and if there's one thing paddling partners should avoid doing, it's standing in the canoe simultaneously. The boat wobbled, I lost my balance and, rather than capsize the vessel, barreled out feet-first—a rather heroic gesture on my part, I thought, though Scott was unimpressed, judging by his derisive laughter. At least the dunking felt good on a warm day. As for the actual rapid, no problem. The bow scooped up a few gallons as it dipped under, but it bounced back up and we bailed out the water downstream.

Unlike some four-lane divided highways, 49 offers access to the creek. It's a scant mile from there to the junction with Okatoma Creek, another 9 miles to Interstate 59, 3 more to Glendale Road and 2.5 to the Highway 42 bypass just below Bowie's juncture with the Leaf. The pretty, woodland scenery and good fishing continue for most of this section, but below I-59 development picks up considerably. A low-head dam of concrete rubble is used to reroute water for industrial use just north of Highway 42. The spot is swift, deep, and dangerous, and a number of deaths have reportedly occurred there. Better to portage around. Huge gravel mining operations have scarred these lower reaches, muddying the water and leaving many borrow pits alongside the channel.

As if that's not enough, in the late 1990s a dam was proposed just above the confluence with the Okatoma. In 1999 the Pat Harrison Waterway District, the cities of Petal and Hattiesburg, and the Forrest County Board of Supervisors teamed up to study a $12–30 million, 1,200–2,000-acre reservoir. Supporters said southeast Mississippi needs the new water source to handle the growth of development. Opponents, such as Dr. Stephen Ross, professor of biological sciences and curator of fisheries at the University of Southern Mississippi, said the dam would harm rare fish species such as the huge Gulf sturgeon and the tiny pearl darter and Alabama shad, which use Bowie for spawning.

The Gulf sturgeon, listed as a threatened species, is a long-snouted, bony-plated fish that can reach 8 feet in length and 28 years in age and can weigh more than 200 pounds, though 40 pounds is considered average. It's mind-boggling to picture such a behemoth in the small Bowie. I remember seeing the shape of a 3-foot-long fish darting in the shadow of my canoe that I assumed at the time was a catfish but realized later could have been a sturgeon. Then again, maybe it was a striped bass; the state record 37.82-pounder was caught in Bowie. Anyway, the Gulf sturgeon leave the sea and head upstream in spring, spawning in mid-summer and returning in September. But don't bother buying any 200-pound test line: They only eat when they're at sea. The fish inhabit the waters between Florida and Texas. Their numbers have dropped to an estimated three thousand or less, which scientists believe is largely due to such habitat degradation as dredging, pollution, decreasing water tables—and dams. Meanwhile, radio-tracking indicates a spawning site right about where the Bowie reservoir was proposed. A dam there would likely destroy one of the few places left where they reproduce.

Another argument against a Bowie River dam is the fact that the Pascagoula is the only major river system in the lower forty-eight states as yet undammed in its main branches (though it has some man-made lakes in its extreme upper headwaters). A dam across Bowie would ruin that distinction. One alternative to a reservoir is to convert the riverside gravel pits into a series of connected ponds that would impound water but not block the streambed. Ross and others would prefer to make the river a showcase by promoting canoeing and similar eco-tourism.

These dilemmas exemplify how lack of recreational use can actually threaten a river. Although serious paddlers naturally fear what can happen to a stream when crowds discover it, also to be feared is what can occur when a stream goes unnoticed and unappreciated. In such a situation there may not be enough voices raised against plans to dam, mine, channelize, or otherwise damage it. One hopes that won't prove to be the case with Bowie.

Bowie routes

1. Seminary-Sumrall Road to Highway 589, 4 miles.
2. Highway 589 to Highway 49, 10.5 miles.
3. Highway 49 to Glendale Road between Glendale and Highway 42 at Hattiesburg, 13.5 miles.
4. Glendale Road to Highway 42 at Leaf River, 2.5 miles.

Area campgrounds

Lake Mike Connor, 8 miles west of Collins off Highway 84 on Lake Mike Connor Road just north of the river. RV and tent camping and an 88-acre state fishing lake. 601-765-4024.

High points

A real deep-woods feel, with good chances for spotting wildlife.

Low points

Gravel mining, a lowhead industrial dam, and a proposed reservoir on the lower river.

Tips

Take a tree identification book to learn more about some of the many species.

Okatoma Creek

Most of Mississippi's neighboring states have whitewater. Alabama, Tennessee, and Arkansas all boast respectable rapids. Louisiana doesn't, but it makes up for it with abundant wetlands. Several Mississippi streams have occasional chutes and dropoffs, but only one is renowned for its whitewater: Okatoma. Even so, the creek doesn't take itself too seriously. The fact is, Okatoma is just a regular Mississippi creek that happens to have some rapids—just four notable ones on the popular 13-mile stretch between Seminary and Sanford. This modest series of adrenaline thrill-providers draws huge crowds, making Okatoma one of the most popular floats in the state. On a summer Saturday, canoe rental companies may easily put in well over five hundred customers. And 95 percent of them will capsize before the trip is done, one outfitter told me. That's not because the rapids are particularly daunting—they're all Class I or, at most, borderline II. Rather, it's because most Deep South floaters lack experience in running whitewater, which is hardly surprising when you consider how little there is in the region to practice on. Besides, for most people, capsizing just means getting pleasantly wet on a warm day.

Most of the 50-mile-long Okatoma is not whitewater at all. It heads up east of Mendenhall and runs southeast toward its rendezvoux with Bowie Creek northwest of Hattiesburg. It's not floatable until the 8-mile stretch from Kola Road just south of Collins to Highway 590 at Seminary, and that stretch is subject to logjams, though there are periodic efforts to clear it out. If you want to float it, check with one of the creek's two canoe outfitters in advance to learn current conditions. There are no rapids, just a pretty, forested creek disturbed only by the hum of traffic from busy, four-lane Highway 49 a short distance to the west.

Seminary is where the crowds converge for the 13-mile run to Highway 598 at Sanford. The first rapid is about a mile below 590. Rock shoals block most of the river just beneath the surface, but a quick glance reveals a fairly easy passage to the left. This run is a fun warm-up for the Chute, 1.5 miles farther on. As with the first rapid, the Chute's outlet is a narrow channel to the left. But then the canoe must make a hard right to negotiate a second drop, all at roller-coaster speed. It's tricky, especially in the slow-turning, non-whitewater vessels most of us use. The third challenge, 2 miles below the Chute, is Okatoma Falls at Fairchild Landing, a straightforward plunge of about 2.5 feet. As long as you keep your bow forward and head down the tongue of the wave, it's usually no problem, though standing waves may toss a few cups of water into the boat. The fourth rapid comes up quickly as the river narrows into a tree-lined gorge. Keep the bow pointed downstream and expect water to splash in over the sides. The stretches between these thrills are surprisingly slow but interspersed with smaller rapids.

The 6-mile stretch from Sanford to Lux offers fewer thrills but still some challenges. Below Lux there are a 1–2-foot waterfall and a couple sets of rapids within the first half hour before the river slows as it curls toward Bowie 1.5 miles away.

The Okatoma's whitewater has more benefits than providing a thrilling ride. The deep pools below the first rapid and below Okatoma Falls are popular swimming holes. Fishing is typically good around any fast water, especially below the Chute, though hordes of paddle-clanging boaters can give fish lockjaw. Go on a weekday and drag a spinnerbait, beetlespin, or black topwater lure through the rapids to tempt one of the 1–3-pound bass common in the creek. Or use fly rod or cane pole for bluegill. As for catfish, monsters up to 52 pounds have been hauled from the creek's deep holes.

If crowds make fish scarce, they make wildlife scarcer. But you can get your animal fix at Trapper's Gator Farm on Highway 15 nine miles southeast of Laurel, or at Collins Exotic Animal Orphanage on Highway 49. The former has such creatures as gators, bear, cougar, deer, and snakes. The orphanage houses similar exotic animals that people bought as pets and abandoned. Each place charges a modest admission fee.

Collins is also home to a poultry processing plant that discharges wastewater into the Okatoma. The company, Sanderson Farms, built a new wastewater treatment plant in the early 1980s. Wastewater goes through three treatment stages between the plant and the creek—an anaerobic lagoon, an equalization basin, and a series of aeration ponds. Each stage filters the water and removes sediments. Plant officials claim the treated wastewater is cleaner than the creek itself, which is possible considering that the creek suffers from other sources of pollution such as towns, residences, farms, and camps. State officials say they have received no complaints about negative effects on water quality from the plant.

Other potential threats to the river have been more severe. In 1974 the U.S. Soil Conservation Service—now the Natural Resource Conservation Service— proposed damming and channelizing the stream on its upper reaches near Magee and installing flood-control devices. In counterpoint, in 1978 the Mississippi Heritage Conservation and Recreation Service recommended the creek be listed as a National Wild and Scenic River, which would protect it from such assaults. Neither proposal came to pass. But public interest in the Okatoma was vividly illustrated in 1995 when a company began mining gravel near the river at Lux without getting a state permit. J. J. Pryor and Hattiesburg Materials, Incorporated, cleared 72 acres of ground and began mining on 50, dredging ponds and installing a gravel-washing operation. Even though the company left a 50-foot buffer zone with a berm between mining sites and the creek, many feared that high water could flood the site, alter the river course, cause severe erosion and siltation, and damage fish habitat. Whether the Okatoma mining operation was too close to the creek was hotly debated. (Unfortunately, there are areas, such as the Amite River in Louisiana, where mining companies leave a buffer of mere inches between gravel pit and river, with no berm or anything else to prevent the inevitable flooding of the site.) After considerable public outcry over the Okatoma, the Mississippi Department of Environmental Quality (DEQ) fined the company $6,000, denied a permit, and ordered restoration of the 72 acres. Monitored quarterly by DEQ, the company planted pine trees and otherwise tidied up the land. The incident highlighted shortcomings in the state's mining laws and prompted calls for stiffer legislation. As late as 1999 such changes hadn't materialized, but the state Scenic Rivers Act did, and the Okatoma gravel mining incident was cited as a factor.

That Scenic Rivers Act took effect July 1, 1999, and allowed residents to recommend streams for inclusion. Six had already been recommended when the legislation was passed, including Okatoma and Black Creek in southeast Mississippi, Wolf River in south-central, Strong and upper Pearl in central, and Buttahatchee in northeast. After the law took effect, more recommendations came in to the Department of Wildlife, Fisheries, and Parks. To qualify, a stream must be listed as a public waterway by the DEQ, which means it must move 100 cubic feet per second at low flow. Virtually all floatable streams meet that standard, and many that are not floatable. State officials then assess the stream to see if it meets a variety of other criteria, from water quality to biodiversity to recreational use. If they approve, an advisory committee is formed, the majority of whose members are landowners along the river. Public hearings are held; then the river is submitted to the legislature for official designation. Once the legislature designates a river, a voluntary stewardship plan is drawn up, with recommendations for protecting and enhancing the waterway. The state may offer economic incentives to landowners to leave a buffer zone of trees along the stream. A buffer helps protect streams from a variety of ills, such as siltation, erosion, pollution, overheating, and destruction of native species. A related forestry bill also passed in 1999, provided landowners with a lifetime $10,000 tax credit off state taxes to plant trees. Legislation was planned to provide tax credits for wildlife and fisheries projects as well. State officials believe economic incentives are the key to protecting rivers and avoiding battles over landowner rights.

Okatoma routes

1. Kola Road south of Collins to Highway 590 at Seminary, 8 miles. Kola Road joins Highway 49 with the community of Kola about a mile south of Collins.
2. Seminary to Highway 598 at Sanford, 13 miles. Outfitters charge a small fee for use of Sanford access points.
3. Sanford to Lux, 6 miles. It's another 1.5 miles to confluence with Bowie.

Area campgrounds

Lake Mike Connor, 8 miles west of Collins off Highway 84 on Lake Mike Connor Road. RV and tent camping and an 88-acre state fishing lake. 601-765-4024.

Outfitters

1. Okatoma Outdoor Post, Sanford, 601-722-4297.
2. Seminary Canoe Rental, Seminary, 601-722-4301.

High points

Whitewater!

Low points

Crowds!

Tips

Learn basic boat-handling skills to negotiate the rapids (see chapter 1). And go on a weekday or during the off-season to avoid the mob.

Tallahala Creek

Tallahala is an unusual creek. Even though it stretches 120 miles across southeast Mississippi, little over 25 miles of it is easily floatable, and even those miles can be difficult in low water. Compare that to Black Creek, which is about 130 miles long but offers 100 miles of canoeing. The Tallahala runs down a narrow corridor of land, bounded on the west by the Okatoma Creek valley and on the east by Bogue Homa Creek—the latter, in places, as close as 5 miles away. As a result, Tallahala has few notable tributaries and never gets a chance to grow. It's not often used by either canoers or motorboaters, despite the fact that it's an attractive stream with good fishing.

Tallahala starts 15 miles west of Enterprise and doesn't pick up tributaries for quite a ways: Nuakfuppa Creek east of Bay Springs, then Tallahoma Creek above Ellisville and Rocky Creek below it. Thus undernourished, the creek limps south on its journey to the Leaf River near New Augusta. It's characterized by big woods, big cutovers, medium-sized sandbars, and lots of peace and quiet.

Despite the stream's scenic qualities, for many people Tallahala is synonymous with pollution. That's because for years the river was grossly polluted by two huge municipal wastewater lagoons and a Masonite mill in Laurel. However, in the 1970s Masonite made significant improvements to its wastewater treatment system, as did the city of Laurel in 1989. Laurel went from lagoons to oxidation ditches, considered state of the art even at the turn of the twenty-first century. In this system, filtered sewage enters an oval ditch with huge steel brushes churning to provide oxygen, creating an optimum environment for microbes to feed on wastes. DEQ officials describe Tallahala pollution as virtually a thing of the past and say the creek meets or exceeds federal clean-water standards.

The creek is not even remotely floatable until Highway 29 east of Ellisville, and even then logjams and shallows dominate on the 4.5 miles between Highway 29 and Augusta Road and the 10 miles from Augusta Road to Moselle-to-Ovett Road. Tallahala is a bit wider on the 5 miles from Moselle-to-Ovett Road to Ovett-Petal Road (known as Morriston Road on the west side of the river), but shallows may require some wading.

At Ovett-Petal Road the Mississippi Department of Wildlife, Fisheries, and Parks has installed a boat ramp, and from here down the creek is usually sufficient for paddling. Motorboaters, however, can't normally get far in any direction without grounding in gravel shoals, which pose little problem to a canoe, though a few fishermen keep small motorboats near their camps for running nearby lines or minnow traps. There are 6.5 river miles to Highway 42, 4 miles from Highway 42 to Thomas Creek Road, then 11.5 miles to Old River Road, the last bridge on the creek. Both Thomas Creek Road and Old River Road join

Highway 29 just east of the creek, so they're easy to find, but their characteristically rural put-ins require some toting to get to the water. Tallahala empties into Leaf River less than half a mile below Old River Road. From there you can paddle half a mile up the Leaf to the boat ramp at Farlow Landing near Memorial Church Road, or 5 miles downriver to the ramp off Highway 29 at Old Augusta.

The stretch from Ovett-Petal Road to Highway 42 makes an admirable, and easy, day trip. A few spring branches feed the Tallahala. One of them, to the right not far below the bridge, alternates between clear, sandy stretches and muddy pools created by a series of beaver dams. In one shallow cove I spotted water boiling up from a saucer-sized circle of sand. Kneeling, I tested it with my finger: ice-cold. Rolling up my sleeve, I plunged my hand into the sandy circle. The liquified sand parted, and I slid my arm well above the elbow in the refrigerated tunnel. When my arm was in as far as the bicep, my fingers touched the end of the tunnel where the spring gushed out.

In unfortunate contrast to such gems, Tallahala sports some depressingly long stretches of cutover with no buffer zone of trees. As a result, tributaries spill muddy water into the river, especially after a rain. The Tallahala is a prime case for legislative efforts to provide landowners with incentives to leave such buffers. Bankside trees not only cut back on erosion, they shade the river and keep it cooler. When the cutovers end, the creek coasts between walls of big trees and high banks. In April and May, flowering mountain laurels glow like cotton candy in the deep shade. The waxy-leafed bushes are blanketed with white pentagonal blossoms half an inch across, speckled with pink, red, and purple. Interspersing this bounty are native azaleas. Sometimes called wild honeysuckle, they sport a pink honeysuckle-shaped flower; there is also an orange variety in southeast Mississippi. Hornbeam trees, sometimes referred to as ironwood, resemble stunted, twisted beech. Sandbars glow golden in the sunshine, and mossy banks drip with cold springs in the shade.

Tallahala provides good fishing for spotted bass, longear sunfish (redbellies), bluegill bream, and catfish. Angle for spotted bass with spinnerbaits on light spinning tackle. For panfish, try fly rods with popping bugs, which also work for bass. Or just use live bait for whatever bites, like the bankside fisherman we saw who caught a good-size channel cat followed by a string of redbellies.

For off-creek entertainment, on Highway 15 three miles south of Laurel is a re-created 1800s settlement, Landrum's Country Homestead and Village (601-649-2546). The 10-acre site includes a village with chapel, general store, gem mine, cabins, jail, and gristmill as well as a camping area with RV hookups. Like the creek, it conjures a simpler, quieter time.

Tallahala routes

1. Highway 29 to Augusta Road, 4.5 miles. Augusta Road runs south from Highway 29 in Ellisville and forks southeast across the creek.

2. Augusta Road to Moselle-to-Ovett Road, 10 miles. Moselle-to-Ovett Road, also called Ovett-Moselle Road, runs from North Pumping Station Road north of Runnelstown west to the community of Union.

3. Moselle-to-Ovett Road to boat ramp at Ovett-Petal Road, 5 miles. Ovett-Petal Road runs from Pumping Station Road west to Macedonia Road, becoming Morriston Road west of the creek.

4. Ovett-Petal Road to Highway 42, 6.5 miles.

5. Highway 42 to Thomas Creek Road, 4 miles. Thomas Creek Road runs west from Highway 29 south of Runnelstown.

6. Thomas Creek Road to Old River Road, 11.5 miles. It's another half mile to the Leaf River. Old River Road runs west from Highway 29.

7. Old River Road to ramp east of Highway 29 on Leaf River at Old Augusta, 4.5 miles.

Area campgrounds

Landrum's Country Homestead and Village, Highway 15, 3 miles south of Laurel. Re-created nineteenth-century village with RV hookups. 601-649-2546.

High points

Secluded stretches loaded with beautiful plants such as mountain laurel and native azalea.

Low points

Long stretches of cutover.

Tips

Go in April or May when the mountain laurels are in bloom.

Bogue Homa Creek

It's not often you find two good-looking streams running side by side just a few miles apart, but that's the way it is with Bogue Homa and Tallahala. The southeast Mississippi creeks are like two sisters in a beauty contest. One is long and blond, the other short and brunette. Both are gorgeous. Tallahala is the taller one, starting 20-odd miles north of Laurel and running due south past Runnelstown en route to Leaf River. Bogue Homa, to the east, gets going at Heidelberg and passes Richton. I call it brunette because it's a blackwater stream, its clear waters darkened by tannic acid. Tallahala is clearer, with a tendency to muddiness after a rain, which gives it a blond complexion. The streams run parallel roughly 5 miles apart on their journey to the Leaf near New Augusta. Though not far east of the metropolitan areas of Hattiesburg and Laurel, neither creek is heavily used—nothing like the whitewater Okatoma to the west. Bogue Homa's biggest calling card for the general public is a man-made lake on its upper extremities. The 1,200-acre Lake Bogue Homa 7 miles east of Laurel just north of Highway 84 offers skiing, fishing, camping, and picnicking.

Bogue Homa is Choctaw for Red Swamp, since bogue means swampy and homa or homo means red. The red probably refers to the tannin-stained waters, which, seen in daylight, give the stream the color of Dr. Pepper. Its tributaries too are blackwater, as though someone spilled a truckload of soda pop upstream.

The Mississippi Department of Wildlife, Fisheries, and Parks has a boat ramp at Highway 42, a fit starting point. Stretches above Highway 42 are theoretically floatable, but even from 42 down, canoeing this small creek is a chore, albeit with great rewards. From Highway 42, Bogue Homa flows 8.5 miles to Old Augusta Road and 3.5 miles to Leaf River.

As with Tallahala Creek, the navigability of Bogue Homa is heavily dependent on rainfall. I checked it one spring day while passing by on Highway 42, and it looked imminently floatable. When I returned to float a week later—a week without rain, that is—it had dropped 2½ feet. The fact that we launched at dusk didn't help matters. Dipping a paddle in that dark river was like burying it in black ink. The water had a sinister laugh as it sizzled among downed logs. The fact that the creek was just inches deep offset some of its menace. We blundered along until we found a likely camping spot at a tributary. Soon we were settled back listening to the water's no-longer-sinister chuckle as a half-moon spilled its light into the canyon of trees where we sheltered.

You won't get far down Bogue Homa before you'll have to get out and tow through sand and gravel shoals and slide over barely submerged logs. Also, this is what I call a pool-and-drop stream: long, still pools alternating with fast chutes. That means you must paddle continually in the pools, then get out and drag through the shallow swifts. In other words, floating Bogue Homa is work, and at first you may be prone to overlook the exquisite water, the darting fish, the absence of humans, the abundant birdsong. I confess I've reached a point in my river career where I try to avoid streams with logjams. I suspect most paddlers feel the same way, with the exception of hardcore fishermen who often find prime fishing in the most wretchedly obstructed places, and even many of them prefer to wade-fish. So, had I known how low and bony the Bogue Homa was going to be, I wouldn't have floated it. But I did, and as it turned out, I was glad of it.

Several miles below Highway 42, the creek begins to widen at last, passing under mossy banks spouting spring water like marble fountains. Wildlife is rich in these big, lonely environs. A big red-and-black pileated woodpecker whirls up from a log. A swallowtail kite soars overhead. A grunt from the forest may be a wild hog; a loud splash either a big turtle or small alligator. The woods assume rainforest proportions. Vine-draped water oaks rise tall as skyscrapers; thick-trunked elms lean like bridge buttresses. Spotted bass race over the sand, gasper gou lumber in front of the boat, and in springtime you'll see bream fluttering on their round gravel beds. Bogue Homa offers good fishing on any sort of light tackle. We saw a few families at their own sandbars, using spinning rods, cane poles, and limb lines for catfish, bream, whatever was biting. Fishing is even better at the mouth of the creek, with 2–3-pound spotted bass and big catfish waiting in line to gobble baitfish.

Some 3 miles below Old Augusta Bridge, the creek hooks to the right under a mountainous red bluff, and a tree-arched tunnel opens onto the big Leaf River, which sidles past a broad sandbar and houses on stilts. There's a boat ramp on the right side of Leaf River just below the mouth of Bogue Homa, but it's private, used by residents of a subdivision. Unfortunately, getting out at Wingate Road just below there involves a brutal climb up a sheer bluff, and the next public takeout is 9 miles farther at a ramp at Highway 15 north of Beaumont. But if you've made it down Bogue Homa, you're fit enough to handle either.

Bogue Homa routes

1. Highway 42 to Old Augusta Road, 8.5 miles. Take-out is poor at Old Augusta Road with no under-bridge parking. The winding country road runs from Richton to Old Augusta.

2. Old Augusta Road to Wingate Road on Leaf River, 4 miles. Wingate Road runs north from Highway 98 at the community of Wingate. It's 3.5 river miles from the bridge at Old Augusta Road to Leaf River, and half a mile to Wingate Bridge. The take-out at Wingate requires a steep, grueling climb. The next public boat ramp is 9 miles farther down Leaf at Highway 15 north of Beaumont.

Area campgrounds

Lake Bogue Homa, Highway 84, 7 miles east of Laurel. Primitive and developed campsites, with 1,200-acre lake. 601-425-2148.

High points

Seclusion, little sign of humans, big woods.

Low points

Shallow water, downed logs.

Tips

Wear your wading shoes.

Pascagoula River

The Pascagoula River is the grand waterway of southeast Mississippi, absorbing a wealth of fine canoeing streams—Chunky, Chickasawhay, Leaf, Bowie, Okatoma, Tallahala, Bogue Homa, Black, Red, Escatawpa—as it culminates in cypress jungle and coastal marsh at the city of Pascagoula. But not only is the Pascagoula River significant by Mississippi standards, it's important for the nation, for it's the only major river system in the lower forty-eight states with no dams on any of its main branches. Though it has some in its extreme upper headwaters—such as Little Black Creek Water Park, Lake Bogue Homa, and Okatibbee Lake—the river and its main tributaries still run free, at least for now. I saw a vivid illustration of the Pascagoula's singular status in an article in the November 4, 1994, issue of *Science* magazine. The article, "Fragmentation and Flow Regulation of River Systems in the Northern Third of the World" by Mats Dynesius and Christer Nilsson, featured a map that showed the lower forty-eight states covered in red, indicating major river systems that have been dammed. Green symbolized undammed river basins, and the only patch of green this side of Alaska and the northern territories of Canada was the Pascagoula.

The 81-mile-long river is already sizeable when it officially begins at the juncture of Leaf and Chickasawhay, and it may seem too wide and strong for some paddlers. But it's a remarkably wild river, bordered for most of its length by the 37,124-acre Pascagoula River Wildlife Management Area and the 9,494-acre Ward Bayou WMA, flanked by the 501,000-acre De Soto National Forest to the west, 940-acre Leaf Wilderness Area to the northwest, 3,273-acre Charles M. Deaton Nature Preserve to the north, 19,273-acre Mississippi Sandhill Crane National Wildlife Refuge to the southwest, and the 18,500-acre Grand Bay Reserve and 7,000-acre Grand Bay NWR to the southeast. Such phenomenal country makes it worth putting up with the occasional motorboat, headwind, mudbank, or monster alligator.

The word *Pascagoula* appears to be a derivation of Native American words *pasca* for bread and *okla* for people. When French explorers visited the tribe in late summer 1699, the Indians fed them bread made from corn and "a grain that grows on canes"—cattails, perhaps—along with buffalo, bear, and deer meat, peaches, plums, watermelons, pumpkins, and a succotash of corn and beans. Men and boys went naked while women wore loincloths made of Spanish moss. They lived in round huts with dirt walls and bark or leaf roofs. The Pascagoulas were generally peaceful except for occasional wars with neighboring tribes such as the Biloxis. Mississippi's coastal tribes headed west after the 1763 Treaty of Paris. Groups of Pascagoulas moved to Lake Maurepas and the Amite River in southeast Louisiana, Red River and Bayou Boeuf in central Louisiana, and on into East Texas and Oklahoma, with the last identifiable tribe members reported in 1914.

That ending—assimilation into other tribes and into rural America—is more prosaic than the "singing river" legends that still circulate around Pascagoula and adorn such edifices as Singing River Hospital and Singing River Bridge. The legends purport to explain a "singing" noise reportedly heard on the river. According to the most common version, when the disease-and war-ridden tribe realized they faced extinction, they decided to commit mass suicide. They held hands and, singing, waded into the water, never to be seen again. A little research reveals similar legends concerning Biloxi Indians, Yazoo Indians, and escaped African slaves in Georgia. The story existed even among the Pascagoulas about an earlier, ancestral tribe. According to that one, the ancestors had emerged from the sea to live a gentle harmonious life, but shortly after Hernando de Soto's army came through in 1539, a missionary appeared and began to teach them the gospel. One moonlit night a mermaid goddess arose from the water and summoned her children, telling them she would never surrender them to a foreign way of life. About the only discernible seed of truth in all this is a 1726 account of several people drowning in Fish River, as the east branch of the Pascagoula was then called. It's possible that incident fueled the legends. As for the mysterious noise, I too have heard the singing, but it came from the thousands of mosquitoes clustered about my tent, not Indian spirits.

The Pascagoula is still wonderfully remote for the eastern United States. And that remoteness isn't accidental; it's the result of vision translated into intricate political maneuvers in the 1970s. State wildlife officials worked with the Nature Conservancy and the legislature to create the Pascagoula River WMA by purchasing 32,000 acres from Pascagoula Hardwood Company. The accomplishment, the conservancy's first land acquisition project in the Southeast, was groundbreaking enough to merit a book, *Preserving the Pascagoula* by Donald G. Schueler (University Press of Mississippi, 1980). Ward Bayou WMA was added twenty years later, and in 1999 the Charles M. Deaton Nature Preserve, named after one of the players in the Pascagoula River WMA story, extended the corridor of wildness northward between Chickasawhay and Leaf Rivers.

Not surprisingly, the Pascagoula offers a wealth of fishing options. Run trotlines or limb lines in the muddy river and backwaters for catfish. Slip up into the clearer water of oxbow lakes and bayous to find bass and bream. Toss a large topwater lure or dangle an artificial worm near a cypress trunk or along the edge of a channel for bass, or bob with crickets or worms for bream.

Paddlers can launch just below the confluence of Leaf and Chickasawhay Rivers at Merrill on the east bank. After a few miles of private land, the Pascagoula River WMA begins, and public land dominates most of the rest of the way. As with the Mississippi River, there are just a few bridge crossings—

Highways 26, 614, and 90 and Interstate 10—and several remote landings, both public and private.

On the 13.5-mile stretch from Merrill to Highway 26, the Pascagoula retains elements of hill country, with high bluffs, pine trees, and only intermittent swamps and bayous among the big, beautiful sandbars. It's 32 miles from Highway 26 to a boat ramp at Highway 614, also known as the Wade-Vancleave Road. About 4 miles downriver from Highway 26 are public boat ramps on each side of the river. Big Black Creek enters from the west 2 miles above Highway 614, carrying with it the waters of Black and Red Creeks from the piney hills of De Soto National Forest.

The Pascagoula grows increasingly swampy below Highway 614 as it enters Ward Bayou WMA. The river curves east and does some serious meandering before turning back south at Cumbest Bluff (where there's a pay boat ramp at a bait shop on the east side) 10 miles below Highway 614. It continues south another 7.5 miles, then seems to come to a dead halt. The illusion of a big river that suddenly ends is eerie. As you approach this apparent dead end, however, you'll see a branch leading to either side. This is the beginning of the east and west rivers.

Below the east-west split, the river scarcely flows at all as it twists through dense woods, cypress, and swamp grass. If you take the west river, in 2 miles you'll pass Ward Bayou and Poticaw Landing on the west with a concentration of camps, houseboats, and a bait shop with a pay boat ramp. From here to Gautier, camping is likely to be muddy. The river is subject to tidal fluctuations, so be sure and tie your boat at night. I learned this the hard way when I hauled my boat 30 feet from the water's edge at bedtime one night and woke the next day to find it floating. The woods eventually give way to marsh grass and serpentine bayous. Drivers on I-10 over the Pascagoula River get a good aerial view of this huge swamp. A couple of miles above I-10 you can take Swift Bayou to the left (south) and follow it to Creole Bayou, which leads to the right under the interstate and back to the main river, thus cutting off one huge bend. On one trip, Scott saw an alligator on Swift Bayou that he claims was longer than his 19-foot boat, giving him a new respect—perhaps dread is a better word—for gators. From here it's a hard pull on windswept water big enough for shrimp boats. Such vessels are a romantic sight; considerably less appealing are the power boats, personal watercraft, ski boats, and so on, which can make the most beautiful waterway miserable for paddlers. I try to avoid big water on summer weekends, when motorboats are most numerous. There are more private for-pay boat ramps and bait shops along the lower river. Less than a mile above Highway 90 a broad channel to the left connects back to the east river. Stay on the west river to take out at a ramp at Highway 90 some 33 miles below Highway 614. Or continue another mile to Shepard State Park, which has a boat ramp, canoe rental and campground. The park lies back off the river on the right.

If you take the east river, you'll paddle some 5 miles before joining a broader channel coming out of several bayous. The east river then runs south alongside the towns of Escatawpa, Moss Point and Pascagoula, with development and industry including Ingalls Shipyard. There's a public ramp under the I-10 bridge off Highway 63, and one in Moss Point just above where Escatawpa River enters from the east a mile below I-10. Two miles farther the east Pascagoula River splits, one channel joining the west river, the other going east and south to a ramp at River Park just north of Highway 90.

If all this sounds complicated, well, it is. Indeed, this is the simplified version. The lower rivers are joined by numerous bayous, creeks, sloughs, and dead lakes. This is one of those cases where a good map is well worth acquiring. Without one, you may wind up turning onto some dead-end channels and having to backtrack—no great disaster, but time-consuming. You may also miss shortcuts like Swift Bayou. The U.S. Geological Survey quadrangle maps for the lower river, from the split on down, are Three Rivers, Pascagoula North, and Pascagoula South; the bulk of the difficult section lies within Pascagoula North. Maps of the complete river, from north to south, also include Merrill, Avent, Benndale, Basin, Easen Hill, and Vancleave. The maps can be purchased in stores or by calling U.S.G.S. Information Services at 1-800-HELP-MAP or 1-800-USA-MAPS. Keep in mind that terrain can change faster than the maps are updated. For instance, the Pascagoula North and South quad maps date to 1979, and some channels may have changed, so an exploratory spirit is always necessary. Maps of the wildlife management area are available by calling 601-947-6376 for the George County portion or 228-588-3878 for the Jackson County portion. However, they're not extremely detailed.

On a swampy river like Pascagoula, it makes a big difference whether you paddle during low water or high. Both seasons have their charms. In the floods of late winter and early spring the river can easily get out of its banks, ideal for exploring. As you paddle along, watch for openings into the woods. Machete and compass come in handy for getting the boat through walls of canebrake, though beware of snakes that like to coil up on bushes above the water. And be aware that a cottonmouth making its lazy way across the surface is not likely to be intimidated by a mere canoe. Poke a paddle at it and you may get to see the white interior of its mouth and its slivered fangs. Such thrills aside, it's enchanting to drift through a flooded forest, especially in late winter and early spring when dogwoods, red maples, and redbuds are in bloom. The narrowest passage may open onto a lake shaded by giant cypress trees and tupelo gums. When camping during high water, you may have to settle for a spot just an inch or two above the level of the river in big woods. But even if the ground is squishy and you're surrounded on all sides by water, you can make a cozy camp, with barred owls for nighttime entertainment. And if the moon is out, some night paddling is in order.

In low water time, such as October, sandbars abound. Even on a sandbar, though, you can tell you're in swamp country by the hordes of mosquitoes waiting in ambush in the willow thickets. The Pascagoula swamp is one place I have found where Avon Skin So Soft lives up to its reputation for repelling mosquitoes. Many outdoorsmen swear by this pungent substance, but in my experience it doesn't work everywhere. In the Pascagoula, though, I discovered to my amazement that simply opening a bottle of it made the mosquitoes vanish. While low water makes it harder to explore the backcountry, it uncovers other wonders, such as a 4-foot waterfall tumbling from a jungled clay bank.

Among other factors for which the Pascagoula is memorable is the likelihood of seeing a swallowtail kite. These graceful, distinctive birds of prey range from extreme southeast Mississippi along the Gulf coast down to Florida and on to southern South America. With slender wings spreading up to 50 inches and edged at the rear in black, and a long, sharply-forked black tail contrasting with white body and forewings, the kites are instantly identifiable. They inhabit wetlands, feed on insects and reptiles, and skim the water to drink. Mainly you'll see them riding the air currents, and when you do, you can rest assured that you are in a fine, wild place.

Pascagoula routes

1. Merrill to Highway 26, 13.5 miles.
2. Highway 26 to ramp at Highway 614 (Wade-Vancleave Road), 32 miles. There are also ramps about 4 miles below Highway 26 on each side of the river

accessible by following wildlife management area signs from Highway 57 on the west or River Road on the east.

3. Highway 614 to ramp at Highway 90 at Gautier on west river, 33 miles. Shepard State Park is about a mile farther; stay near west bank, cross under the railroad trestle and turn into west alcove about 100 yards farther. It's about 200 yards to the park ramp.

4. Highway 614 to ramp under I-10 on east river, 26 miles.

Area campgrounds and outfitters

Shepard State Park, 1034 Graveline Road, Gautier, 228-497-2244, campground with hookups, canoe rental, boat ramp leading to West Pascagoula River.

High points

Massive wetland semi-wilderness, great for exploring.

Low points

Wide river more suited to johnboats than canoes.

Tips

Take a good map.

Black Creek

Black Creek is Mississippi's premier canoeing stream. That's not just a statement of personal taste. Consider:

- For most of its length, the roughly 130-mile-long southeast Mississippi creek is ideal canoeing size, not so small you're constantly battling logjams nor so big you're dodging speedboats and headwinds.
- The current is just right, neither foaming whitewater nor stagnant bayou, lively enough to keep you alert without distracting you from the scenery.
- Black Creek is located largely in the 501,000-acre De Soto National Forest. In essence, that means most of the surrounding wilderness is yours to camp in, hike in, and enjoy.

Canoe instructor Lane Boler of Liberty gives paddling pointers to Patrice Huff of Rosetta on Black Creek.

• As testimony to the excellence of this stream, a 20-mile section is a designated National Wild and Scenic River. Also, part of the creek lies within Black Creek Wilderness Area, and a 41-mile hiking trail roughly parallels it.

To sum up, on Black Creek you can paddle for days and remain within a Deep South wilderness of towering pine trees, gushing springs, glistening sandbars, and occasional cypress swamps. Nor does this glory end with a whimper. Running in a southeasterly direction south of Hattiesburg, Black Creek joins the equally lovely Red Creek to form Big Black Creek, which empties into the mighty Pascagoula River with its awe-inspiring swamps. To float from, say, Big Creek Landing—the uppermost put-in within the national forest—to the city of Pascagoula on the Gulf Coast is to see Mississippi geography writ large, a tour from piney peaks to land's end.

Black Creek is called black because of its tannin-stained waters. The tannic acid comes from a blend of acidic vegetative matter. Blackwater streams abound in varying shades across the Deep South from southeast Mississippi to southeast Georgia. The latter's upper Suwannee River, for instance, resembles cola, while Red Creek is more like honey. Black Creek's tannic luster is highlighted by small white sandbars beneath green forest walls speckled in the springtime with creamy white blooms such as titi bushes, catalpa trees, and Virginia willow, and pink with mountain laurel, native azalea, and occasional mimosa. Curly-barked river birches bow before tall spruce pine, water oak, hickory, ash, and their royal kin. Sweet-smelling coastal rosemary and edible sawbriar shoots garnish the forest's edge, and gravel bars reveal geologic history with fossilized tiny crinoid plants, relics from the epoch when this region lay undersea. There's no sea-salt now in the ice-cold springs that tumble from clefts in the pine-strawed bluffs. As you drift along the creek agape at these wonders, you may miss the well-camouflaged non-poisonous diamondback water snakes curled in the lower limbs of overhanging bushes—6-footers aren't uncommon—but you're less likely to overlook a pair of nervous mallards swimming up ahead, especially when they panic and fly back upriver in such haste you almost feel their feathery wingbeats near your cheek. The clear stream abounds with bream and bass, both of which can be caught on ultralight rigs with green-and-black beetlespins, fly rods with popping bugs, or cane poles with worms and crickets. Farther downriver toward the Pascagoula, switch to limb hooks with stinkbait or chicken livers for catfish.

There are other wild foods if you know where and when to look. Late August and early September is time for muscadines. The luscious wild grapes grow along virtually all Mississippi streams, but they're most accessible along waterways like Black Creek, which has plenty of sandbars. Muscadine vines, which have characteristic grape leaves, climb trees along the riverside to absorb sunshine. When they dangle directly over the water, it's nearly impossible to get the fruit. But when they hang over bare ground, you can fill a bucket. The prime method is to shake the vines, which causes the fruit—along with dirt, bark, and fire ants—to rain down around you. Throw sticks at the uppermost reaches to knock down the rest. Some people spread a bedsheet on the ground for easier collecting.

Pawpaws get ripe the same time muscadines do. The small trees, with leaves similar to those of hickory, thrive in the shade of tall hardwoods along riversides. Their oblong, greenish-skinned, creamy-fleshed fruit tastes like a cross between pear and banana. Harvest by shaking the trees and picking the fruit up off the ground, taking care not to get bonked on the head. Quince and hardy oranges are ready to pick in the fall. Being sour, they fare better as jelly, though some relish the tart taste, especially with salt. Persimmons lose their bitterness after the first frosts of late November. The trees are easily identifiable since leaves fall off while the orange fruit still clings to the limbs. Few fruits are more bitter than an unripe persimmon, few more delicious than a fully ripe one. Wild winter huckleberry, which is actually a blueberry, produces in February and March and grows right on the river bank. Other wild blueberries mature from April to June. Mayhaw, a tree that produces a tart red berry used for jelly, is ready in early April. It prefers swampy areas. Wild strawberries spring up in sunlit areas in April and May, though they have little flavor. Much tastier are dewberries, which are especially prolific along sandbars beside rivers at the same time of year. Wild cherries drop in late April. They tend to be tiny, but trees that get plenty of moisture may produce fruit big enough to snack on. Blackberries abound in May and June in tangled, chiggery, snakey thickets. From May through July, American plums can be found in sunny margins such as the edges of clearings; sloe plums, dusty blue-gray in color, come ripe in the fall. Crabapples are sweet enough to eat by June or July. Mulberries, which grow on trees and are beloved by birds, are edible in July. Maypop, a lemony fruit with lots of seeds, ripens on ground-running vines throughout the summer and stays ripe into the fall. Elderberry bushes, which favor moist soil, produce bold white flower clusters starting in May, and tiny black berries from late July into early September. The berries are edible, but they leave an inky stain and cause an allergic reaction in some people. They can be boiled with sugar for ten minutes to make juice and are used for wine. Fruits just scratch the surface of edible wild foods. Others include cattails, pecans, walnuts, acorns (palatable when the tannic acid is leached out), arrowhead root, daylilies, sawbriar shoots, dried goldenrod seed, and countless more. Unfortunately, there are virtually no field guides available for edible plants of the Deep South. One reason may be the liability. For instance, it's possible to mistake poisonous gallberries for blueberries, wild carrots for hemlock.

The uppermost Black Creek put-in is at Churchwell Road (Camp Dantzler) 8 miles above Big Creek Landing. The bridge lies outside the borders of the national forest, and the first 5 miles or so of creek below it pass through private land, mostly forested. The national forest's Big Creek Landing, located on the south side of the river, marks the western terminus of Black Creek Trail, which rambles in and out along the stream's south side en route to its eastern end at Fairley Bridge. U.S. Forest Service maps of the De Soto National Forest and of Black Creek in particular are helpful in getting to the put-ins, locating the trail, and otherwise understanding the countryside; they're available by calling national forest headquarters at 601-928-4422.

From Big Creek Landing to Old Highway 49 at the town of Brooklyn stretch 5 lovely, meandering miles. (New Highway 49 crosses the creek less than a mile above Old 49, but the Old 49 take-out is much better.) Black Creek Canoe Rental does a steady business at Brooklyn, and nearby Paul B. Johnson State Park provides a convenient basecamp for day-trippers. There are also campsites aplenty as you continue down the creek. The stream runs between broadening sandbars and high bluffs on the 5-mile leg from Brooklyn to Moody's Landing, which is located on the north bank on Forest Service Road 301. The stream is narrow and shallow enough in places to

Group floats are popular on Black Creek, like this Franklin County High School field trip.

require tricky maneuvering, even the occasional portage, but not enough hardship to make you question the worth of the trip. Of course, you may find, as I did, a massive tree blocking the river, requiring you to swim your boat under or tote it around. Such drawbacks merely add zest. Less appealing is the proximity of the U.S. Army's Camp Shelby just a short distance to the north. The thunder you hear may be artillery.

After the 10 miles from Moody's Landing to the boat ramp off Highway 29 at Janice Landing, Black Creek becomes a designated National Wild and Scenic River, and the 5,050-acre Black Creek Wilderness Area sprawls around the 5-mile stretch from Janice to Cypress Creek Landing. Less than a mile below Janice, Beaverdam Creek enters from the south, an impressive little brook worth exploring on foot, either by wading or following the segment of Black Creek Trail that loops around it. About 4 miles farther down Black Creek, Cypress

Creek runs in from the north just above Cypress Creek Landing off Forest Service Road 305. Hickory Creek enters from the north about a third of the way along the 5-mile reach from Cypress Creek Landing to Fairley Bridge, which marks the eastern end of Black Creek Trail. All of these landings—Big Creek, Moody, Janice, Cypress Creek, and Fairley—have U.S. Forest Service primitive campgrounds, not that you need them if you're canoe camping.

Outdoorsmen with several days to spend may face a difficult choice between hiking the trail and floating the creek. Each is worth a visit, but with a canoe you can allow time for day hikes and enjoy both environments. The going is easy and pleasant on the wide, mostly flat path, which has wooden footbridges over the innumerable streams that course through the forest. Still, waterproof boots are advisable; in high water some boardwalks go under. Much of the forest is stately and grand, with big hardwoods, large sloughs, and species of trees ranging from swamp-loving tupelo gum to hilltop-hugging longleaf pine. The trail in places follows Black Creek and tributaries, offering some excellent views. No motor vehicles of any kind, not even pack animals, are allowed on the trail. Some visitors may be concerned about traveling during deer hunting season. I would recommend wearing something bright orange, such as cap or vest, for safety's sake, but in other ways hunting season offers certain benefits even if you're not a sportsman. The presence of hunters and hounds gets wildlife moving, and you're more likely than ever to see creatures. I was sitting by the campfire one frosty morning when I heard distant hound music. My buddy, Dan Banks, spotted movement in the rain-swollen river, and we hurried to the bank as a doe, only her head showing, made steady progress straight across the foamy brown current and disappeared into the woods on our side. A half-hour later two dogs arrived at the far shore. The first came to the edge and jumped right in. The second hung back for a minute, then followed. They swam straight across the 100-yard wide, bank-to-bank flood, and soon resumed howling as they picked up the scent.

The river widens a bit on the 8 miles from Fairley to Highway 26 with the addition of Deep Creek from the east, Barney Branch from the west, then Mill Creek and Flat Branch from the east. A few miles below Highway 26, on the 19-mile run to Highway 57, Black Creek exits the national forest, but the change is not dramatic. More noticeable is the creek's gradual evolution toward swampiness. Below Highway 57 it slows, and soon you see more cypress than pine, with Spanish moss dangling over the browning current. Springs continue to freshen the river, but they leak from low slippery-clay shelves rather than high red-clay bluffs, and they sizzle with mosquitoes. It's 13 miles from Highway 57 to the juncture with Red Creek, 5 more from there to Pascagoula River, and 3 miles to a ramp at Highway 614 (Wade-Vancleave Road).

I had the privilege of paddling this lower stretch in the dark one time. Traveling in sea kayaks, Scott and I reached Highway 57 around 3:30 P.M. and calculated that we were a day behind schedule on our journey from Brooklyn to Pascagoula, so we decided to continue to the Pascagoula River without stopping. As it got dark, navigating among the logs and submerged branches became intuitive. You can't very well hold a flashlight and wield a double-bladed kayak paddle at the same time, so we relied on night vision, responding to wisps of shadow and glimmers of light on the surface of the river. Cypress trees canopied the river, blocking the last dusk light. Suddenly the water exploded just ahead of me like a cannon shot. I started, then laughed: a beaver, more scared than I. It was probably cruising blithely along, little expecting to glance back and see a big, silent kayak bearing down. Then I spotted what appeared to be a log in front of the boat. As I neared, it sank without sound or ripple and did not resurface. Alligator. There seemed to be some gray mass up ahead. Before I had time to investigate, my kayak slammed head-on into a tree which lay across the river. The current swept me sideways against it, into a mass of vines and branches. I thrust the boat forward, hoping to find a passage but rammed another log. Behind me Scott stopped when he heard the commotion and pulled out a flashlight. While he played his beam over the fallen tree, I kept watch on the network of branches, which looked awfully snaky. Scott found a way through, a 2-foot-wide opening just past the treetop, and we continued. After we reached the convergence of Red and Black Creeks, the river broadened and we didn't have to worry much about snags anymore. The moon, just past full, rose over the water, and barred owls talked the language of the swamp. Side by side in silence we plied our kayaks down the broad, moonstruck river through the black forest toward the wide Pascagoula.

Black Creek routes

1. Churchwell Road (Camp Dantzler) to ramp at Big Creek Landing, on south bank of river, 8 miles. Churchwell Road runs south to the creek from Old Highway 49. To get to Big Creek Landing, follow County Road 334 (Brooklyn-

Carnes Road) half a mile west of Brooklyn, go west on County Road 335 (Carnes-Rockhill Road) 2.5 miles to Forest Service Road 335E, and go north to the landing.

2. Big Creek Landing to Old Highway 49 at Brooklyn, 5 miles. New Highway 49 crosses the creek less than a mile above Old 49, but the Old 49 take-out is better.

3. Brooklyn to Moody's Landing on County Road 301 east of Brooklyn on the north bank, 5 miles. The Forest Service charges $3 per day for parking at Moody's.

4. Moody's Landing to ramp at Janice Landing off Highway 29, 10 miles. (From Moody's Landing to Fairley's Bridge, approximately 20 river miles, Black Creek is a designated National Wild and Scenic River.) The Forest Service charges $3 per day for parking at Janice.

5. Janice to Cypress Creek Landing on F.S. Road 305B south of F.S. Road 305, on the north bank, 5 miles. The Forest Service charges $3 per day for parking at Cypress Creek Landing.

6. Cypress Creek Landing to ramp at Fairley Bridge Landing at Fairley Bridge, 5 miles. Fairley Landing is located at the end of F.S. 374A off F.S. 374 which runs south from County Road 318 just west of the bridge. The Forest Service charges $3 per day for parking at Fairley.

7. Fairley Bridge to ramp at Highway 26, 8 miles.

8. Highway 26 to ramp at Highway 57, 19 miles.

9. Highway 57 to ramp at Highway 614 (Wade-Vancleave Road) on Pascagoula River, 21 miles. There's also a state ramp on the west side of the creek just below the juncture of Red and Black Creeks 13 miles below Highway 57.

Outfitters

1. Black Creek Canoe Rental, Brooklyn, 601-582-8817.

Area campgrounds

1. Little Black Creek Water Park on Little Black Creek Road between Purvis and Lumberton. This Pat Harrison Waterway District has developed camping and cabins with a 600-acre lake, formed by damming Little Black Creek, a tributary to Black Creek. 601-794-2957.

2. Paul B. Johnson State Park, 319 Geiger Lake Road just east of Highway 49 south of Hattiesburg. 601-582-7721.

3. Big Creek Landing, U.S. Forest Service primitive campground on Forest Service Road 335E off F.S. 335, 5 miles west of Brooklyn, located on the south bank of Black Creek. Camping is free. 601-928-4422 (Forest Service headquarters).

4. Ashe Lake, Forest Service primitive campground on F.S. C308E 2 miles south of Brooklyn off Ashe Nursery Road. Camping is $7 per night. There's also an 8-acre lake and restrooms.

5. Moody's Landing, Forest Service primitive campground on F.S. 301 on the north bank of Black Creek. Camping is $7 per night.

6. Janice Landing, Forest Service primitive campground along Black Creek at Highway 29. Camping is $7 per night.

7. Cypress Creek Landing, Forest Service primitive campground along Black Creek off F.S. 305. Camping is $7 per night.

8. Fairley Bridge Landing, Forest Service primitive campground on F.S. 374A south of the bridge on the west side of the creek. Camping is $7 per night.

High points

Unrivaled scenery, perfect canoeing size, national forest.

Low points

Occasional fallen logs, crowds on summer weekends.

Tips

Take hiking boots for day hikes on nearby Black Creek Trail.

Red Creek

Red Creek heads up around Lumberton and flows southeast, roughly paralleling Black Creek to its north until the two creeks merge to form Big Black Creek and then enter the Pascagoula. Red Creek is shorter and shallower than its sister stream, and passes through less national forest, but it's still a canoeing gem. Because of their names, it's logical to wonder if Red Creek is a bit lighter in color than Black. Based on my observations, it is. But it may be less the color of the water than the fact that Red Creek is shallower and sandier. Thus, when its tannic-acid-stained water flows a few inches deep over white sand, it looks light amber compared to Black Creek's maple syrup color.

Red Creek is first floatable at Highway 26 west of Wiggins, though paddlers may still encounter some shoals and logjams. By Highway 49, some 9.5 miles down, it's pretty open. The creek's only outfitter, Red Creek Camp and Canoe Rental, is located on the southeast side of Highway 49 and has a campground. Another campground, Perk Beach, is located across the creek, plus there's one just north of Wiggins at Flint Creek Water Park.

At Highway 49 Red Creek is still small but rarely requires portaging. Studded with exquisite sandbars, it flows 6 miles to the rather remote City Bridge, then 15 more miles to Highway 15 at Ramsey Springs. A couple of miles before Highway 15, it enters De Soto National Forest, and exits about 3 miles below the bridge on the 15-mile stretch to the community of Vestry just east of Highway 57. The creek also runs through a substantial portion of the 91,139-acre Red Creek Wildlife Management Area. Below Ramsey Springs, the stream widens almost imperceptibly, deepening and darkening until, past Vestry, bayous appear with mammoth cypress trees. It's another 5 miles from Vestry to the bridge at Highway 57. From there to the juncture with Black Creek are 8 miles, then 5 to the Pascagoula River and 3 more to Highway 614 (Wade-Vancleave Road). Below Highway 57, Red Creek lies within the realm of the Pascagoula swamp. Floating this stretch during high water is a ticket to some great backwater exploration. The final mile or so before the juncture with Black Creek flows within the Pascagoula River Wildlife Management Area. When the creek is out of its banks you can paddle into the forest and explore at will, a delight provided you have a compass and machete.

Red Creek is the perfect foil to the image many non-Mississippians have about the state. When I took two northern friends—Dave Lambert from Michigan and his son Seth from Nebraska—down Red Creek, they were expecting mud, mosquitoes, moccasins, and moonshiners. What they found was white sand, fewer mosquitoes than they have in Michigan, an abundance of non-poisonous critters, and not a single *Deliverance*-type character. However, the forest wasn't quite as impressive as I would have preferred, for while big woods lined both sides of the creek, we could usually see through them to more open land— presumably pasture, pine plantation, and cutover. The forest simply forms a

Seth Lambert of Lincoln, Nebraska, tries his hand at fly-fishing in the clear waters of Red Creek.

dense corridor. I'm thankful for that, anyway, since logging to the bank causes erosion and siltation. Thus the creek is pretty much protected. Plus, pine trees grow so fast that in no time that openness will fill in. But it doesn't quite conjure the deep-woods feeling you get on Black Creek. Even so, "I've never seen so many trees in one place—ever," Seth told me after an exploratory hike.

I've heard mixed reviews of Red Creek fishing. Some anglers claim it's good. A Mississippi Department of Wildlife, Fisheries, and Parks brochure ranks it as generally poor due to the shallowness of the stream. I'd have to concur with the department. Seth used a fly rod while his father employed a spinning outfit and I worked a spincast. We even put some hooks out at night. Conditions seemed perfect, but on a four-day float we came up with just six keepers—five bass and a bluegill—despite using every lure in the box as well as live and cut bait. I talked to other fishermen who had poor luck on the same weekend, so maybe it was the phase of the moon or the barometric pressure or whatever other mysterious forces dictate fish-biting habits. Still, we caught enough to supplement our diet. Fishing improves below Highway 15 as the creek deepens and provides better habitat for spotted bass, bluegill, and catfish. Use topwater lures and jigs for bass, stinkbait and livers for catfish, worms and crickets for bream.

A canoe circles past a massive cypress tree on a bayou off Red Creek.

Fishing aside, the creek is satisfying from a paddler's perspective. Dave had canoed many a whitewater river in Montana but still seemed challenged by Red Creek's obstacle course of submerged logs and branches, hairpin bends, and sandy shoals. These are intermixed with long, still stretches just right for lazying. In the aquarium-clear water you can see creatures on the creek bottom several feet down, such as snakes wriggling along the sand and big turtles gliding like raptors.

Unlike Black Creek, Red Creek doesn't have its own parallel hiking trail, but Tuxachanie Trail comes close, within 5 miles in fact. The 23-mile path, located a mere 30-odd miles north of Gulfport, provides a wonderful sampling of coastal pine savannah, characterized by sandy soil, longleaf pine trees, and broad views. The route has been declared a National Recreation Trail. The mostly flat path is actually more convenient than Black Creek Trail since it has a 12.5-mile loop on the east end and crisscrosses Bigfoot Horse Trail, allowing for day-hike possibilities. Outdoorsmen who want to mix floats down Red Creek with hikes on Tuxachanie Trail can find a convenient base at the P.O.W. Camp, a small lake and primitive campground located along the trail not far south of Red Creek. As with the creek, I used the trail to demolish some Mississippi stereotypes, in this case with a fellow who was born and raised in Los Angeles and worked in New York City. At age thirty Brian Moore had never been camping, so I took him to the Tuxachanie. He did experience some terror at the sound of a beaver smashing the water with its tail near our tent and the loud footsteps of a squirrel scampering across dry leaves as we hiked. But he marveled at the intricate details within the "cathedral of pines," as he called it: the miniature canyon carved by Bigfoot River (a small, sandy creek), a woodpecker's relentless hammering, white fungus growing on deadwood, clusters of insect-devouring pitcher plants. For a map of the trail or of the De Soto National Forest call Forest Service headquarters in Biloxi, 228-928-5291.

Red Creek routes

1. Boat ramp at Highway 26, 3 miles west of Wiggins, to Highway 49 just north of Perkinston, 9.5 miles.
2. Highway 49 to City Bridge, 6 miles. From Highway 49, 2 miles south of Perkinston, take Sunflower Road east to Sunflower Church, turn left, go 2 miles and left again on City Bridge Road; bridge is 2 miles farther.
3. City Bridge to Highway 15 at Ramsey Springs, 15 miles.
4. Highway 15 to Vestry, 15 miles. To get to the Vestry take-out, take the first road southwest off Highway 57 just south of Black Creek.
5. Vestry to Highway 57, 4 miles.
6. Highway 57 to Highway 614 (Wade-Vancleave Road), 16 miles. It's 8 miles from Highway 57 to the juncture with Black Creek, 5 miles to the Pascagoula River and 3 miles to Highway 614. There's a state boat ramp on the west side just below the juncture of Red and Black Creeks.

Outfitters

Red Creek Camp and Canoe Rental, Highway 49 at Biloxi, 601-264-4783.

Campgrounds

1. Flint Creek Water Park, Highway 29 North, Wiggins. 600-acre lake, four water slides, developed camping. 601-928-3051.
2. P.O.W. Camp off Forest Service Road 402E just north of F.S. 402 midway between Saucier and Highway 15. Free primitive camping beside 7-acre fishing lake along Tuxachanie Trail. 228-928-5291 (Forest Service headquarters in Biloxi).

High Points

Beautiful amber-clear water.

Low Points

Shallow and narrow in spots.

Tips

Don't depend on fishing for your food supply.

Escatawpa River

Like Black and Red Creeks, Escatawpa River is a blackwater stream, its waters stained by natural tannic acids leached from vegetation. But Black and Red enter the Pascagoula from the west, while Escatawpa comes from the east. The 125-mile-long stream, which is floatable for half its length, heads up along the Mississippi-Alabama state line. Topographic maps indicate it starts in Alabama, but the U.S. Army Corps of Engineers puts its headwaters near the community of Copeland, Mississippi, southeast of Waynesboro. Regardless of who can claim the exact birthplace, the upper two-thirds of the river lie in Alabama, flowing generally south parallel to the state line. It angles into Mississippi at Highway 98 and eventually hooks west into the Pascagoula River at Moss Point.

If Black and Red Creeks are the color of iced tea, the upper Escatawpa is more like strong black coffee. Bordering porcelain-white sandbars and gnarled cypress roots, the dark river gleams like an antique mirror in an old mansion. One fellow described it as spooky. My wife called it miraculous. Either way, it's a wonder to behold. An unfortunate blemish on this riverine beauty is the abundance of litter. It's worse around bridges, where people apparently toss it out, but it washes down to mar even the most remote stretches.

There's a popular swimming hole at the put-in at Lott Road, a county road north of Highway 98. On the 7 miles from Lott Road to Georgetown Bridge Road, the stream is small enough to require some drags over sandy shallows and tight squeezes among logs. This stretch can be a problem in late summer and early fall when water levels are low. Puppy Creek enters from the east just above Georgetown Bridge, boosting river width as it continues 13.5 miles to Highway

98. Brushy Creek flows in from the west 10.5 miles below Georgetown, another sizeable creek that enlarges the Escatawpa considerably. Brushy Creek, which runs about 6 miles from Brushy Creek Road to the Escatawpa, is canoeable if there's sufficient water and you don't mind some pullovers. Escatawpa Hollow Camp and Canoe sprawls out along the east bank just past Highway 98, providing the only access.

As the Escatawpa widens, the intensity of its blackness diminishes. Still, it continues lovely and wooded on the 6 miles from Highway 98 to Howell's Bridge at Highway 612 and the 8.5 miles from Highway 612 to Tanner Williams Road. Sandbars remain pleasantly small. Shady red-maple arbors at the edge of the river on the lower ends of sandbars provide great hammock spots. You can sling a hammock in the shade just inches over the cold, running river for a water-cooled, bug-free shelter even in the heat of summer.

While the Escatawpa is hardly treacherous, it demands precise maneuvering in the bends where swift currents rush among fallen logs. That's fun to some and toil to others. I mistakenly insisted on stationing my wife at the stern so she could practice her steering. I spent years figuring out paddle strokes, but I saw no reason why Angelyn couldn't learn all that by, say, lunchtime. I explained everything, then turned around and left the steering to her. As she wrestled to guide the straight-keeled 17-foot boat, the woodland quiet was punctuated with splashes, thuds, mutters, and an occasional screech. But we didn't turn over, and by late afternoon she was dodging logjams handily. However, when she recalls the trip, that session is not the high point.

Canoe outfitters tell me that some of the worst problems come from conflicts between male and female partners. In a typical scenario, the man knows just enough to get into trouble. What he can't handle with skill he'll solve with muscle. Capsize is likely, and the aggrieved woman swears off canoeing forever. I'm glad I haven't been guilty of such behavior—at least not recently.

The Escatawpa grows noticeably swampy on the 10 miles from Tanner Williams Road to a boat ramp at Highway 614. Bayous and oxbow lakes provide good side trips. Showy white spider lilies and titi (pronounced tie-tie) bushes bloom in late spring and early summer. Titi, also known as leatherwood, has drooping, finger-shaped clusters of white blossoms; it grows thick along river banks. Spider lilies stand upright, their three to seven white petals sparkling with leggy fringe. They flourish in lower, swampy areas such as the shores of oxbow lakes.

A sea kayak probes marsh country of lower Pascagoula River.

Below Highway 614, on the 22.5-mile stretch to a ramp at Pollock Ferry Road, sandbars diminish, banks sag, and the river is wide enough for motorboats. As a result, fewer people paddle down here. This stretch is low-lying enough for flanking areas to merit names such as Red Oak Swamp, Reed Brake Swamp, and Island Swamp. Big Creek flows in 12 miles below Highway 614, then Jackson Creek 4.5 miles farther down, both from the east. There's a for-pay take-out, Presley's Outing, on the oxbow lake at the mouth of Jackson Creek, 16.5 slow miles below Highway 614. This oxbow, known as Goode's Mill Lake, is a popular water skiing spot, so paddlers beware. I-10 crosses the river a couple of miles farther. This lower river is the least appealing section to paddlers due to industry and motorboats, but ironically to the south and east lie the 18,500-acre Grand Bay National Estuarine Research Reserve and the contiguous 7,000-acre Grand Bay National Wildlife Refuge. This impressive swath contains coastal bays, saltwater marshes, maritime pine forests, pine savannas, and pitcher plant bogs. It harbors creatures like the Alabama redbellied turtle, Bachman's sparrow, speckled burrowing crayfish, crawfish snakes, glass lizards, and diamondback terrapins, plus plants like sundew, wild orchids, Chapman's butterwort, pineland bogbutton, night-flowering wild petunia, giant spiral ladies-tresses, and Harper's yellow-eyed grass. The reserve and the refuge—which are closed to residential and industrial development but open to fishing and hunting—serve to protect a habitat that has shrunken drastically in recent years.

After Pollock Ferry the river turns west toward Moss Point, expanding into 2-mile-long Robertson Lake on its final 11-mile run to the Pascagoula River. There are public boat ramps in Moss Point just above where the two rivers join and at River Park north of Highway 90 in Pascagoula, as well as private marinas. Unfortunately this urban stretch of river has been notoriously polluted. It ranked number 44 on the Environmental Working Group's list of the fifty most polluted waters in the nation based on U.S. Environmental Protection Agency statistics from 1990 to 1994. Dioxin from chlorine bleaching at the International Paper Company paper mill at Moss Point prompted the Mississippi Department of Environmental Quality to post fish consumption advisories. The plant modified its process, and the advisory was lifted in 1995. A mercury advisory for bass and large catfish consumption remains in effect from the state line south to I-10, but mercury apparently comes more from atmospheric sources—pollution wafting across the nation—than local industries. Low dissolved oxygen levels—caused by release of wastewater with organic matter from the paper mill and a fish oil processing plant, among others—continue to be a problem in the lower river.

But the water quality remains good upstream. In fact, DEQ officials call the upper Escatawpa one of the cleanest streams in the state. The fishing is good as well. Bass fishermen use white or chartreuse spinnerbaits on the uppermost stretches, jig-and-pig and small topwater lures or crankbaits on the lower. Cane-pole fishing for panfish and catfish is effective as well. Spring and fall are best times to wet a hook. Anglers should remember that the creek flows through both Alabama and Mississippi, and buy licenses accordingly.

Escatawpa routes

1. Lotts Road to Georgetown Bridge, 7 miles.
2. Georgetown Bridge to Highway 98, 13.5 miles. The only take-out is at Escatawpa Hollow Camp and Canoe (see below).
3. Highway 98 to Highway 612 (Howell's Bridge), 6 miles. There's a steep carry and limited parking at Highway 612.
4. Highway 612 to Tanner Williams Road, 8.5 miles. Tanner Williams Road runs east from Highway 613 at the community of Harleston.
5. Tanner Williams Road to public boat ramp at Highway 614, 10 miles.

6. Highway 614 to ramp at Pollock Ferry Road northeast of Orange Grove, 22.5 miles. There's a for-pay take-out at Presley's Outing 16.5 miles below Highway 614 on Presley's Outing Road at Goode's Mill Lake where Jackson Creek runs into the Escatawpa on the east side.

7. Pollock Ferry Road to Pascagoula River, 11 miles. There are public boat ramps in Moss Point just above where the Escatawpa and Pascagoula rivers join, and at River Park north of Highway 90 in Pascagoula about 5 miles below the juncture, as well as private marinas.

Outfitters

1. Escatawpa Hollow Camp and Canoe, 15551 Moffat Road, Wilmer, Ala., 334-649-4233. It also has a campground.

2. Sunshine Canoes, 5460 Old Shell Road, Mobile, Ala., 334-344-8664.

Campgrounds

1. Shepard State Park, 1034 Graveline Road, Gautier. Campground with hookups, canoe rental, boat ramp leading to West Pascagoula River. 228-497-2244.

High points

Stunningly beautiful blackwater contrasts with sugar-white sandbars.

Low points

Litter; motorboats and pollution on lower river.

Tips

If you plan to fish, keep in mind that the river crosses from Alabama into Mississippi; you may need fishing licenses from both states.

N

LOUISIANA

ALABAMA

Wolf River

Biloxi River

59

49

10

90

McLEOD WATER PARK

Jourdan River

DAVIS BAYOU

BILOXI BAY

Bay St. Louis

Pass Christian

Gulfport

Biloxi

Deer Island

Pascagoula

Round Island

MISSISSIPPI SOUND

Cat Island

Ship Island

Horn Island

Petit Bois Island

BAY OF ST. LOUIS

6. Coastal Waters

Gulf Islands National Seashore

Mention the Mississippi Gulf Coast and you probably don't think of paddling. More likely you picture casinos, hotels, restaurants, beaches, traffic, and a phone book nearly as thick as Jackson's. "The Coast" is an almost continuous strip of towns from Waveland to Pascagoula, but there are places to paddle. Prime among them is Gulf Islands National Seashore, headquartered at Ocean Springs. The park provides canoeing at Davis Bayou and sea kayaking to the barrier islands of East and West Ship, Horn, and Petit Bois. There are other islands as well, so options for coastal paddlers range from an afternoon's easy paddle to a saltwater expedition.

The park at Davis Bayou on the east side of Ocean Springs is a green pocket of marsh and piney woods barely a mile across but with winding bayous, a good place for casual exploring. The park's entrance fronts Highway 90, or take Government Street east through the scenic little town and turn right at the park boat ramp sign. There are actually four bayous within the park, each a finger of the Mississippi Sound. You can't paddle more than half a mile in any direction without getting outside the park's boundaries, usually into residential areas. From the park boat ramp, Halstead Bayou wiggles west past the campground, Stark Bayou runs north to a park road, a smaller bayou meanders east beside the William M. Colmer Visitor Center, and Davis Bayou opens out to Biloxi Bay, with Deer Island barely a mile away.

You can drive to the visitor center or paddle up to it, and it's well worth a stop. The beautifully rustic, spacious building features boardwalks overlooking the bayou, Walter Anderson artwork, and a bookstore with a selection of titles on nature, travel, and history that will make you reach for your wallet. All four bayous are easy paddling except Davis, which is up to half a mile wide and subject to strong winds. But when the breeze is light, you can paddle inland to the east and north for several miles, past developed areas, then the Sandhill Crane National Wildlife Refuge, under a railroad trestle and up to Highway 90. The wildlife refuge, headquartered at 7200 Crane Lane north of Gautier (228-497-6322), features a visitor center and short nature trail amid 19,273 acres of coastal savannah. The endangered sandhill cranes, which are rarely seen, resemble great blue herons but are distinguishable by a red crown and long curving tail feathers.

All told, the Davis Bayou area offers a neat sampling of marsh. Though rarely out of sight of houses or roads, it's home to ospreys, pelicans, and hermit crabs (not to mention mosquitoes and sandflies). There's fishing from a pier by the boat ramp, in the shallow bayous, or farther offshore. There are also picnic areas, a nature trail, and developed campsites in a lovely setting, which is unfortunately noisy at night because of the proximity of railroad tracks.

If you feel adventurous and the weather's calm, you can paddle to Deer Island. A canoe can handle the task, but a sea kayak is even better. From the Davis Bayou boat ramp, paddle south, then west onto Davis Bayou past a bird-crowded sand spit, and out into Biloxi Bay. Down the coast to the right stand casinos and high-rise hotels. The island lies due south across a channel often plied with boats. You may see a shrimp boat churning out to sea dragging blue nets, a rip-roaring speedboat, or a graceful sailing yacht. It takes about half an hour or so to reach the island, which is 5 miles long and a quarter mile wide. A strip of sand crowned by pine forest and palmetto, it's privately owned but uninhabited and undeveloped, at least as of this writing. You can poke along the inside shore in a canoe; a sea kayak will enable you to paddle out to the offshore side. The water around the island is remarkably shallow, advantageous for paddling since it's inaccessible to motorized craft, though sand flats can be troublesome even to paddlers at low tide. Once you're on the outside of the island, the pine forest blocks out most of the coastal urbanization. You may find bottlenose dolphins cavorting around you even though the water's only a few feet deep. Somehow the sight of dolphins suggests oceanic depths, not kiddie-pool shallows. Their big bodies glisten darkly, their blunt foreheads taper abruptly to nar-

Sand beaches contrast with hotels and casinos at Gulf Coast near Ocean Springs.

row snouts, and each time they surface they blow with a low and contented sigh, accompanied by squeaks, squawks, and grunts. I tried once to swim with them, or rather wade, but each time I approached, they vanished and resurfaced at a safe remove. I wanted to grasp a damp dorsal and go for a ride, but I don't blame the dolphins for not obliging. As you round the western side, casino hotels rise beige, pink, and green beyond the tree line. The scene grows magical in the afternoon light. Crowds of seagulls spin confetti dances over the shoals at the western end of the island. A pelican soars past, heavy-bodied and smug. A silhouetted man in a bateau flings a net into the shallows, watched by two smaller silhouettes in the rear of the boat. The Biloxi area has changed dramatically in the past few years, but as far as I'm concerned, the real lure of the Mississippi Gulf Coast is still out on the salt where dolphins tumble instead of dice.

It takes considerably more skill and courage to paddle to Horn Island, 10 miles from Davis Bayou. It's amazing to consider that the late Ocean Springs artist Walter Anderson rowed there repeatedly in a 10-foot dory. True, he capsized several times, but it never deterred him. His boat, on display along with his art at the Walter Anderson Museum in Ocean Springs, is testimony to a brave and determined man. Anderson is renowned for his beautiful art based largely on the Gulf Coast's marshes, beaches, and barrier islands, with scenes of herons, fish, crabs, alligators, and other creatures. Born in 1903, he spent weeks at a time on barrier islands like Horn, where he immersed himself in art and nature. Once he even lashed himself to a tree to ride out a hurricane. His art is as wild as the man, as the exhibits show. The room in which Anderson lived has been attached to the museum, its walls and ceilings covered with an astounding array of nature scenes. Tragically, Anderson was schizophrenic, repeatedly admitted to the state mental hospital at Whitfield, often at his own request—a seemingly classic case of a man whose genius was inseparable from madness. He died in 1965 of lung cancer. His story is told in the wonderful book *Approaching the Magic Hour: Memories of Walter Anderson* by his widow Agnes Grinstead Anderson (University Press of Mississippi, 1989).

It's also amazing to consider that Native Americans canoed to Horn and other barrier islands. Even today, many native people paddle dugout canoes on saltwater throughout the world, albeit usually with an outrigger attached to minimize the chance of rolling. For us moderns, though, it's daunting enough even in a sea kayak or catamaran. A lot can happen at sea, even on a relatively short crossing. Sudden winds, whitecapping waves, jellyfish stings, equipment breakdown, and so on can turn a few hours' paddle into a survival situation. Kayakers who take on such a crossing should be well-equipped with such items as a portable VHF radio and emergency flares, and well-versed in techniques such as low and high braces and Eskimo rolls. Since some of the islands are not visible until you're several miles offshore—especially to low-seated paddlers—a deck-mounted compass, hand-held GPS, and good maps or charts are advisable, not to mention good navigational skills. Hurricane season extends from June through November, followed by winter gales, then spring rains, so weather forecasts are important. Kayakers should also carry extra supplies, especially drinking water, in case of the not-unlikely event of getting stormbound for a few days.

In addition to the difficulties of crossing, Horn Island, like all the barrier islands, has outrageously fierce biting insects, withering heat, and, in the winter, unvarnished cold. Such hardships are the price you pay to visit this astonishing wilderness of beaches, dunes, forest, marsh, and lagoons. Horn Island is a powerful experience for those who get there by whatever means—kayak, sailboat, or motorboat. The most direct starting point is the water tower at Belle Fontaine Point on South Belle Fontaine Drive off Fountainbleau Road between Ocean

Springs and Gautier; from there it's approximately 6 miles due south. Leaving from either Davis Bayou to the west or Pascagoula to the east adds a few more miles. Horn, 13 miles long and up to ¾ of a mile wide, is uninhabited except for a ranger's house mid-island. Primitive camping is permitted on Horn, Petit Bois, and East Ship. None has water except Horn (at the ranger's station mid-island) and West Ship, so carry your own, and plenty of it. Prepare for extremes of sun, thirst, insects, rain, and wind.

Horn Island is the only place I've seen a truly blood-red moon. We were camped among the dunes in November when through the trees to the east I saw a red light which, to my surprise, turned out to be the rising moon, just past full. It went through shades of orange and yellow before reaching a silvery white overhead. Its glow combined with lights from the coast, especially Ingalls Shipyard at Pascagoula, to brighten the night sky and the water. Even without the moon, the view of the coast lights from the barrier islands is enchanting, as is the view from the south side to the unlighted Gulf.

Horn Island is home to wild hogs, bald eagles, ospreys, deer, rabbits, raccoons, snakes, and alligators. I called up a baby gator in an interior lagoon one time, and Scott saw a 10-footer swimming off nearby East Ship Island. The U.S. Fish and Wildlife Service used Horn Island as a sanctuary for endangered red wolves from 1989 to 1997, producing numerous pups, which were transferred to other remote areas of the Southeast. Only a few paths cross the island. You'd think a trail wouldn't be necessary on such a narrow island, but the interior is a wilderness of lagoons, marshes, and thickets. There are plenty of poisonous snakes, so watch your step. The trails lead through slash pine forest past swampy sloughs and emerge on the sprawling dunes of the south side. Here you can walk beside the clear water of the open Gulf, picking up shells and letting the smell of brine and the feel of sea breeze unlock memories. On both the blue Gulf side and the amber-green Mississippi Sound side, Horn Island boasts miles of empty beaches—empty, that is, except for washed-up refuse. Among the countless items I've seen are a girl's saddle oxford, a car bumper, garbage cans, buckets, tires, hard hats, deflated air mattresses, and sections of washed-away dock. Most of that probably came from the coast, while occasional coconuts suggest more distant ports. But the views offset the detritus—shrimpers and sailboats gentling in the breeze, low-flying pelicans in V formation, smooth-barked pine trees gnarled by wind. The setting sun unrolls your shadow down the beach, whose white sand turns gold with sunset, fading to silver and blue. Evening beauty gives

Round Island offshore from Pascagoula makes a good place to rest and inspect gear.

way to insect hell, though, unless you're camping in cold weather. And even a cold night may lead to a mild morning where swarms of mosquitoes bounce against the tent mesh, accompanied by no-see-ums and, later, biting flies. Such conditions make you glad to get out on the water.

If you launch at Pascagoula or Gautier, Round Island provides a good break point 3.5 miles out, slightly less than halfway to Horn. The island is a half-mile long wedge of sand and pine trees. Part is privately owned and part belongs to the City of Pascagoula. The city's portion includes the site of an old lighthouse that was blown apart by Hurricane Georges in 1998; at this writing efforts were under way to restore it. Three miles east of Horn Island lies Petit Bois Island—French for "little woods," well-named since the 7.5-mile long, 1,466-acre isle has just 10 acres of forest. Petit Bois lies about 8 miles south by southeast from Pascagoula.

Five miles west of Horn Island is 2.6-mile-long East Ship Island, 10 miles due south of Biloxi. When French explorers led by Pierre Le Moyne, Sieur d'Iberville arrived in 1699, East and West Ship Islands were one piece of land, and offered a good enough harbor to earn the name Ship Island. Leaving his three vessels at the island, Iberville, his brother Jean-Baptiste Le Moyne, Sieur de Bienville, and some of the men took longboats around to the mouth of the Mississippi and rowed upriver. The explorer Rene Robert Cavelier, Sieur de La Salle had already come down the Mississippi in 1682, and Iberville was following up from the lower end. After exploring upriver into what is now Mississippi and Louisiana, they returned to Bayou Manchac. The bayou ran by the current site of Baton

Rouge, Louisiana, named after the red pole there that marked the territorial dividing line between the Houmas and Bayogoulas. An Indian guide told Iberville that Bayou Manchac provided a shortcut back to the Gulf, so leaving Bienville and the rest of the men to take the longboats on down the Mississippi, Iberville and a few others headed down Manchac in a pair of bark canoes. They found the bayou so logjammed that in one day Iberville counted fifty portages on a 21-mile stretch. But the waterway did merge with the Amite River—which was swarming with alligators—and thence to Lake Maurepas, Lake Pontchartrain, and the Gulf. Iberville's team made it back to the rendezvous at Ship Island shortly before the other men. Before returning to France, Iberville built a fort at Biloxi Bay. He came back to the Gulf Coast late in the year to continue the process of exploration and settlement.

On the west side of the island—what is now West Ship Island—U.S. troops began building a fort in 1859 to guard that back-door, Lake Pontchartrain passage to New Orleans, but construction was interrupted by the Civil War. Before the war, brown bricks were ferried over from the Slidell, Louisiana, area. After the Confederacy seceded, the U.S. Army had to ship red bricks from New England. Visit the fort today and you can see the start of the Civil War clearly marked in the fort by a line several feet off the ground where brown bricks were replaced by red ones. At one time 22,000 soldiers bivouacked on the island while sixty warships ranged in the surrounding waters—not a good time to paddle, I daresay. The fort was protected by 8-foot-thick walls and sixteen cannons with ranges of up to 5 miles. A top layer of sod allowed rainwater to percolate into pipes and thence into 15,000-gallon tanks for drinking. The Confederates captured the fort briefly but lost it after a bloodless twenty-minute battle with Union ships. Unfortunately, all of the cannons but one were later sold for scrap iron. The remaining 50,000-pound behemoth on top appears to guard the harbor.

In 1946 a hurricane cut Ship Island in two, but wave action filled the gap with sand. In 1969 Hurricane Camille split the island again, much more emphatically. In 1998 Hurricane Georges washed completely over East Ship Island, clearing the underbrush out of the woods and lopping off the western end. Such events are a few of the many that illustrate the changeability of barrier islands. Fort Massachussetts, for instance, was built 500 feet from the western end of Ship Island; 130 years later that shore extended more than a mile westward. Petit Bois Island used to be part of Alabama's Dauphin Island, which is now 5 miles east.

The Isle of Caprice, located between Horn and Ship, held a casino resort in the 1920s; it's now nothing but a submerged sandbar. Such changeability is a good argument against developing barrier islands.

Paddlers who want to experience a barrier island without a difficult and possibly perilous crossing can catch an excursion boat to West Ship Island from the docks at both Gulfport and Biloxi (1-800-388-3290 toll-free, 228-864-1014 locally; tours run March through October). In less than an hour from departure, excursion boat passengers glimpse shimmering white beaches. Then Fort Massachussetts looms into view. A half mile east of the fort, on the north end of the island, is the replica of an old lighthouse built by Friends of Gulf Islands National Seashore. On the picture-perfect south beach, visitors read, sleep, swim, sunbathe, toss food to gulls, fish in the shallows, and let the subtropical breeze blow their landlubberly worries away. The rest of the treeless island remains untouched since few tourists care to wade through swamp crisscrossed by alligator trails. Behind the grassy dunes, tracks of raccoons and birds imprint the sand. Gator trails lead into the muck and grass-clogged water of the interior. The north side of the island has narrow beaches and is rarely visited. Here you can sit quietly and watch gulls gather in the shallows and listen to the music the wind makes when it spills off the continent and strums the Mississippi Sound.

Five miles west of West Ship Island and 7 miles south of Gulfport lies Cat Island, named for its raccoons, which French explorers mistook for cats. Unlike the other barrier islands, which are linear, Cat Island is wildly irregular. The result is a number of coves that make paddling all the more interesting. As of the year 2000 the privately owned, 2,100-acre island was being considered for potential purchase by the National Park Service for inclusion in the Gulf Islands National Seashore, which includes not only the Mississippi islands and Davis Bayou area but parts of Perdido Key, Alabama, and Santa Rosa Island, Florida.

There are plenty of fishing options at Gulf Islands National Seashore. At Davis Bayou, people angling from the pier put bread balls on bream hooks and jiggle them near the bottom to catch flounder, which can be plate-sized. Sparkle beetles are another good flounder lure. Since the bayou opens onto the saltwater, there's also the chance of hooking varieties like redfish. Paddle inland on the bayou to find freshwater species like bream and bass. Weedless spoons and spinnerbaits are good for both redfish and black bass. Another option is a cast net, sometimes called a "mullet gun" on the coast. Casting is an art that involves throwing a net out into the water in hopes it lands in a circular "silver dollar" shape rather than a deflated "pork chop." When pulled in, the bottom of the net draws inward. In clear water you can see your target, and depending on the mesh size you can catch species ranging from shrimp to mullet. Offshore and near barrier islands, fishermen go for redfish, sheepshead, red snapper, red drum, cobia, and sand sharks. Cast nets catch bait such as mullet or pogies, good for bull reds. These big fish hang out around structures such as rock riprap, feeding on small fish. Using heavy-duty rod, reel, and line, wade out and cast toward the rocks. When a bull red hits, work it away from the rocks since the fish will use them to break the line. Big reds swallow the bait and the hook sticks deep in the gullet, so keep pliers handy. To butcher redfish, don't bother to skin, scale, or gut; just cut a slab off each side, then barbecue scale-side down with salt, pepper, lemon juice and, optionally, butter. When they're done, scoop the fillets right off the armor-like shell.

Like it or not, the gambling industry has transformed the Gulf Coast. Once-sleepy towns are now home to such developments as the $650 million Beau Rivage casino and 1,780-room hotel at Biloxi, which sports a 100-foot glass atrium with fully grown trees, a yacht marina, a Cirque du Soleil showroom, a health spa, 12 restaurants, and high-end retail shops. Billboards line the interstate announcing attractions at casinos. At the turn of this century, the Isle of Capri, Casino Magic, and Grand Casino Biloxi combined had more than 200,000 square feet of casino space, nearly 2,000 hotel rooms, 14 restaurants, more than 60,000 square feet of meeting space, showrooms, theaters, health clubs, spas, gift shops, and arcades. And things were still growing. Highway 90 from Long Beach to Ocean Springs at times looks more like Las Vegas than south Mississippi. What sets it apart, of course, is the Gulf of Mexico, the beautiful white beaches and great seafood restaurants. Government officials have done a good job of providing public beach parks with attractive pavilions, bathrooms, and piers. You can launch a sea kayak from countless places. The growth means jobs and millions of dollars of tax revenue. But all that high-cost development is vulnerable to hurricanes and erosion. In Louisiana, coastal erosion gobbles the equivalent of a football field every fifteen minutes. It not only devastates seafood and wildlife but eventually may affect ports, construction sites and transportation routes in neighboring Mississippi. The gambling-fueled Gulf Coast boom could prove as fragile as barrier island sand. One hopes the marshes, estuaries and islands will survive.

Outfitters

Natural Adventure Touring Kayaks, 21640 Tucker Road, Long Beach MS 39560, 228-452-0118 or 228-452-7666. The company rents a variety of kayaks and canoes and provides sea kayaking instruction as well as guided tours of marshes, backwaters, and islands.

Area campgrounds

Gulf Islands National Seashore headquarters, Ocean Springs. Full hookups. 228-875-9057.

Shepard State Park, 1034 Graveline Road, Gautier, 228-497-2244, campground with hookups, canoe rental, boat ramp leading to West Pascagoula River.

High points

The lure of the sea, the smell of salt, the breeze in the sea oats, and the joys of walking a beach or paddling around in the marsh.

Low points

Overdevelopment makes traffic thick on land and water.

Tips

Take earplugs when camping at Davis Bayou to cut out nighttime train noises; be well-equipped and well-practiced before kayaking beyond Deer Island.

Biloxi River

Coast streams are typically short. In the space of a few miles they can expand from narrow creek to wide estuary. That's certainly the case with Biloxi River. Cross it on Highway 49 north of Gulfport and you see a small, tumbling, woodland stream. Cross it on Interstate 10—barely 10 miles away as the crow flies—and you're eyeing a huge estuary of Back Bay of Biloxi. The main canoeing stretch, 10.5 miles from Old Highway 49 to Three Rivers Road near Wool Market, offers a few hours of paddling or a day of lazing, with several miles of national forest and thirty gorgeous sandbars. It's a beautiful float, to be sure, though hard going in low water.

The river is actually 52 miles long, heading up just south of Highway 26 between Poplarville and Wiggins. It remains creek-sized until it's joined by Little Biloxi River, a mere 11.5 miles from the mouth. The best put-in is at Old Highway 49 a mile west of four-lane 49. The Old 49 crossing is located just inside the western border of De Soto National Forest. Less than a mile downstream you'll pass a national forest campground on the north bank, though there's little sign of it from the water since it's atop a bluff. It's a good place for a base camp but unfortunately offers no access to the river unless you want to tote your gear through the woods and down the bluff. Access at four-lane Highway 49 is about as bad.

The first half of the stretch runs through national forest and contains shoals and logjams. Don't even try it in low water. The Biloxi is, however, a classic bass stream. Topwater lures, crankbaits and beetlespins catch both redeye and largemouth. Redeye bass lurk in the upper stretches where the water is cooler, such as near springs. The creek also sports gorgeous, iridescent bluegill and chinquapin bream. Pull up at deeper pools in bends and fish with worms, minnows, or crickets. Catfishermen use limb lines or jug fish. The upper stream is also great for wade fishing, using ultra-light rigs or even fly-fishing tackle.

Piney woods continue outside the national forest boundaries, but it doesn't take long to find development. A casino golf course stretches a long way down the west bank, scenic in its own way with its sweeping greenswards among groves of tall pines. Unfortunately, golf courses have been criticized for their heavy use of lawn-type chemicals which can run into rivers. Little Biloxi River enters from the west 9.5 miles below Old 49, a mile from the take-out. You can paddle about a quarter mile upstream on the small, canopied creek before logjams block the way. The Biloxi is notably wider as it wends the final, slow mile to Three Rivers Road. At the take-out there is a huge stretch of sand beach that lures crowds on weekends and summer days.

When I floated the Biloxi, I did everything backward: I paddled upstream, in late winter, in the rain. That's a combination I recommend, crazy as it sounds, for it enabled me to avoid several problems. Because of the season and the precipitation, the huge sandbars at Three Rivers Road were deserted. By going upstream, I avoided the pullovers found on the upper reaches. And I didn't have to bother with a shuttle, which was a good thing since I was alone and there was

Golf course construction equipment stands on the bank of Big Biloxi River north of Gulfport.

no canoe rental service available (one was advertised in the phone book but was not in business). It took me many years to discover paddling upstream is not nearly as hard as it seems. It is work, but no more than, say, digging azalea holes for my wife. And it doesn't require another vehicle or person for shuttling, just you and your canoe.

Though this was the outskirts of Gulfport, all I saw was woods. Red maple trees glowed like Rome apples, covered with tiny angel-wing fruits. Holly trunks also showed patches of red. Above the mouth of Little Biloxi, the Biloxi narrowed considerably, with more current. Its tea-colored waters spouted past sugarcake sandbars where wild blueberry bushes dangled white blossoms like tiny china cups. As the rain pattered my poncho, not a creature showed, only occasional birdsong chirruping from the pine forest. I passed the golf course and, when my muscles had had enough, turned downstream and drifted. In the misty-wintry air, I admired the way the wooden gunwales of my dark green canoe mirrored the brown of birches against a background of pines. For a day trip, this was hard to beat.

Below Three Rivers Road, the river enters the heavily developed urban areas outlying Wool Market and Gulfport. In the 6.5 miles from Three Rivers Road to

I-10, it expands dramatically as it meets the brackish backwater from Back Bay. Here fishermen can catch both fresh and saltwater species. At Back Bay, the Biloxi merges with Tchoutacabouffa (Chu-ta-ca-BUFF) River, which is even shorter than the Biloxi and also expands from a tiny creek to a huge estuary in the space of several miles.

If there's sufficient water, the Tchoutacabouffa provides a 5-mile float through national forest from Highway 15 to C.C. Road in the De Soto National Forest. The catch is it's hard to tell when there is sufficient water because the put-in is a small tributary, Hurricane Creek, and the take-out is plenty wide; what's in-between remains out of sight. Even checking with local sources can leave you high and dry, as I discovered when Steve Cox and I set off down Hurricane Creek with a boatful of camping gear. Our optimism quickly wilted as the stretch down Hurricane Creek to the main stream turned into a mile or so of constant pullovers. And the so-called main stream, to our dismay, was not one bit better. We dragged our barge through sandy shallows, down narrow chutes, over logs and along a slippery clay bed—and I mean slippery. The soles of neither Steve's rubber boots nor my tennis shoes could keep us from taking some unheroic spills. At least we found a decent campsite, a tiny sand island surrounded by rivulets of babbling water. We spread our sleeping bags under the half moon and tried not to think about the next day. In the morning we resumed our toil. The creek didn't begin to widen until we neared the take-out. When there's enough water, I'm told, this is a great float with good light-tackle fishing. Several miles below C.C. Road the Tchoutacabouffa widens into the huge estuary visible from the Interstate 10 bridge.

Biloxi routes

Old Highway 49 to Three Rivers Road, 10.5 miles. To get to Old 49, from Highway 49 just north of the river go west, then back south. Three Rivers Road crosses the river east of Lyman.

Area campgrounds

Big Biloxi Campground, U.S. Forest Service campground overlooking Biloxi River on De Soto Park Road just west of Highway 49. Camping is $13 with hookups, $7 without. There's also a nature trail, bath house with showers, picnic area, and pavilion. 228-928-5291 (Forest Service headquarters in Biloxi).

High points

Surprising slice of woodland beauty hard against urban sprawl.

Low points

The 10.5-mile day trip may require portages on upper portion.

Tips

Paddle upstream from Three Rivers Road. It's a great workout, you'll avoid any portages, and there's no shuttling involved.

Wolf River

Wolf River is the showpiece of coastal streams, offering 35 miles of near-pristine paddling down a challenging and exquisite river. That's more than half the river's 66-mile length. The stream heads up west of Lumberton but doesn't become navigable until the Silver Run community southeast of Poplarville. It flows south by southeast until it crosses I-10, after which it swings west and broadens into marsh as it empties into St. Louis Bay. Not only is the Wolf fine in its own right, it's a microcosm of other Mississippi piney woods streams. The ever-changing Wolf has sections reminiscent of virtually every other river in the southern half of the state. At Silver Run, it looks much like the Bogue Chitto River. Yet it's clear and tea-colored like Red Creek. Then it narrows and runs under big, overarching trees like Magee's Creek. Later it becomes wider but still shady like Bowie Creek, opens onto big gravel bars like the Tangipahoa River, with occasional logjams like the Amite, plunging rapids like Okatoma, high mossy bluffs like the Chicka-sawhay, multicolored clays like Bayou Pierre, sudden drops like Strong River, and wide, muddy reaches like the Leaf. Just when you feel overwhelmed by the constant sense of déjà vu, the Wolf takes on an appearance all its own, such as narrowing from 100 feet wide to 10 feet as it rushes down a clay chute. As with the weather, if there's a part of the Wolf you don't like, just wait: It will soon change.

There's a sense of adventure just in finding some of its remote put-ins, like Silver Run or Cemetery Road. There's no substitute for a copy of *Mississippi Road Atlas* or *Mississippi Atlas and Gazetteer* in locating these spots. But the real sense of excitement begins when you launch the boat and slide away from shore. Multitextured smells, sights, and sounds surround the gloriously simple yet impossibly complex path of water through its tunnel of green forest and blue sky.

In addition to the aesthetic qualities, the 13-mile stretch from Silver Run to Highway 53 is challenging—swift, crooked, narrow, and tricky. The ability to read a river is a much-needed skill on the Wolf, which frequently offers just one path for a canoe to squeeze through. I made the mistake of taking a long, straight-keeled, 17-foot Sawyer down the Wolf. Steve Cox and I rounded a tight, sharp bend, the current barreling toward a sweeper, a chest-high horizontal log protruding over the water. If we'd been in a more maneuverable boat we might have avoided it. As it was, I could only watch in horror as Steve prepared to have the top half of his body sheared backward. Did the McComb architect face decapitation, or merely a broken back? Fortunately he has good reflexes. He put his left foot against the log, which spilled us both into the cold river and half-swamped the boat. Steve took off after his paddle while I struggled to haul the canoe out of the current. I didn't mind the dunking, considering the alternative of hauling Steve's carcass through the woods. We continued to bump logs, scrape over sandy shoals, and brush against bushes as we strove to handle the canoe. I recommend a more maneuverable boat if possible.

The upper river provides typical creek-fishing: bream (bluegill and longear), bass, and some catfish. Toss bass lures such as spinners or topwater baits to still pockets at the edge of swifts, or use beetlespins or live bait for bream or catfish. The Wolf is also a good fly-fishing stream since it's shallow enough to wade. Those shallows can cause some dragovers during the dry season. They also enable four-wheelers to ride in the river as well as on forest trails paralleling the stream on both banks for miles. Four-wheeler riding is a fun sport to plenty of people, and the all-terrain vehicles provide access to remote areas. They're also invaluable to hunters for hauling deer out of the woods. But the wide, knobby tires disturb gravel and sandbars, silt up the stream and erode the banks, plus the noisy buzz is irritating to people seeking woodland quiet.

The upper river features fine, small sandbars backed by thickets of muscadine, wax myrtle, red maple, and Chinese tallow trees (a non-native species unfortunately proliferating on southern waterways). Behind this green tangle rise giants like water oak, pine, and magnolia trees. Sandbars grow bigger below Highway 53. On a moonlit night these expanses resemble a Colorado snowfield. But the morning sun can quickly change them into a reflector oven.

It's 8 miles from Highway 53 to Wolf River Park on Cemetery Road, a privately run primitive campground on county-owned 16th Section land. This is a good place to leave your vehicle, for a small fee. It's another 3.5 miles to Cable Bridge Road, where there is no public takeout, though Wolf River Canoe and Kayak (see below) maintains a gated landing. The river passes through a conservation easement on this stretch from Highway 53 to Cable Bridge Road, 300 feet wide along each bank. International Paper Company donated the land to the nonprofit Conservation Fund in 1999. The act was hailed as a milestone in state conservation efforts and one hopes will augur many more. The easement not only gives the public access to the streamside land but prevents logging, gravel mining, construction, and other development that could damage the stream.

Below Cable Bridge, as the river widens, deepens, and slows, the canoeing feels more coastal. Gone are clay chutes and rapids. What's left is a contemplative paddle past big sandbars and through beautiful woodland and marsh scenery. I-10 crosses the stream about 8 miles below Cable Bridge, and it's another 2.5 miles to Wolf River Canoe and Kayak headquarters. This company rents boats and offers guided paddle trips through the marshes in and around St. Louis Bay. From there it's a mile to Bells Ferry Road, where the access is poor; 3 miles to Kiln-Menge Avenue, where there is a riverside lounge with boat launching for a fee; then 4 miles to a boat ramp at Hampton Road, the last takeout on the river. Bayou Acadian merges from the east just above Hampton Road.

There's plenty of opportunity for poking around in these marshes, even in the bay itself, wind and motorboat traffic permitting. But motorboats can be obnoxious on summer weekends and especially on holidays. Scott Williams was sailing in Bay St. Louis one Labor Day weekend and encountered aggressive, drunken speedboaters and personal watercraft users that made him fear for the safety of his vessel. One speedboater refused to give way in a tight squeeze under a drawbridge until ordered to do so by the drawbridge operator, and two personal watercraft users roared so close to the sailboat that their wakes drenched Scott and his companions. Nor are secluded bayous necessarily safe. One personal watercraft operator careened up Bayou Portage at top speed despite a no-wake zone and refused to pull over when a marina owner threatened to call the law. Unfortunately, paddlers are at the mercy of such people. On the other hand, on off-season weekdays you may find the entire bay virtually deserted, not to mention the backwaters. At such times the area is bewitching.

The Wolf River, not surprisingly, was named for the red wolves that once roamed the South. By 1980 their numbers had dwindled to fourteen. The U.S. Fish and Wildlife Service captured all of them alive in hopes of preventing extinction, breeding them in captivity for later release to places like Horn Island. Now there are a few hundred. Red wolves do not fit the traditional picture of big, savage canines. At 30–80 pounds, they're larger than coyotes but considerably smaller than the better-known grey or timber wolf. They're extremely shy and don't even hunt in packs, feeding mainly on small game. There has never been a reported case of an attack on humans, officials say. I was fortunate enough to see a couple of red wolves, not in the wild but in a pen at Land Between the Lakes National Recreation Area, Kentucky. It was feeding time, and a wildlife official stepped into the pen and banged on a metal dish. The animals emerged from a burrow and began darting back and forth under the trees, torn between hunger and fear of spectators. Looking at this nervous pair, I couldn't imagine them as menacing. Even when I stared at them, they seemed out of focus, like puffs of smoke in the woodland shadows, always on the verge of vanishing. Sometimes I think our rivers are like that.

Wolf routes

1. Silver Run to Highway 53 just south of Sellers, 13 miles. The Silver Run bridge is just west of the intersection of Silver Run Road and Perkinston Silver Run southeast of Poplarville.

2. Highway 53 to Cemetery Road, 8 miles. Cemetery Road runs west from Highway 53 a few miles south of the Wolf River bridge. A sign on Cemetery Road marks the entrance to Wolf River Park, a privately run campground where fees are charged for entry and camping.

3. Cemetery Road to Cable Bridge, 3.5 miles. There is no public takeout at Cable Bridge. However, Wolf River Canoe Rentals maintains a takeout there. Cable Bridge Road runs west from the intersection of Northrup Cuevas Road (which joins Highway 53 near Lizana) and Wolf River Road.

4. Cable Bridge Road to ramp on Hampton Road south of De Lisle, 18.5 miles. The river passes two other roads, Bells Ferry Road and Kiln-Menge Avenue, but Hampton has the best access with a public boat ramp. Wolf River Canoe Rental headquarters and takeout is located 8 miles below Cable Bridge Road at the end of Tucker Road off Red Creek Road, accessible from the I-10 Long Beach exit.

Outfitters

Wolf River Canoe and Kayak, 21640 Tucker Road, Long Beach, 228-452-0118 or 228-452-7666. The company rents a variety of kayaks and canoes and provides sea kayaking instruction as well as guided tours of marshes, backwaters, and islands.

Area campgrounds

1. Wolf River Park, fee primitive campground along the river on Cemetery Road.
2. U.S. Forest Service campground on Biloxi River just west of Highway 49. Full hookups. 228-928-5291 (Forest Service headquarters in Biloxi).
3. McLeod Water Park, 8100 Texas Flat Road, Kiln. Primitive and developed campsites on Jourdan River southeast of Kiln. 228-467-1894.

High points

Swifty, twisty creek is a fun challenge to paddling skills.

Low points

Four-wheelers on upper river, motorboat traffic around Bay St. Louis.

Tips

If possible, take a boat that handles easily since the river requires quick, sudden turns.

Jourdan River

The Jourdan River is scarcely a river at all, more of an estuary of St. Louis Bay. With virtually no current, it's just right for exploring from a base camp, namely McLeod Water Park. The park, located southeast of Kiln, is the highest public access point on the river, yet even here the Jourdan is wide and deep enough for large motorboats. The river is born just a few miles upstream from the park at the juncture of Catahoula Creek and Bayou Bacon. Farther north, where those streams cross Highway 43 between Kiln and Picayune, they're tiny brooks, and it's amazing to think they can become a river the size of the Jourdan in such a short span. All told, the distance between the juncture of Catahoula and Bayou Bacon and the outlet in St. Louis Bay is scarcely 20 miles, making Jourdan a candidate for the shortest river in Mississippi.

The Jourdan offers an interesting lesson in geography. If you take Interstate 12 east of Hammond, Louisiana, you're driving through mud and cypress country. But when you cross into Mississippi on I-10, a funny thing happens: Mud turns to sand; murky waters run clear; pine trees creep down to river banks. While Louisiana's Tchefuncte River to the west is muddy and brown, the Jourdan has gem-clear water, sugar-white sandbars, and clean-smelling pines. Maybe it's the artesian springs, or the shift from Mississippi River floodplain to coastal geography. Regardless, it makes for some interesting paddling—if you don't mind company. For the Jourdan's biggest problem is its popularity. This pretty, pine-clad stream is traversed by personal watercraft and water skiers as well as canoers. McLeod Water Park is likewise overly popular, and understandably. Named for turn-of-the-century settlers, the 328-acre park is a comfortable, down-home place where you'll nearly always smell charcoal burning, see children romping—and hear radios playing. That can be pleasantly homey when the radios are at a distance, but not if you have the misfortune to be camped next to a crowd of teenagers in party mode. The park is owned by Pearl River Basin Development District and operated by Hancock County, with fees charged for camping and boat launching. The tent camping area is located on a sandy peninsula among pine and bay trees. You can launch a canoe from virtually any site as well as a park boat ramp.

To explore the Jourdan, just set off upriver—paddling is no problem against the slight current—where the scenery is best and motorboat traffic least. The park's 1¼-mile no-wake zone helps slow big-boat traffic. Narrow side passages lead to oxbow lakes, and paddlers can poke into them to find quiet, lonely waters ringed by forest. The park encompasses an oxbow lake accessible by just such a channel. A nature trail also wends through the swampy forest around the oxbow lake if you want to explore on foot. The park is so close to Bay St. Louis that the river rises and falls with the tides, making it a good place for both fresh and brackish-water fish species. I talked to one fisherman who told me he caught a bass, bream, redfish, speckled trout, and flounder in one day on the same lure, a black and white Strike King spinner. Farther downriver, during September and October, bank fishermen throw catfood and rabbit food into the water to entice shrimp, then haul them in with cast nets. These shrimp can reach a foot long and are best stuffed or fried butterfly style.

The Jourdan hosts abundant birdlife, from massive ospreys to lanky great blue herons. Night is a good time to paddle to see other wildlife. Flashlight beams may pick up a beaver gliding nearby or a big-eared doe floundering neck-deep before climbing the low bank into the woods. It's also fun to cut the lights and use the dim reflection of night sky as guide. Dark forest lines either side, and the twisting channel sometimes leaves you wondering which way to turn, but not for long. The night thrums with crickets, the swish of paddles, the occasional sigh of a breeze. The backwaters look sinister in the darkness, a likely place for the creature from the black lagoon, but it's a pleasant fear: Despite its monster mask, the swamp is benign. Meanwhile back in camp, raccoons will clean your dishes for you if you set them back in the woods. They won't even wait till you go to bed; you'll likely hear them grunting and scuffling in the darkness. Flash-lights will send them scurrying, at least temporarily.

This used to be the heart of turpentine country. In the last century, turpentine collectors cut cavities in longleaf and slash pine trees near the roots, obtaining the resin in boxes but often killing the trees. In 1901 federal forestry officials de-veloped a method similar to obtaining maple sap for syrup: Collectors would use a V-shaped blade to cut the inner bark of a tree about once a week, gathering the resin in a cup without killing the tree. The resin was then distilled and stored in oak barrels. Albert and Virginia McLeod, for whom the park is named, ran a sawmill, general store, and turpentine plant in the early 1900s, employing some five hundred people. Mr. McLeod died in 1931, but his wife, known as "Aunt Gin," operated the old store until her death in 1973 at age ninety-five. The park was developed in 1975.

Jourdan routes

Launch at McLeod Water Park west of Highway 43 south of Kiln, and explore upstream in the negligible current, then return to camp.

Campground

McLeod Water Park, 8100 Texas Flat Road, Kiln, 228-467-1894. Primitive and developed sites located on the river.

High points

Lovely coastal scenery.

Low points

Noisy park, motorboat traffic.

Tips

Explore every side channel wide enough for a canoe.

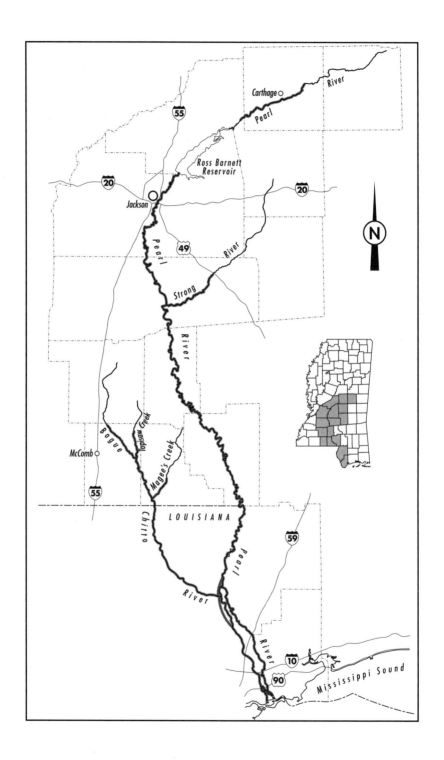

7. The Pearl River Basin

Pearl River

At more than 400 miles long, passing from Choctaw country through the state capital down to the coast, the Pearl River is one of the state's most significant waterways. It's not a typical canoeing river, but it is both interesting and challenging. Challenges include logjams on the upper reaches followed by dwindling current as the river approaches Ross Barnett Reservoir; long stretches of big river with infrequent access below Jackson; and some of the most impressive swamps in the state as it nears the coast. The payoff for tackling such a river is a real sense of isolation and an abundance of wildlife rarely encountered on more accessible waters.

The Pearl begins in a swamp and ends in one. It starts in Neshoba County where the clear waters of Nanih Waiya (Choctaw for rock river) Creek trickle beneath the shade of cypress and tupelo gum trees at Nanih Waiya State Park off Highway 393 (Mound Road) some 20 miles northeast of Philadelphia. According to legend, Choctaw ancestors emerged from a cave penetrating a wooded hill beside the creek. To the west, along Highway 393, stands Nanih Waiya Indian mound, a village center two thousand years ago but now just a big green hill in a pasture. Below Highway 393 a number of creeks—Big Slough, Old Creek, Fox Branch, Bogue Chitto (not to be confused with Bogue Chitto River, which feeds the Pearl far downstream)—come together to form the Pearl. The Mississippi Department of Wildlife, Fisheries, and Parks has cleared and marked a canoe trail along the 15-mile stretch from Highway 393 to a ramp at Burnside

Lake Water Park just past Highway 15. This float, which runs through Nanih Waiya Wildlife Management Area, is an overnighter. It may have logjams in low water, and during flood the water spreads far out into the woods, making navigation a challenge despite aluminum tree markers. U.S.G.S. quad maps for this segment are Noxapater and Philadelphia.

Below Highway 15, the Pearl continues as a small, meandering creek for 2.5 miles to Highway 19, about 20 more to Highway 16 at Edinburg (with the Mississippi Band of Choctaw Indians Reservation along the south bank for the second half of that stretch), and another 8 or so to Battle Bluff Road just south of the community of Sunrise. While parts of the upper Pearl may be floatable during high water, during normal conditions the highest put-in is at Battle Bluff Road. The 10-mile stretch from there to Highway 35 south of Carthage is still likely to be rife with logjams, however, and even the 10-mile stretch from Carthage to a ramp near Highway 25 may pose obstacles of sandy shoals and fallen trees during low water. The Pearl widens and slows at the mouth of Tuscolameta Creek just upstream from Highway 25. Logjams cease to be a problem, but lack of current translates into deadwater paddling on the 10 miles to Leake County Water Park or the additional half-mile to a lowhead dam. Motorboats travel this stretch too, though not as many as on the river below the lowhead dam, which is wide open all the way to Ross Barnett Reservoir. The 33,000-acre reservoir is floatable if you are willing to deal with powerboats and windy lake conditions. There are numerous ramps around the reservoir.

Powerboats thin out on the 9-mile day float from the Ross Barnett dam to Lakeland Drive (Highway 25). On the west bank below Lakeland Drive sprawls LeFleur's Bluff State Park. Park trails lead to the river but there is no canoe access. LeFleur's Bluff has thirty campsites with water and electricity, a series of oxbow lakes, nature trail, and golf course. Also at the park is the Mississippi Museum of Natural Science (601-354-7303), which moved to new facilities there in the year 2000. The museum features fantastic exhibits representing natural habitats found throughout the state. At the edge of the park, 2 miles below Lakeland Drive, a lowhead dam at the Jackson Water Works pumping station blocks boat traffic. At this writing, a proposal was being debated to create an 11-mile-long lake on the Pearl in this area.

The city and the reservoir have had a substantial impact on the river. For years the Pearl below Jackson was severely polluted. However, those problems were substantially improved with the construction of a regional sewage system and wastewater treatment plant, according to the DEQ. Another problem for many landowners along the Pearl is erosion. When the outflow gates at Ross Barnett Reservoir slam shut after a flood, water levels in the Pearl plummet as much as 20 feet in three days. The saturated, suddenly exposed banks collapse, dropping live trees and tons of soil into the river, a huge problem for landowners. Reservoir officials note that after a late-spring flood the reservoir must retain enough water to supply the Jackson area through the summer, and that may require shutting the floodgates and causing a fast drop downriver. They also point out that fallen trees and caving banks occur above the reservoir as well, which suggests the problem may be partly natural.

From a paddler's perspective, the distances between access points below Jackson can be daunting. From Highway 80 at Jackson to Gatesville Road east of Crystal Springs, for instance, lie 41.5 miles of river. Three other bridges cross the segment but provide no access. This situation is not uncommon with a waterway like the Pearl, which is a big river with steep banks flanked by oxbow lakes, sloughs, and swamps. Distances between put-ins range from 5 miles to more than 50 on the lower river: 5 miles from Gatesville Road to Hopewell; 10 miles from Hopewell to Highway 28; 27 miles from Highway 28 to Wanilla Water Park; 14 miles from Wanilla Water Park to Atwood Water Park at Monticello; 50 miles from Atwood to Columbia Water Park; 5 miles from Columbia Water Park to Highway 98; 57 miles from Highway 98 to Bogalusa, Louisiana. En route to Bogalusa, the Pearl gradually widens as it courses through increasingly remote farm, pasture, and timberland. Paddling is fairly simple, with few obstacles and a good current. Occasional fishermen may motor by in johnboats.

Wildlife is plentiful along these stretches. I've rarely seen more wildlife on a canoe-camping trip than I did on the 50-mile stretch from Monticello to Columbia. We started late in the evening, and in the morning we got our first glimpse of deer. Five does browsed in a low spot, and when my red canoe hove into sight, with the dip-splash sound of well-worn wooden paddles, they looked up, tall ears alert. After watching us a while, they bounded lazily up the high bank, white tails flapping. Birdlife was just as abundant. At seemingly any given moment, a great blue heron was leading our way downriver. Flocks of ducks skittered out of hiding places. Crows stirred up a ruckus. And we passed a serious buzzard hangout where dozens roosted in trees and spread their wings on a sandbar. Hawks took reluctant flight with tough-guy dignity. Wild turkeys tiptoed noisily in the dry leaves. A fat beaver, surprised at his snack, plunged down the bank and disappeared into the turgid brown water. When it came to humans, the river was windswept and lonely: just one old fisherman who commented happily on the plentiful ducks. Next morning as we sipped coffee in camp, a band of deer appeared on the far bank, a cow-horn spike with harem. They milled around, disappeared, returned. Apparently they wanted to cross, and we were in the way. Other deer snorted behind us in the willows and sycamores. Deferring to the deer, we launched our canoe, only to see plenty more whitetails, including a magnificent four-point with Christmas-tree tines. Roused from his nap, the buck glanced at us haughtily and pranced into the forest. Maybe the weather had stirred the animals up. Maybe their numbers were indicative of the state's overpopulation of deer. Maybe they were trying to get in some last-minute rambling before gun season, which was to open the following weekend. Unfortunately for hunters but happily for the deer, there's no public hunting land on the Monticello-to-Columbia strip.

You can get a bird's-eye view of this remarkable country at Red Bluff on Highway 587 between Monticello and Columbia. The scenic backroad passes by the stupendous bluff, with a view east to Columbia and beyond. The massive, multihued clay bluff reveals a valley wild, lonely, and rough as a cob, a perfect hiding place for deer. Red Bluff is one of those improbable wonders stuck by the side of a country road, unheralded by signs, parking area, or designated trails. You're driving along Highway 587 just northeast of Morgantown and there it is: a vertical painted desert dropping hundreds of feet down, colorful as neapolitan ice cream. Pink predominates, but there is also purple, yellow, white, gray, blue, and red. The colors are so sweet you have to envy earthworms. The sandy dunes resemble desert, but down below, Red Bluff Creek leads into a sweetbay jungle. The stream flows under a railroad track, down a wooden chute, through the woods, and out to the Pearl, where wide sandbars harbor interesting rocks. I talked to a man who watched his Sunday school teacher drown there. The teacher and his wife of six weeks were playing around by the Pearl where Red Bluff Creek empties into it, and she threw some sand in his hair. He leaned over to wash it out in the river and fell in, or perhaps the sand caved under him. Unable to swim, he never came up. Even people who know how to swim should take care in the Pearl, as sandy shallows can drop off precipitously into black depths.

Below Bogalusa, the river begins to split as it fans out into swamps and marshes. Also complicating navigation on these lower segments are various

Scott Williams enjoys a hammock in the Honey Island Swamp along the lower Bogue Chitto and Pearl Rivers.

man-made projects. About 10 miles below Bogalusa, a barge canal, blocked by a lowhead dam, branches off to the southwest at Pool's Bluff Sill, where there's a boat ramp below the dam. On the barge canal there are also ramps at Lock No. 3 east of the intersection of Louisiana Highway 21 and Highway 16, and farther south at Lock No. 1 east of Highway 41 between Talisheek and Hickory, Louisiana. These ramps make possible starting points for swamp exploration, and barge traffic is scarce these days.

Fourteen miles below Pool's Bluff Sill on the main river, Wilson Slough angles off to the right, or southwest. "Slough" is misleading since this is actually a big waterway. Until Corps of Engineers diversion efforts in the late 1990s split the water between Wilson Slough and the main Pearl River, the slough captured most of the flow. Now, when it leaves the main Pearl, Wilson Slough passes through a man-made weir en route to the West Pearl. This weir, which drops 17 feet over a 100-plus-foot-long stretch, was redesigned to be safer after a paddler drowned in it in 1998, but take care should you venture this way. (If you do, options include portaging around the weir, or turning right on Government Ditch just above the slough and winding through the swamps to Cannon Lake and back to Wilson Slough.) A better bet for paddlers is to avoid Wilson Slough altogether by continuing down the main Pearl, now noticeably narrower, toward Walkiah Bluff Water Park, which is located on the east bank 4 miles downstream from the split. A surprisingly strong current can make paddling to the park boat ramp a tricky proposition; if the current shoves you past, just turn and paddle up close to the bank. Five miles below Walkiah Bluff, the river splits again. The left branch, which leads to Pearlington, dwindles away in low water, while the right branch, Holmes Bayou, angles southwest for 4 miles to the West Pearl, then the barge canal just beyond. You can turn right onto the canal and paddle half a mile to the ramp at Lock 1, located off Highway 41. Or continue to a ramp under Interstate 59 about 6 miles farther, some 15 miles below Walkiah Bluff. By this point, the river is big and powerful. Headwinds sweeping up from the Gulf of Mexico can create whitecaps such as you'd expect to see on a large lake. From I-59 it's 7 miles to a ramp at Davis Landing and three more to Crawford Landing near I-10; both landings are located off Louisiana Highway 1090. From Crawford it's 5 miles to a ramp at Indian Village east of Highway 190 and another 2.5 miles to a ramp at Highway 90 on the West Pearl. To avoid the big river and see more swamp, paddlers can branch off to the east 1.5 miles below Davis Landing and travel down the West Middle Pearl, the Middle Pearl, or any other of the numerous bayous to Highway 90 roughly 11 miles away. Boat ramps are located at all the Highway 90 bridges, and east-west bayous make it possible to paddle from one bridge to the other with the exception of the one over the West Pearl.

Not surprisingly, good maps are recommended for tackling the lower Pearl. A description of the main routes doesn't do justice to the incredible labyrinth that includes Mississippi's Old River Wildlife Management Area, Bogue Chitto National Wildlife Refuge, and Louisiana's Pearl River Wildlife Management Area. Old River WMA is located in Pearl River County, comprising some 15,000 acres of mostly hardwood bottomland. Camping is permitted anywhere inside the WMA, though a free permit is required; for permit, basic map, and other information, call 601-772-9024. The 37,000-acre Bogue Chitto National Wildlife Refuge extends some 21 miles along both sides of the river from just south of the St. Tammany Parish line to the juncture of Holmes Bayou with West Pearl River. Primitive camping is permitted within 100 feet of Bogue Chitto River, Wilson Slough, and West Pearl River south of Wilson Slough, as well as refuge lands along East Pearl River and Holmes Bayou. The refuge publishes a basic map of the area; call 504-646-7555. The 34,000-acre Pearl River WMA continues to the south and includes the ramps at I-59, Davis Landing, Crawford Landing, and

Highway 90. For a detailed map of the WMA call 225-765-2800. This WMA also extends 5 miles south of Highway 90 where the marsh fades into Little Lake, which opens onto the Rigolets, a passage linking Lake Borgne with Lake Pontchartrain. U.S.G.S. quad maps of the lower river, starting from Bogalusa and going south, are Bogalusa East, Henleyfield, Industrial, Hickory (Louisiana), Nicholson, Haaswood (Louisiana), Rigolets (Louisiana) and English Lookout.

An April 12, 1993, Associated Press wire story illustrated how tricky the lower Pearl River swamps are. The article told of a turkey hunter who got lost in Honey Island Swamp—the 250 square miles of wilderness along the lower river near the mouth of the Bogue Chitto River—and couldn't get out for a week. Having talked to others who have gotten turned around there, if not so dramatically, I sometimes wonder if anyone has ever traveled in Honey Island Swamp without getting lost at one time or another. If you take plenty of food and gear and allow several days for exploration, getting lost doesn't have to be a problem. When Scott and I paddled through Honey Island Swamp, we didn't even bother with good maps. We just followed the Bogue Chitto River into the swamp and turned off onto the first channel. For the next two days we didn't know, or care, exactly where we were, happy just to explore as we worked our way generally south. Bayous branched and branched again, and we generally took the smaller forks to avoid motorboats. Forest gave way to marsh, and we ultimately emerged at Highway 90, following side channels to get to the bridge where Scott's truck was parked. That "method" may sound crazy to some, but it's worked for me in several large swamps. With sufficient provisions and time, you can wander at will and still find your way out, concentrating on your surroundings rather than your location on a map. A perhaps more sensible way to travel is with a plastic-coated U.S.G.S. quad map in front of you, and a GPS as well. Some people prefer to forgo navigation and take a guided trip, like those listed at the end of this section. I recommend you do what you feel most comfortable with. But no matter how you do it, it's thrilling to venture into a narrow, jungly passage in the heart of the swamp. Indeed, it can be thrilling in more ways than one. Scott told me of a surveyor working in Honey Island Swamp who felt something like a fly in his beard as he peered through his instrument. He swatted repeatedly and finally looked up to see a cottonmouth snake coiled on a palmetto striking at his face. Only his beard saved him.

The 1953 novel *The River Is Home* by Patrick Smith and the 1964 folklore collections *Pearl River: Highway to Glory Land* and *Next Door to Heaven* by

S. G. Thigpen portray the rustic lifestyle of earlier times along the lower Pearl. In the sparsely populated virgin forest with crystalline streams and towering long-leaf pines, settlers hunted, fished, trapped, gardened, and raised livestock. But lurking in the backwaters were bandits such as Pierre Rameau, known as "King of Honey Island," and the James Copeland gang. Then came the Civil War, when the countryside was plagued with Jayhawkers: thugs and deserters who preyed on families whose men were off fighting the war. Yellow fever outbreaks were so terrifying that people panicked and fled at an hour's notice. Seeds of change were sowed early on since logging was the main way to make cash. As a result, trees started falling, and a huge timber industry evolved, stripping the countryside of its majestic forests. Logs were floated downstream in vast rafts as some of the then-largest sawmills in the nation sprang up along the lower Pearl at towns like Pearlington and Logtown. By the late 1800s, however, these logs had jammed up at the shoals on the East Pearl, which was then the main river, below Holmes Bayou. Boat traffic began going down Holmes Bayou and other westerly routes, which the Corps of Engineers dredged to make more navigable. As a result, more and more water flowed out of the main river and into the West Pearl, which had once been a minor route. The Corps also built a barge canal on the west side of the river; it not only blocked the Bogue Chitto's natural flow into the Pearl with a lowhead dam, it siphoned water off the main river, speeding up the current. Among the results, Wilson Slough, which flowed from the main river into the West Pearl, enlarged while the main river and its swamps on the Mississippi side virtually dried up, leaving Walkiah Bluff Water Park high and dry. In an attempt to rectify this situation, at least partially, the Corps of Engineers redirected water in the late 1990s to reduce the flow down Wilson Slough and increase it down the main river at least as far as Holmes Bayou. The result of all this, from a paddler's standpoint, is a confusing swamp made even more confusing by all these man-made changes—changes that will no doubt continue to occur.

Probably the most dramatic change of all was the John C. Stennis Space Center. In the early 1960s, when the space race was sizzling, NASA selected 128,000 acres in south Mississippi for a rocket-testing site. The area was considered near-ideal for testing rockets. It's far enough from populated areas to provide a buffer for the awesome noise levels. At 125 decibels, the sound of test rockets can reportedly kill people and destroy buildings at close range. Despite its isolation, the area is accessible by water—for transporting huge rocket chambers on barges—

and by highway. Plus the climate permits year-round testing. To local residents, the economic prospects of a rocket facility were enticing, but the change was disturbing too. The buffer zone encompassed 695 homes, 14 churches, 2 schools, 17 stores, and many other buildings, including the entire town of Logtown and other communities, according to the book *Way Station to Space: A History of the John C. Stennis Space Center* by Mack R. Herring. It was a testament to Stennis's skills as a statesman that he sold the project to local residents and helped protect them from exploitation at the same time. Construction was a formidable task. The swamp swarmed with salt marsh mosquitoes, so bad the workers couldn't stand it until aerial spraying of insecticides. As many as 85 snakes were killed during one day, though only 2 people were bitten and none died. By 1996, however, the designated swamps and woods had been transformed into a world-class technological center. The remarkable thing about all this is that, from the perspective of a paddler on the river, there's little evidence the space center even exists. Even today, despite all the changes, the Pearl River swamps seem more stone age than space age.

The Pearl got its modern-day name from French explorers who discovered pearls near the mouth of the river. A mother-of-pearl industry continued into the early twentieth century as mussel fishermen went out on the river in flat-bottom boats and caught their prey with long-handled scoops such as those used on the coast for oystering. They'd bring their catch to shore and boil them in pots to remove the meat, which would be used for fish bait, while the shiny inner shells were sold to companies that converted them into buttons. In this era of mainly plastic buttons, mussel fishing has faded along Pearl River, though the business still thrives in the Kentucky Lake area where brail boats—brail refers to the hooked lines used to drag the lake bottom—still catch mussels for use as buttons.

If Pearl River mussel fishing has diminished, other fishing is going strong. In spring high water, tributaries tend to clear up faster than the main river, and that's when anglers catch all sorts of fish at the mouths of streams where clear and muddy water mix. Live crawfish or crawfish-type lures are best then since that's what fish are feeding on naturally. Worms are also good. For bass you can also use artificial bait like shiny spinnerbaits or small beetlespins on ultralight rigs. From such spots you may pull out Kentucky redeye, black and striped bass, bluegill, redbellied and goggle-eye bream, as well as catfish and white perch. When the river tops its banks, you can catch catfish in the still backwaters by baiting droplines or trotlines with Octagon or Ivory soap, which slowly melts, luring small to medium channel cats with its tallow content. Bloodbait works on the same principle. Buy it ready-made or make your own by soaking a piece of sponge in pork or beef blood. As the water levels fall and stabilize in the summer, catfishing is good in the river on catalpa worms, pond perch, and spot-tailed minnows. Catch your own spot-tails by baiting a minnow trap with dog food or cheese and cornmeal and placing it on the downside of a sandbar. Then set your catfish hooks on the river bottom or just off it in places such as the downstream side of a fallen treetop. For summer bass, use white buzzbaits and spinners. In the fall when the river is low, go to topwater lures, retrieving slowly since the fish are slow to move in cold water. In the swamp and marsh country below I-59, just about any bass lures will catch the smaller black bass known locally as green trout, along with redfish and speckled trout. Saltwater species sometimes make their way far upstream. In June 1992 some Walthall County fishermen were seining for bait in the river near Columbia, 130 river miles from the mouth, when they hauled in a tiny flounder. Biologists say it's common for flounder to follow a "saltwater wedge" pushing into river mouths at certain times of year. Other species that sometimes wind up in fresh water include mullet, striped bass, skipjack herring, tarpon, snook, and needlefish.

Unlike the Pascagoula River, the Pearl has few easily canoeable tributaries. There are Strong River, which comes in from the east near Georgetown; the Bogue Chitto River, which enters from the west below Bogalusa; and two Bogue Chitto tributaries, Topisaw and Magee's Creeks. However, the Pearl is fed by many creeks that are enjoyed by local folks willing to deal with logjams and shallows for some good fishing or outdoor adventure. For example, the Yockanookany (Yock-a-NOOK-anee) enters from the north above Ross Barnett Reservoir between Highway 25 and Leake County Water Park. It's a fine fishing creek, but pack a chain saw with the tackle box. An easier way to see it is to paddle up from the Pearl, where you can experience a half-mile or more of quiet water and deep woods before coming to the first fallen trees. Much the same can be said for more tributaries downstream, like Fair River, Silver Creek, and White Sand Creek in the Monticello vicinity, Louisiana's Pushepatapa (Push-pa-TAP) Creek near Bogalusa, and Hobolochitto Creek (Ho-bo-lo-CHIT-to, named for a Choctaw chief named Hobolo) near Picayune, among others. These are lovely little streams but can make for hard going, especially during low water. For instance, I showed up at the Hobolochitto—locally known as the Boley—

one fine fall day ready to paddle and found it so shallow that four-wheelers were riding down the middle of the creek, and even at the last take-out it appeared formidably logjammed. With sufficient water, though, the shallow, sandy West Hobolochitto is floatable on its lower reaches. From Highway 43 northwest of Picayune to Highway 992 on the west side of town is a distance of 2.5 miles. The East Hobolochitto joins a half-mile above Highway 992, making the creek slower and muddier. From Highway 992 it's 4.5 miles to Palestine Road west of town, the last take-out before the Boley empties into the Pearl River another 5 miles downstream.

Pearl routes

- **Upper Pearl River**
  1. Highway 393 to ramp at Burnside Water Park just below Highway 15, 15 miles.
  2. Highway 15 to Highway 19, 2.5 miles.
  3. Highway 19 to Highway 16 at Edinburg, 20 miles.
  4. Highway 16 to ramp at Battle Bluff Road, 8 miles. The Battle Bluff ramp is located on a small road northwest of bridge, just south of the Sunrise community off Highway 16.
  5. Ramp at Battle Bluff Road to ramp on Highway 35 just south of Carthage, 10 miles. The Carthage ramp is accessible from the southeast side of the bridge.
  6. Carthage to ramp at Old Highway 13 just east of Highway 25, 10 miles. The Old 13 bridge is closed, but a ramp is located on the southeast side.
  7. Old Highway 13 to ramp at Leake County Water Park, 10 miles. There's also a ramp on the southeast side of the lowhead dam a half mile farther. Both the water park and the lowhead dam are located west of Highway 25 on the south side of the river.

- **Middle Pearl River**
  1. Ross Barnett Reservoir dam to Highway 25 (Lakeland Drive), 9 miles. There are ramps on both sides of the river just below the dam. It's another 2 miles from Highway 25 to a lowhead dam at the Jackson Water Works pumping station and another 4 miles to Highway 80, but the lowhead dam is a difficult obstacle, and this stretch of river nearly dries up in low water.

- **Lower Pearl River**

1. Highway 80 to Gatesville Road bridge just east of Gatesville, 41.5 miles. Access is difficult at Highway 80 because of steep banks and rutted road, but people do use the river for four-wheeler riding and picnicking. Florence-Byram Road, Rosemary Road, and Moncure Road all cross the river on this stretch but lack access.

2. Gatesville Road to ramp at bridge on Harrisville-Hopewell Road just east of Hopewell, 5 miles.

3. Hopewell to ramp at bait shop on Highway 28 just east of Georgetown, 10 miles.

4. Highway 28 to ramp at Wanilla Water Park, 27 miles.

5. Wanilla Water Park to ramp at Atwood Water Park on Highway 84 east of Monticello, 14 miles. Mill Road crosses the river 5 miles below Wanilla, but there is no access.

6. Atwood Water Park to ramp at Columbia Water Park, 50 miles. Columbia Water Park is located off Highway 35 west of Columbia on the east side of the river.

7. Columbia Water Park to ramp at Highway 98, 5 miles. The ramp at Highway 98 is located via a road on the southeast side of the bridge.

8. Highway 98 to Louisiana Highway 10 at Bogalusa, La., 57 miles. At Bogalusa, a road on the northwest side of the bridge leads to a ramp underneath, while a road southeast of the bridge leads to a ramp in Mississippi's Old River WMA just downriver. There's also a high-water ramp east of Angie, La., 27 miles below Highway 98.

9. Bogalusa to Pool's Bluff Sill, 10 miles. At Pool's Bluff there's a ramp below the lowhead dam, or sill, east of Louisiana Highway 21. The sill is located at the head of the barge canal which branches west off the main river. Portage around the dam if you take out here.

10. Pool's Bluff Sill to ramp at Walkiah Bluff Water Park on the east bank of the river, 18 miles. Walkiah Bluff Water Park is located on Walkiah Bluff Road west of Highway 43 north of Picayune.

11. Walkiah Bluff to ramp at Lock 1, 10 miles. Going downriver, take Holmes Bayou to the southwest 5 miles below Walkiah Bluff. Holmes Bayou joins the West Pearl in 4 miles, then the barge canal just beyond. To get to boat ramp, turn right onto barge canal and paddle half a mile to Lock 1, located off Highway 41.

12. Lock 1 to ramp under I-59 on West Pearl, 6 miles. The I-59 ramp is located off the exit 5 miles north of the intersection of I-59 and I-10.

13. I-59 to ramp at Davis Landing on the West Pearl River off Louisiana Highway 1090, 6 miles.

14. Davis Landing to Crawford Landing off Highway 1090 just above I-10 on the West Pearl, 3 miles. It's also possible to take the east branch 1.5 miles below Davis and paddle 11 miles down the West Middle and/or Middle Pearl to ramps at Highway 90.

15. Crawford Landing to ramp at Indian Village off Highway 190, 5 miles.

16. Indian Village to ramp on Highway 90, 2.5 miles.

Outfitters

1. Indian Cycle, Fitness and Outdoors, 125 Dyess Road, Ridgeland. Rents canoes for use on upper Pearl (and just about anywhere else in the state). 601-956-8383.

2. Bluecat's Canoe Tours, Pearl River, La., 504-863-0628 or 504-649-2804. Tours of Honey Island Swamp.

3. Canoe and Trail Adventures, 6976 General Haig St., New Orleans, La., 504-283-9400. Tours of Honey Island Swamp.

Area campgrounds

1. Leake County Water Park off Highway 25 east of Ludlow, northeast of Jackson. There are also campsites at the nearby lowhead dam. 601-654-9355.

2. Coal Bluff Water Park off Highway 25 a few miles downstream from the lowhead dam northeast of Jackson. 601-654-7726.

3. LeFleur's Bluff State Park, 2140 Riverside Drive, off Exit 98B, Jackson. Trails lead to the river but there is no canoe access. 601-987-3985.

4. Atwood Water Park, Highway 84 East, Monticello, 601-587-2711 or 601-587-7732.

5. Walkiah Bluff Water Park west of Highway 43 north of Picayune. The park is operated by Pearl River County, 601-798-1339.

High points

Vast stretches with little sign of humans.

Low points

Long distance between bridges makes day trips scarce.

Tips

Learn to appreciate the sweeping views on this big, powerful river.

Strong River

Strong River begins in the Bienville National Forest near Morton and flows southwest past Puckett and Mendenhall before reaching Pearl River. Only about a third of its length is canoeable, the 25 miles or so from D'Lo Water Park near Mendenhall down to the Pearl, and even the upper parts of that are too shallow at times. But if you ever hear the thunder of the rapids just above D'Lo Water Park—and some other places along the river—you'll agree the Strong is well named. In February 1990, for example, flash-flooding on a tributary forced several hundred Mendenhall residents to flee their homes, taking shelter in a National Guard armory and a church. The tributary, which empties into the Strong about half a mile from town, rose about 2 feet in seven minutes, piling into the flooded Strong and flowing backward. On other occasions, I've been told, teams have had to rescue experienced paddlers who ran into trouble in high water. Even in more normal conditions, the river can deceive. I met a man who as a boy was with a group of paddlers when his canoe flipped and he went under. When he tried to surface he found himself blocked by branches. He was about to run out of air when his buddy reached down and grabbed him by the collar, hoisting him to safety. Lest you conclude this is a raging river, however, bear in mind that most of the time it's placid, more so than many state streams, in fact. There are long stretches with virtually no current at all, with only occasional shoals and falls for brief excitement.

The river is usually floatable at D'Lo Water Park off Highway 49 northwest of Mendenhall. The park—known locally as "the rock"—has a campground and provides canoe rental and shuttle service. From the park boat ramp to Chapel Bridge near Pinola is 11 miles. Merit Bridge, a historic iron bridge, crosses 5 miles below the park but offers no public access. In the dry season this stretch of river may be shallow and require a good bit of towing. Otherwise it's just slow, coast-

Even dogs like the usually mellow Strong River near Mendenhall.

ing between walls of immense hardwood forest with few sandbars, inhabited by shy beavers, sunning turtles, and gliding cranes. Just before Chapel Bridge is a river-wide rapid that can be exciting and fun, provided there's enough water to get over it. The roar sounds intimidating, especially if the river is up a bit, but the main hazard is getting stuck on the rocks and having to wade your boat through. It's worth scouting from the bank to pick the best course. In our group, some went to the right and got temporarily stuck on the rocks, while others went over the center without problem.

It's 3 miles from Pinola to Highway 28, where access is steep. Dr. Guy and Tay Gillespie operate Strong River Camp and Farm for Boys and Girls (601-847-4440) at Highway 28. The summer camp for children eight to twelve years old was established in 1920 by the Vicksburg YMCA, later sold to the Jackson YMCA, then to Mrs. Gillespie in the early 1970s. The children canoe and camp on the river, including a four-day float at the end of the summer.

The 9-mile run from Highway 28 to Bridgeport Road starts with a long rapid, then subsides into more quiet, leisurely water, perfect for silent contemplation as you dip your paddle into the mostly still surface beneath towering hickories, water oaks, and cypress trees. Sandbars, nearly nonexistent on the upper river, become noticeable at last. Scenic bluffs tower over the south bank about 5 miles below Highway 28, and hundreds of vultures roost around a big old tree nearby.

From Bridgeport Road, where access is nearly as difficult as at Highway 28, it's just 3.5 miles to Pearl River. There used to be a take-out just across the Pearl at Georgetown Water Park. But that park has closed, which means the nearest access is 1.5 miles up the Pearl to a bait shop boat ramp at Highway 28, or 25 miles down the Pearl to Wanilla Water Park.

The Strong's slow, often shallow nature makes casual fishing hit-or-miss. Hand-grabbers occasionally pull out some big catfish around D'Lo Water Park and elsewhere, and trotliners and bass fishermen report some success, but I also know experienced fishermen who have come away empty-handed after a hard day's angling. To me the Strong is best for daydreaming. Its big, quiet woods and generally unobstructed paddling make it perfect for thoughtful conversation and plans for future trips.

Strong routes

1. Ramp at D'Lo Water Park to Chapel Bridge, 11 miles. D'Lo Water Park is located off Highways 49 and 149 northwest of Mendenhall. Chapel Bridge is off Highway 43 north of Pinola. Merit Bridge crosses 5 miles below D'Lo Water Park but there is no access.

3. Chapel Bridge to Highway 28, 3 miles. Access is steep at Highway 28.

4. Highway 28 to Bridgeport Road, 9 miles. Bridgeport Road connects Highways 28 and 478. From Bridgeport Road it's 3.5 miles to Pearl River, where the next take-out is 1.5 miles up the Pearl River at Highway 28, or 25 miles downriver at Wanilla Water Park on the west bank just north of Wanilla.

Outfitters and campgrounds

D'lo Water Park, off Highway 49 northwest of Mendenhall, rents canoes and provides shuttle. 601-847-4310.

High points

Beautiful hardwood forest.

Low points

Long stretches with no current.

Tips

Use this river to unwind and clear your mind.

Bogue Chitto River

The Bogue Chitto River of southwest Mississippi begins in Lincoln County with tiny east and west forks that come together like a wishbone to form a single stem. At first a logjammed creek, it extends southeast into Pike County where it widens into one of the prettiest and most popular canoeing rivers in Mississippi. It angles across Walthall County, passes into Louisiana north of Franklinton, curves southeast and reenters Mississippi at the Pearl River. All told, that's well over 100 miles of river, and for most of that length the Bogue Chitto is perfect paddling size: not so small that you're constantly dragging over logs, yet not so big that you're forever fighting headwinds. It's relatively fast, too, with sharp bends and submerged logs: Snooze at your peril on a Bogue Chitto float!

The river abounds in wildlife, with only occasional human disturbance. The water is fairly clear, the bottom sand and gravel. Sandbars alternate with big woods. Those woods particularly impressed a Canadian paddler I know. "Going down that river was in fact like wilderness," Lawrence Pitcairn of Winnipeg, a former member of the Canadian national kayak racing team, told me after a day-float. "There were hardly any people and very little development on the shores." Few trees in his home territory match the size of our southern giants, like the beeches, river birches, magnolias, sycamores, water oaks, bald cypress, and tupelo gums lining the stream. "Although I realize the countryside is developed around the river, on the river itself there really isn't much development," Lawrence said, referring to the beef cattle, dairy, and poultry farms in the surrounding countryside. "It's nice. You get the impression of being way out, and that's what counts."

The river's name is Choctaw for "big swampy"—chitto means big, bogue means swampy. But the Bogue Chitto is not really swampy until more than 100 miles from its source when it joins the Pearl River north of Picayune. The wetland that extends from there to the coast is indeed a big swamp, and perhaps what the Choctaws had in mind. There are other Bogue Chittos in Mississippi, incidentally, including Bogue Chitto creeks northwest of Jackson and southeast of Starkville, a Choctaw community and another creek near Philadelphia (the Choctaws pronounce it "Boke Cheeto"), and a community on Highway 51 south of Brookhaven.

On the river, there's little point in launching a boat above Alford's Bridge in northern Pike County, and even then you can expect plenty of logjams before reaching Highway 570 five miles downstream. Still, it's a sweet stretch. Its shady reaches form a realm of green shade and chatterbox water that seems like a preview of heaven. Birch and sycamore trees reach across the river in places to form a canopy. The water is usually clear enough to spot fish darting from sandy shallows to opaque depths. But don't be sweet-talked by all this gentleness. Eddie McCalip, who lives near the river, told me about a close call he had when canoeing with a friend in high water. The current swept them against a log, the buddy jumped onto it, and the boat flipped. The current pinned Eddie against the log. The friend tried to pull him out, but the river was too strong. "I had to let myself go under the log," Eddie told me. "That was one of the hardest things I've ever done." He slipped under, knowing the river might decide to keep him. When he bobbed up on the far side, he owned a new wisdom. "I learned one thing about the river," Eddie said. "It's the boss. If you try to beat it, you'll lose."

The water level was normal when Eddie and I encountered a logjam just above Highway 570, but we still had problems. Completely blocked, the river piled a hard current against the barrier. High banks and massed roots discouraged portaging. We pulled over to assess the situation. We knew the current would press the canoe against the log sideways. In such situations, it's important not to lean upstream, since the boat can tilt and fill. If that happens, it can become a permanent fixture in the Bogue Chitto, concreted in place by the jackhammer current. As with many anticipated dangers, though, this one turned out to be not so bad. A submerged stob—the tip of a vertical branch or stump— slowed the canoe and cushioned the impact. What looked like peril turned into toil as we climbed onto the log—gingerly, since such spots can be slick—and lifted the canoe over. Soon we were back on the river, sweaty but unharmed. Such obstacles are common on this upper stretch. It's best to approach them slowly, allowing the current to swing the boat alongside if there's no way through. Lean toward the log and, once stabilized, assess the situation. If you

Charles Sharp of Pike County points his pirogue down the Bogue Chitto River east of McComb.

have to get out onto the log, make sure it's not rotten. Usually you can simply slide the boat over and get back in—which isn't so simple if the boat contains a couple hundred pounds of gear, I grant you. Some obstacles aren't so obvious. Just below that logjam, Eddie and I ran onto an unseen stob in smooth, open water, and suddenly we were stuck, swinging back and forth, leaning danger-ously to one side. We managed to muscle off, reminded that it's the easy spots that will get you.

There aren't too many logjams on the 4-mile stretch between Highway 570 and Highway 44 east of McComb. The stretch is a fine one, but you're likely to hear the sound of machinery from Sanderson Farms, a poultry processing plant just visible from the river. In 1993, when Sanderson Farms built the plant, some area residents expressed concern about possible river pollution. But the com-pany built a $3 million, state-of-the-art, four-stage treatment plant to handle the 700,000 to 800,000 gallons of water it discharges each day. Before waste-water leaves the plant, blood is removed for use in animal feed, and solids are filtered out. The water from the poultry processing operation and from cleanup passes into a large, plastic-lined, fenced-in lagoon. The liquid is capped with a layer of tar and hay to keep out air and light, which allows it to decompose anaerobically. From there it's piped into a 15-foot-deep aerobic basin, which is constantly stirred and pumped with oxygen by a rotating boom. Next the liquid passes into a 17-foot-deep clarifying tank. Any remaining particles settle and are returned to the aeration basin. Finally the water flows through a chute under ultraviolet lamps, which sterilize bacteria to keep them from reproducing. The resulting flow, which is crystal clear, enters the Bogue Chitto underwater to be out of sight. The outflow is monitored daily by a company environmental supervisor and periodically by the Mississippi Department of Environmental Quality. The system is also equipped to handle emergencies like power failures. An emergency basin can handle up to fifteen days of flow. If a power outage lasted longer than that, processing would shut down.

A more subtle threat to Bogue Chitto and most Mississippi streams is non-point pollution—runoff from no particular point or source such as a heavy industry, rather the leach of sewage and other pollutants from camps, farms, gas stations, and so on. Another widespread problem is mercury. Scientists say mercury enters the atmosphere as industrial pollution and spreads across the continent. The most pristine areas of the world are not immune. Ironically, it's often the cleaner streams that are most likely to be affected. Murkier rivers in the Mississippi Delta, for instance, haven't shown elevated levels because the chemical makeup of the soil prevents buildup. Streams like the Bogue Chitto flow through piney-woods terrain with acidic soils that react with mercury and release it into the water. The neuro-toxin builds up in fish, particularly older ones, and DEQ has issued advisories against eating large quantities of such fish on a regular basis.

The Bogue Chitto does provide good fishing. Eddie McCalip's father, Ed, has fished the river all his life, angling for largemouth bass in the swifts, setting trotlines and droplines for catfish in deeps. He recalls as a boy hooking a catfish with a head as wide as a watermelon. The fish straightened his hook and escaped. "He must have gone 70, 80 pounds," Mr. Ed said. Flatheads of 50 or more pounds have been caught, though most are much smaller. The river also harbors channel cats and a few blues. Catfish action is good just about anytime, whether the water is clear or muddy. Local fishermen prefer natural bait such as crawfish and spot-tailed minnows, which can be seined in the river. Savvy catfishermen also use a type of worm apparently found only in the Bogue Chitto and other streams in the lower Pearl River basin. The worms, known locally as mudworms, make great bait but aren't widely known. The bluish-gray, square-bodied worms live in leafy muck alongside spring branches. Dig them with a potato fork in the early spring and you've got bait aplenty. At up to 2 feet long, a single worm can bait ten to fifteen hooks. But if you're digging and you see one, grab it quickly or it will vanish underground. I checked with fishermen from other areas and they weren't familiar with the creatures. A biologist looked it up and said it appears to be in the genus *haplotaxina*. One old-timer, Charlie Carter of Tylertown, told me, "Way back yonder folks would say, 'There's a good crop of mudworms because the hogs are fat.' Hogs would root in the mud, look like they'd be standing on their head in the hole because they'd be eating those worms. That was 70 years ago. They're excellent fish bait because that is a natural."

The Bogue Chitto offers excellent fishing for largemouth and Kentucky redeye bass, and redbellied and bluegill bream. Bogue Chitto bass like topwater lures such as Tiny Torpedoes, white buzzbaits with red eyes, and white spinnerbaits. Bream go for beetlespins, crickets, worms, and, especially, crawfish in early spring when the mudbugs are naturally active. Bass and bream are most likely to bite in the clearer-water conditions of late summer and fall. River bass typically go 1 to 2 pounds, though lunkers up to 7 pounds get caught. Crappie can be caught on pink and black or chartreuse and black jigs. Cast out in a deep pool and reel in slowly. For better chances rig the jigs tandem style, or two on one line about 6 inches apart.

The 7 miles between Highway 44 and Holmesville contain a few easy pullovers, where you must slide your boat over logs. At this writing plans were in the works to build an electric power plant on the east side above Holmesville. The plant will use natural gas to fire turbines. As the heat dissipates, it will convert water piped from the river into steam to turn more turbines, generating 800 megawatts of electricity, which will be sold to power companies that transmit it to customers. The water will be filtered before being released back into the river. The plant will occupy 40 acres, with the remaining 160 acres for a buffer.

Holmesville, now a rural community, was the first town in Pike County, established in 1816 as a county seat. Pioneers from Georgia, Tennessee, and the Carolinas built a log courthouse complete with a jail, stocks, hanging tree, and whipping post. In 1848 the courthouse burned and was followed by a brick building that still stands today. With the advent of the railroad in the 1850s, officials decided to shift the county seat west to the tracks, so the towns of Magnolia and Summit competed for the privilege. A court ruling favored Magnolia, and a courthouse was built there in 1875. That building, which burned in 1882 and was rebuilt in 1918, is on the National Historic Register and is a Mississippi landmark. McComb, meanwhile, went on to become the largest town in Pike County, which was named for explorer Zebulon Pike of Pike's Peak fame. Access is good at the Holmesville bridge, and there's a ramp at U.S. Highway 98 four miles farther on. Below Holmesville, Topisaw Creek enters from the east.

Below the mouth of the Topisaw, the Bogue Chitto becomes downright cordial as it slides toward U.S. 98 and 2 miles farther to Bogue Chitto Water Park. But people aren't always so cordial. Problems started in the 1970s when the Pearl River Basin Development District established the water park and the river became wildly popular with tubers and paddlers. Some citizens opposed the park, fearing overuse would spoil the river. By the late '70s and early '80s it looked like they were right. On a given summer weekend, up to two thousand people would float the river—mainly from Highway 98 to the water park boat ramp—with the inevitable excesses of litter, profanity, and drunkenness. Landowners protested, saying river access should be limited. Prior to 1970, public waterways in Mississippi were governed by an 1896 statute which defined navigable waterways as at least 25 miles long and capable of floating a steamboat carrying 200 bales of cotton for thirty consecutive days. In 1970 the state Supreme Court upheld a Pearl River County Chancery Court decision that declared Hobolochitto Creek private. The court ruled that the old statute "was intended to exclude small private creeks and streams, non-navigable in fact, and to declare navigable only streams actually capable of being navigated by substantial commercial traffic." In an attempt to clarify the issue, the state Legislature adopted an act in 1972 that stated the public had access to rivers that averaged 3 feet in depth along the thread of a channel for ninety consecutive days. The issue would not be resolved, however, for another twenty years.

In the meantime there were injury lawsuits, such as one for $14 million filed in 1984 by a man who dove from a cliff between Highway 98 and the Bogue Chitto Water Park, breaking his neck. He sued Pike County, the Pearl River Basin Development District, and the owner of the land where the injury occurred, claiming they failed to warn river users of the danger. A judge dismissed the district and the landowner from the suit, leaving the county to settle out of court. The landowner, meanwhile, spent tens of thousands of dollars in legal fees. (And though warning signs are now posted on the cliff, people continue to dive.) Outraged landowners prevailed on the sheriff to bar access to the river on grounds that it was not a public waterway. The issue went back to court, and in 1988 a Pike County chancellor ruled the river to be private. The case went to the state Supreme Court, which in 1991 ruled the Bogue Chitto to be a navigable waterway open to the public.

The ruling affected all rivers with a minimum 100 cubic feet per second flow, which includes streams considerably smaller than the Bogue Chitto. The Commission on Environmental Quality publishes a map and a list showing all public waterways in the state. According to the law, on public waterways "the citizens of this state and other states shall have the right of free transport in the stream and its bed and the right to fish and engage in water sports." The court did not define "bed," however. Most take it to mean the ground beneath the surface of the water, but some argue that it means the area covered by seasonally high levels, which would include sandbars. A court may someday have to resolve that—or maybe not. If river users would show respect for landowners—don't litter, get drunk, shoot guns, and so on—conflicts could dissolve. Even a landowners' attorney was a longtime Scout leader who took Boy Scouts on lengthy float trips, camping on sandbars as needed. The real issue, he told me, is common decency.

Once the public got word they weren't likely to be arrested for trespassing, they returned to the river, and by the late 1990s problems had resumed. Law enforcement reacted, with plainclothes officers making numerous arrests on summer weekends, and county boards of supervisors passing ordinances restricting guns, glass, styrofoam, and, in dry Walthall County, alcohol. Over Labor Day weekend in 1999, someone drove nails into logs in the Bogue Chitto—an act that lawmen said constituted aggravated assault since the nails were evidently placed there to injure people. At least two people were scratched on the spikes, which also gashed at least one canoe and deflated inner tubes. The logs, with protruding nail heads inches below the surface of the water, were found in the river for about a 300-yard stretch north of the mouth of Topisaw Creek between Holmesville and Highway 98. Since the Holmesville to 98 stretch is less heavily floated than 98 to Bogue Chitto Water Park, there was less damage than there might have been. No one was ever caught.

Despite summertime crowding, the Bogue Chitto Water Park is a showcase with gorgeous woods, secluded campsites, rustic cabins, pavilion, hiking trail, picnic areas, and fine river views. There are canoe rental companies just outside the gates. The park is located south of Highway 98 between McComb and Tylertown. A sign on 98 just west of the river bridge points the way. There is a

$2-per-car entrance fee at the park. Launch fee is $2.50 per boat, $1.25 per inner tube. Camping is $12 per site with full hookups at all eighty-one sites, $8 for primitive camping. Four cabins and a boxcar are available at $45 per night on Fridays and Saturdays and $30 other times. Reservations are required on the cabins at all times, but on the campsites only on major holidays. Pavilion rental is $45. For more information call 601-684-9568.

Below the water park there used to be a locally renowned 3-foot waterfall, but the clay-rock shelf that formed it has eroded to a whisper, a good example of the changeable nature of Deep South rivers. The high, forested banks provide a deep-woods feel, augmented by the presence of creatures like ospreys. At 2 feet tall with a wingspread of up to 6 feet, these majestic birds of prey are sometimes mistaken for eagles. However, they're readily distinguishable by their white fronts with slight mottling at the chest, while their bent-tip wings and backs are brown. Binoculars reveal a white head with a dark brown bandit mask across the fierce yellow eyes. Be glad when you see an osprey because they're not found far inland. They breed from Alaska across to Newfoundland and on down the East Coast to Florida and the Gulf Coast. They winter from the Gulf Coast and California south to Argentina, so in pristine areas of south Mississippi you may see them year-round. They live exclusively on fish, and their skills will make you jealous, but ospreys have tackle that we just can't buy. The soles of their feet are lined with spiny projections that give them a firm grip on slippery prey. When an osprey spots a fish near the surface, it swoops down, hovers, then plunges feet-first into the water, grasping the fish in those spiny talons. When you see one rise with a wriggling bass in its claws, you have been blessed.

The 5 miles between Bogue Chitto Water Park and Walker's Bridge Memorial Water Park just below Highway 48 in Walthall County constitute perhaps the finest stretch on the river, a picture of what a canoeing stream should be—narrow enough to provide shade, tricky enough not to be dull, and with little sign of human presence until just above Highway 48, where camps appear. No wonder ospreys like it. Half a mile below the Highway 48 bridge on the west bank, Walker's Bridge Water Park has a fine boat ramp and picnic area but no other facilities. The park is located half a mile south of Highway 48 between Magnolia and Tylertown. A sign points the way off 48, but there is no sign showing the entrance, which is near a group of residences.

Though black and turkey vultures are seen on all Mississippi rivers, they are unusually plentiful on the stretch below Walker's Bridge. They are a holdover from the days when there was an island they called their own. I've seen them perched in trees and standing in the sand by the hundreds, their wings spread to diffuse heat, grunting and hissing. The channel changed and the island merged with the shoreline, but buzzards are still around, and old-timers say it's been that way for decades. Biologists agree that it's normal for vultures to have long-established areas for roosting and resting. There are several differences between black and turkey vultures, the most obvious being their heads. Black vultures have black heads, while turkey vultures have reddish pates like turkeys. Turkey vultures also have narrower wings and tail than blacks. Turkey vultures may not be as regal as ospreys, but they're just as big. Black vultures are a bit smaller. Scientists have determined that turkey vultures locate carrion by smell while black vultures rely on vision, in case you've ever wondered.

Offsetting the relative homeliness of buzzards are wildflowers growing along the river, which is now wide enough to receive full sun. One of the most obvious blossoms on the Bogue Chitto is the cleome, or spider flower, which blooms from June through November. The plants rise 2 to 3 feet from the muddy edges of sandbars and from midriver stumps, their green leafy stalks topped with clusters of pinkish-purple oval petals and deep-purple stamens radiating out like spider webs. Even people not attuned to wildflowers can't miss these beauties.

Camps and riverside residences become more abundant in Walthall County as the river widens on the 6 miles from Walker's to Stallings Bridge west of Lexie, and on the 3 miles down to Dillon Bridge west of Highway 27, the last bridge before Louisiana. River roads roughly paralleling the Bogue Chitto to the west connect the roads on which Walker's, Stallings, and Dillon Bridges are located. Many of the riverside houses are attractive, expansive brick or rustic wood, sheltering beneath water oak and beech trees. At some, white plastic pipe funnels Artesian springs into the river, a cozy sound. Just above Dillon Bridge, a pipe left stranded in midriver when the bank moved south now spouts a geyser of springwater out of the river. In the stretches of unkempt woods between camps, spruce pines grow among the more common loblollies. Loblolly pines are so named because they fare well even in damp soil, "loblolly" being an old-fashioned term for a low, wet place. They're seen all over Mississippi and are easily recognizable by their 6–9-inch needles—longer than shortleaf, shorter than longleaf—and by their thick scaly bark. Spruce pines also like damp soil, particularly along rivers, but their needles are shorter at 1½ to 3 inches and their bark is silvery-gray and smoother, suggestive of an oak trunk. Magee's Creek, a fine floating stream in its own right, enters from the east a half mile above Dillon Bridge. By this time the Bogue Chitto is starting to look like a pretty wide river. Shade is a thing of the past, but so are river-wide logjams. Swift, log-studded bends look more dangerous than they did upstream, deeper and darker, but the channel is broad enough to provide an easy route most of the time.

At Dillon Bridge are two canoe rentals with campgrounds. Take-out at the bridge is difficult so it's worthwhile paying to use a ramp. A mile or so below the bridge, the Bogue Chitto leaves Mississippi for its passage through southeast Louisiana, including 3.5 miles from Dillon Bridge to Highway 438 at Warnerton, 6 miles from Warnerton to Highway 38 west of Clifton, 9 miles from Clifton to Highway 10 just west of Franklinton, 13 miles from Franklinton to Highway 437 southwest of Enon, 17 miles from Enon to Highway 21 between Sun and Bush, and 3 miles from Highway 21 to the West Pearl barge canal east of Sun. At the barge canal turn left, or north, and paddle less than a mile to Lock 3, where there's a ramp. Or turn right onto the barge canal, portage around a lowhead dam to the left, and continue to follow Bogue Chitto River through the swamp. The river wends some 10 miles to Wilson Slough, which becomes West Pearl River. Turn right and paddle some 14 miles past the mouth of Holmes Bayou on the east to the intersection with the barge canal, where you can turn right onto the canal and go half a mile to a boat ramp at Lock 1, located off Louisiana Highway 41. See Pearl River section for the rest of Pearl River. U.S.G.S. quad maps (Industrial and Hickory, Louisiana) are recommended for the lower Bogue Chitto since plenty of channels branch off. Indeed, it's in these "big swampy" environs that the river truly lives up to its Choctaw name.

Bogue Chitto routes

1. Johnston Station Road (Alford's Bridge) east of Dixie Springs in north Pike County to Highway 570 east of Summit, 5 extremely logjammed miles.
2. Highway 570 to Highway 44 east of McComb, 4 miles.
3. Highway 44 to Holmesville, 7 miles. The Holmesville bridge is located on Pike 93 Central north of Highway 98.
4. Holmesville to ramp at Highway 98, 4 miles.

5. Highway 98 to Bogue Chitto Water Park, 2 miles. The water park has a ramp on the west bank.

6. Bogue Chitto Water Park to ramp at Walker's Memorial Water Park just south of Highway 48 (Walker's Bridge), 5 miles. To get to the park, take the first road south on the west side of the river. At this writing there is no sign, so watch for the paved drive among several residences about half a mile from Highway 48.

7. Walker's Park to Stallings Bridge Road west of Lexie, 6 miles.

8. Stallings Bridge to Dillon Bridge west of Highway 27 south of Lexie, 3 miles. Magee's Creek, a good floating stream, enters from the east a half mile above Dillon Bridge.

9. Dillon Bridge to Highway 438 at Warnerton, La., 3.5 miles.

10. Highway 438 to Highway 38 west of Clifton, La., 6 miles.

11. Highway 38 to Highway 10 just west of Franklinton, La., 9 miles.

12. Highway 10 to Highway 437 southwest of Enon, La., 13 miles.

13. Highway 437 to Highway 21 between Sun and Bush, La., 17 miles.

14. Highway 21 to Lock 3 on West Pearl barge canal east of Sun, La., 4 miles. Turn left, or north, at barge canal 3 miles below Highway 21 and paddle less than a mile to Lock 3, where there's a ramp.

15. Barge canal (via Bogue Chitto and Pearl) to Lock 1, 24 miles. When Bogue Chitto enters barge canal, turn right onto canal, then portage around lowhead dam to left. Go 10 miles to Wilson Slough and turn right. It becomes the West Pearl River. When it intersects with the lower end of the barge canal in about 14 miles, turn right and go half a mile to a boat ramp at Lock 1 located off Louisiana Highway 41. To continue down the Pearl River, see Pearl River section above.

Outfitters

1. Bogue Chitto Choo Choo, near entrance to Bogue Chitto Water Park, 601-249-3788.

2. Canoe and Trail Outpost at Dillon Bridge, 601-876-6964.

3. Ryals Canoe and Tube Rentals, outside Bogue Chitto Water Park, 601-684-4948.

4. Sweetwater Park and Canoe Renting, Dillon Bridge, 601-876-5474.

5. Canoe and Trail Adventures, 6976 General Haig St., New Orleans, La., 504-283-9400.

Area campgrounds

1. Bogue Chitto Water Park, Dogwood Trail off Highway 98 just west of River, 601-684-9568.

2. There are several privately operated campgrounds east of McComb, including some at canoe outfitters.

High points

Clear water, exceptional scenery, abundant sand and gravel bars.

Low points

Excessive, sometimes unruly crowds on summer weekends.

Tips

Don't underestimate this river. It's tricky: fast and studded with logs and stobs.

Topisaw Creek

Topisaw is an absolutely beautiful little stream, but whether or not it's canoeable is debatable—indeed, has been debated before government officials in Jackson. It is now considered legally navigable from the confluence of its two forks down to its mouth at Bogue Chitto River in Pike County, but the stream is more suitable to a lightweight kayak or sit-on-top than a full-sized canoe unless you don't mind getting out a lot.

The two forks begin in southeast Lincoln County and run together in northeast Pike County. Above the forks, where Highway 570 crosses the Topisaw, cluster the numerous rustic cabins of Felder's Campground, where an old-time Methodist camp meeting is held every August. Just below the confluence of the forks, at Turnpike Road—the first put-in—stands a massive, $140,000 bridge completed in 1999. The previous bridge sustained damage in high water earlier that year when driftwood broke a concrete piling. Although Topisaw is normally just inches deep, high water can send downed trees barreling down the creek with destructive force. During construction, county engineer Nick Rutter found another problem: The east bank had moved 80 feet. To keep the current from undermining the bridge, workers built upstream jetties planked with creosote timbers and backed with rock riprap. The jetties block the current and send it past the bridge. The project illustrates the potential power in even a small creek like Topisaw. Normally, though, the creek is as sweet and clear as quince jelly, bordered by small sandbars draped with lush muscadine vines and backed by deep forest. Local folks float and fish in a variety of small boats, including johnboats, pirogues, canoes, and kayaks. Some kayakers come from as far off as Louisiana to negotiate the creek's swift, narrow turns.

Three miles below Turnpike Road, Highway 44 crosses the creek. Access here is difficult with "no parking" signs near the bridge and a steep, tight squeeze down the bank to the water. From Highway 44 to Brent Road is another 4 miles, and from Brent Road to Leatherwood Road 4.5 miles. The Topisaw enters the Bogue Chitto a half-mile below Leatherwood Road and continues 2.5 miles to a ramp at Highway 98.

The stretch from Brent Road to the Bogue Chitto was used as a test case when public access was still a legal issue. The year was 1990, and landowners were up in arms, saying they suffered abuse from disrespectful canoers and tubers. One landowner, Bill Stroble—who later became a member of the Pearl River Basin Development District's board of directors—said canoers cursed him when he asked them to leave his property, mooned his wife, and left bags of garbage along the creek. He contended the Topisaw was too small to be navigable since even during normal water levels canoers cannot float far without dragging, thus setting foot on private property. Stroble asked me, as a newspaper reporter, to test his thesis. Since I'd only floated the Topisaw a few times and hadn't memorized all its crooks and turns, I recruited a pair who paddled it on a regular basis, while I went along in another canoe with a novice. The pair familiar with the creek managed it with no portaging. My partner and I, however, had to portage five times, scraped bottom an additional eleven times and capsized once when we ran up under some overhanging limbs and my inexperienced boatmate grabbed them to stop our momentum. As requested, I described our findings at a Mississippi Commission on Environmental Quality hearing in Jackson that year. After listening to testimony from landowners, outfitters, and paddlers, the commission revoked the public status of Topisaw Creek and Bogue Chitto River pending the outcome of a lawsuit before the state Supreme Court. The high court, of course, later ruled them navigable, but disputes over public access continued. In May 1999, for instance, a landowner erected a fence that blocked access under Leatherwood Bridge, removing it only after the Pike County Board of Supervisors filed a lawsuit in chancery court.

Paddlers aren't the only ones who enjoy the creek. Four-wheelers buzz up and down the shallow, sandy Topisaw, to the dismay of paddlers and landowners alike. Of course, such categories are not clear-cut. Landowners often canoe too, as well as ride four-wheelers. The issues are complex, and landowners have a right to feel angry when they or their property are mistreated. It's a shame that the public's right to enjoy a beautiful stream like Topisaw gets compromised in the process.

But people continue to enjoy it in one way or another. Fishermen set trotlines and droplines, catching blue and channel catfish on catalpa worms and pond perch. Catfish as big as 25 pounds have come out of deep holes in the typically shallow Topisaw. Bass fishermen use rubber worms—crawfish is an effective color—as well as small spinnerbaits, beetlespins, and topwater lures like Tiny Torpedoes. Since Topisaw is in essence an extension of the Bogue Chitto, fish swim up from the bigger stream to shelter in occasional pockets.

Topisaw routes

1. Turnpike Road to Highway 44, 3 miles. Turnpike Road runs east from West Topisaw Road north of the Pricedale community. Access is difficult at Highway 44, with nowhere to park but the roadside, and steep banks.

2. Highway 44 to Brent Road, 4 miles. Brent Road crosses West Topisaw South, a road paralleling the creek to the west.

3. Brent Road to Leatherwood Road, 4.5 miles.

4. Leatherwood Road to ramp at Highway 98 on Bogue Chitto River, 3 miles. Topisaw empties into Bogue Chitto River half a mile below Leatherwood Road.

Outfitters

1. Bogue Chitto Choo Choo, near entrance to Bogue Chitto Water Park, 601-249-3788.

2. Ryals Canoe and Tube Rentals, outside Bogue Chitto Water Park, 601-684-4948.

Area campgrounds

1. Bogue Chitto Water Park, Dogwood Trail off Highway 98 just west of River, 601-684-9568.
2. Some canoe rentals also have camping areas.

High points

Clear, shallow water and lovely sandbars.

Low points

Often too shallow or narrow for easy passage.

Tips

Use a small, lightweight boat such as a river kayak, sit-on-top, or pirogue.

Magee's Creek

With water as clear as a Montana brook, rambunctious bass, and deep, shady woods, Magee's Creek is a sparkling jewel of a stream. Though a little over 30 miles long with just 12 miles of canoeing, it's as pretty a creek as you're likely to see anywhere. This tributary to the Bogue Chitto River starts in northeast Walthall County and becomes floatable at Holmes Water Park on Highway 198 West in Tylertown. It runs 6 miles from there to the community of Lexie off Highway 27 south of town, and another 6 to Dillon Bridge on the Bogue Chitto. Actually, the 6 miles from Tylertown to Lexie are navigable thanks mainly to the efforts of paddlers and outfitters who periodically hew a passage through the occasional logjams. This stretch is twisty and narrow and may pose problems in extreme low water. The smaller and more maneuverable the boat, the better. The clear, shallow stream passes beneath spring-dampened clay banks and massive, overarching hardwood trees, its lively current bubbling into champagne rapids at occasional chutes and drops. It widens gradually by Lexie, but not by much. The take-out at Lexie is at a rural bridge just east of Highway 27. Sandbars increase as the creek meanders southwest. Just before Highway 27 it passes the plank remains of the foundation of an old grist mill. Highway 27 offers difficult access on the northeast side. However, it's just a couple more miles to the Bogue Chitto River, and less than a mile to Dillon Bridge. Access at Dillon Bridge, possible on the northwest side, is rough too, but there are two outfitters nearby with boat ramps as well as canoe rentals, shuttle service, and campgrounds.

Like every waterway, Magee's (also spelled Magees and McGee's) has its problems, including conflicts between landowners and floaters, litter, and nonnative species. The human conflicts are an extension of those found on the Bogue Chitto River. Problems swelled in 1996 with a July 4 altercation between a group of tubers stopping on a sandbar and a local family having a cookout across the river. The clash turned into a fistfight, with charges and countercharges filed. Landowners banded together seeking stricter regulations governing the river, and county supervisors approved. The regulations prohibit alcohol, firearms, trespassing, and glass or styrofoam containers on Magee's Creek and Walthall County's portion of Bogue Chitto. Canoe rental companies were required to register and number boats and tubes and equip boats with litter bags. During peak use times in the summer, deputies and wildlife conservation officers stop floaters to check for violations, a practice that has drawn both complaints and praise. Opponents say such enforcement harasses innocent people; supporters say it reduces rowdiness. I floated a summer Saturday one time, and a parade of drunken, yelling, boat-banging paddlers ruined the fishing as well as the peace and quiet of the river. On the countless times I've floated the creek on weekday or during the off-season, however, it's been deserted.

As for litter, I confess I've probably trained myself to overlook it. But when I took an African journalist down the creek in 1994, I heard a less jaded viewpoint. Peter Ngomba Efande, visiting from Cameroon, West Africa, praised the creek to the skies, calling it "a dream come true." "But my beaming smiles toured sour; empty beer cans and worn-out tires littered the river at annoying intervals," he wrote in a *McComb Enterprise-Journal* column. At least it didn't completely spoil his trip. "Despite the litter that left a bitter taste in my mouth, canoeing could be exciting as well as thrilling," he concluded.

Fortunately, paddlers pick up litter as well as cut out logjams. Wilmon Van Dan, who owns Canoe and Trail Outpost at Dillon Bridge, patrols the creek regularly and takes groups to help. On a typical cleanup day, twenty-two volunteers picked up twenty-five to thirty bags of trash as well as old tires. In 1996, then-governor Kirk Fordice signed a proclamation recognizing Van Dan and the New Orleans Sierra Club for their efforts. Van Dan also monitors a Tylertown sewage lagoon outflow just below Holmes Water Park. He's found Magee's to be "a good, clean stream" over the years, and says it's as pretty as rivers he has paddled out west.

Like many streams in Mississippi, Magee's Creek is slowly being occupied by non-native plant species. One beautiful piece of woods north of Holmes Water Park is clogged with acres of privet hedge, which grows so fast and dense it can outrun pine trees and make woods impenetrable. Elephant ear plants appear in intervals along the stream as well. Though beautiful—toss some water on the big leaves and watch it pearl up—they slowly expand their range. San Marcos River, Texas, is a case in point, lined with elephant ears for miles. Other problem plants on Mississippi streams are Chinese tallow trees and kudzu. The tallow tree, also known as popcorn tree for its puffy white fruit, is sold as an ornamental because of its gorgeous fall colors, but it easily spreads into the wild and runs rampant on sunny riverbanks, crowding out native plants. Kudzu, used as a forage and soil conservation cover crop in the 1930s, is most common in north Mississippi, but I've seen it as far south as the banks of Wolf River near the coast.

Plants aren't the only invaders. In 1992 a fisherman caught a weird, toothy fish in Magee's Creek. The hand-sized creature was blue-green and speckled on the upper half and orangish on the bottom, with delicate silvery scales and a forked tail. Caught on a red beetlespin a quarter mile from the Bogue Chitto River, it sported a row of teeth in its lower jaw that made people suspect it was a piranha. However, an ichthyologist determined the fish was a similar-looking pacu, known in the aquarium trade as a "plant piranha" because it feeds on vegetation instead of flesh. Pacus have even been caught in lakes near McComb and Hattiesburg. Aquarium owners typically release them when they get too big for the tank—a bad idea ecologically since alien species can reduce populations of endangered native species. Fortunately, a good hard winter typically kills the tropical invaders.

Far more common are bass. With its fast, clear water running by still, deeper pools, Magee's Creek is a classic bass stream. The fish go for all sorts of lures, including topwater plugs like Devil's Horse, white spinnerbaits, floating minnows and beetlespins. Most creek bass weigh about a pound, though lunkers up to 5 pounds have been caught. Magee's also yields feisty bream and catfish.

Holmes Water Park in Tylertown does not allow camping, but it's a great place to picnic or bank-fish. It's also a popular spot for ball games and various community activities. At Thanksgiving 1999 the park hosted an interracial, interdenominational community church service with more than two thousand people present. At Christmas the park is decorated fantastically. And each June it's the site of the Walthall County June Dairy Festival, which is like no other dairy festival I've ever seen. In addition to events like a pretty cow contest and karate demonstration, there are the much-touted turtle races. One year organizer Dubs Mounger hired a race physician, "Dr. Bari DeLeon" of the Galapagos Islands—who looked suspiciously like Barry Dillon of Tylertown but spoke with a Spanish accent. The illustrious DeLeon claimed to have been "tortoisevictorian" at Harvard, but his reputation took a hit when Mounger claimed to see him accept a $5 bribe from a contestant. Mounger instructed lawmen to escort DeLeon to the stage for public questioning. "I don't recall taking anything, and if I did, I do recall giving it back," DeLeon insisted. This hilarious exchange, which went on for quite a while, was broadcast on the radio and reported in the newspaper—all of which suggests that, despite occasional conflicts, area residents are as sweet-tempered as their creeks.

Magee's routes

1. Holmes Water Park in Tylertown to rural bridge just east of Highway 27 at Lexie, 6 miles.
2. Lexie to Dillon Bridge on Bogue Chitto River, 6 miles. Magee's enters the Bogue Chitto just under a mile above Dillon Bridge, where access is difficult; canoe rentals are located above and below the bridge. Highway 27 crosses Magee's Creek little over a mile above the mouth, but access there is difficult too.

Outfitters

1. Canoe and Trail Outpost at Dillon Bridge, 601-876-6964.
2. Sweetwater Park and Canoe Renting, Dillon Bridge, 601-876-5474.

Area campgrounds

1. Bogue Chitto Water Park, Dogwood Trail off Highway 98 just west of River, 601-684-9568.
2. The two canoe rentals have camping areas.

High points

Steep bluffs with springs; canopy formed by huge, overarching trees.

Low points

Crowds on summer weekends.

Tips

Navigation is tricky on this fast, narrow, twisting creek, especially on the upper stretch, so stay alert.

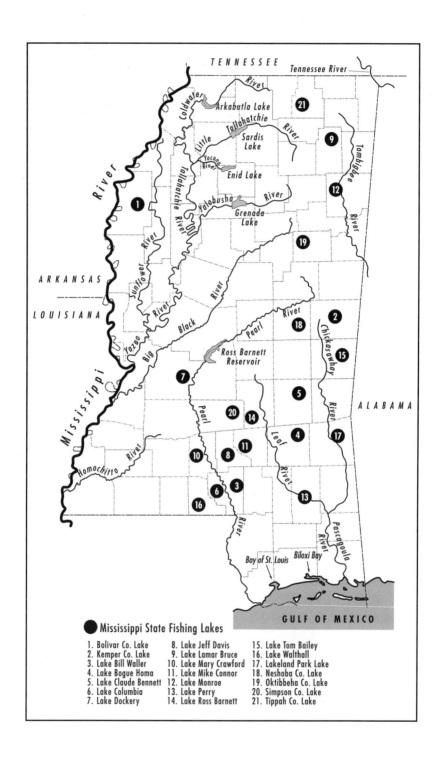

TENNESSEE

Tennessee River

ARKANSAS

LOUISIANA

ALABAMA

GULF OF MEXICO

Coldwater River
Arkabutla Lake
Tallahatchie
Little
Sardis Lake
Yocona River
Enid Lake
Yalobusha River
Grenada Lake
Tallahatchie River
Sunflower River
Black River
Yazoo River
Big
Mississippi River
Homochitto River
Pearl River
Ross Barnett Reservoir
Pearl River
Leaf River
River
Chickasawhay River
Tombigbee River
Pascagoula River
Bay of St. Louis
Biloxi Bay

● Mississippi State Fishing Lakes

1. Bolivar Co. Lake	8. Lake Jeff Davis	15. Lake Tom Bailey
2. Kemper Co. Lake	9. Lake Lamar Bruce	16. Lake Walthall
3. Lake Bill Waller	10. Lake Mary Crawford	17. Lakeland Park Lake
4. Lake Bogue Homa	11. Lake Mike Connor	18. Neshoba Co. Lake
5. Lake Claude Bennett	12. Lake Monroe	19. Oktibbeha Co. Lake
6. Lake Columbia	13. Lake Perry	20. Simpson Co. Lake
7. Lake Dockery	14. Lake Ross Barnett	21. Tippah Co. Lake

8. Lakes

When people say "canoeing" in Mississippi, they usually think of rivers, not lakes. Yet lake canoeing is probably the easiest, most accessible way to go, and can be just about as much fun as a river day trip. Canoes are available for rent at some lakes, and a typical fee of $15 a day or $3 an hour may be as cheap as shuttling two vehicles around for a river float with your own canoe. One drawback to day trips on a stream is the hassle: By the time you load your boat, park one vehicle at a lower bridge, and drive to an upper one, then do the same thing in reverse at the end of the journey, you may have spent as much time as you did on the water. Lake canoeing eliminates all that. You drive in, pay your fee if there is one, throw the boat in the water, and go. When you've gotten your outdoor fix you return to the starting point. It's no-hassle floating.

There are drawbacks to lake paddling, of course. A public lake usually offers less solitude than a river (though not when the summertime weekend hordes hit the popular canoeing streams). Ski boats, speed boats, and personal watercraft can be irritating, even dangerous. But it's not so hard to avoid skiing areas, and by staying out of the main thoroughfares you can avoid being bounced excessively. The best wildlife viewing is in the backwaters and coves anyway, where powerboats slow down if they venture at all.

Otherwise, a canoe is just right on a lake. It can be a perfect fishing vessel. Or it's good just for some family paddling, punctuated by a picnic on shore. Lakes also offer an ideal spot to practice paddling skills. There's nothing like a broad expanse of open water to hone correction strokes, which allow you to keep the canoe straight without swapping sides with the paddle. Once mastered, they are smooth and effortless, and will also be a big help on a river. And a lake trip offers gorgeous views of open water, forested shores, and long-legged herons standing sleepy in the sunlight.

As canoers glide along and a motorboat churns by, the paddlers have a right to feel smug. After all, they're getting their exercise, burning no fuel, and they didn't spend thousands of dollars on boat, motor, trailer, and accessories. And unlike motorboats, a canoe can slip up to browsing deer, dozing alligator, or romping raccoon without alerting them.

There are several categories of lakes in Mississippi, including state fishing lakes, state parks, national forest lakes, national wildlife refuges, reservoirs, water parks, and natural lakes such as oxbows. Tennessee-Tombigbee Waterway lakes are profiled in chapter 4.

State Fishing Lakes

The state's twenty-one fishing lakes, administered by the Mississippi Department of Wildlife, Fisheries, and Parks, are less elaborate than state parks. While some have camping facilities and other amenities, others offer little more than a boat ramp. They're often located in out-of-the-way areas and thus less likely to be crowded. As the name suggests, they're mainly for fishing. As a river-oriented person, I've never gotten the hang of fishing state lakes, and plenty of other fishermen are in the same boat. These man-made bodies of water defy natural laws of lake formation. The deeps are in the middle, not along the bank, and you've got to have a good mental (or physical) picture of the bottom to know where the channels and dropoffs are. The way to fish such lakes, I'm told, is to do so often enough to learn them, and use such devices as electronic depth finders and fish locators. Yet there's plenty to enjoy without wetting a hook. Alligators, deer, turkeys, squirrels, snakes, herons, egrets, turtles—most of the creatures that call Mississippi home can be found around state lakes. No doubt they've learned there is nothing to fear from those fishermen on the water intently casting for bass or white perch. The state also did well by putting picnic areas, pavilions, swimming areas, campgrounds, and boat rentals at many locations. These places are well worth a visit by people who don't even own a rod and reel, who just want to paddle or walk around, watch for critters, picnic in the shade, and feel the breeze off the water.

Fees are charged for various uses, usually on the honor system. Entrance and fishing cost $2, or $5 with boat launching, and $8 for camping. Though the lakes have managers with office phone numbers, they're usually outside working, especially since some have charge of more than one lake. Most rent johnboats but not canoes.

Here are the lakes:

Bolivar County Lake, 512 acres (662-759-6444), is the only state fishing lake in the Delta. It's located 15 miles west of Cleveland off Highway 8. It offers boat rental, camping with hookups, concessions (vending machines), picnic tables, and restrooms. No skiing is permitted.

Kemper County Lake, 652 acres (601-743-5505), is located in east-central Mississippi 3 miles northeast of DeKalb off Highway 397. It has beach, boat rental, camping with hookups, concessions, pavilion rental, restrooms, and swimming. Skiing is permitted daily from noon to sunset.

Lake Bill Waller, 200 acres (601-736-1861), nestles 12 miles southeast of Columbia in the Marion County Wildlife Management Area. It's considered one of the state's top bass fishing lakes since it's produced 14-pound Florida bass. The stump-filled lake caters strictly to fishermen, with no facilities except boat rentals, restrooms, and the standard boat ramp. However, its sister lake down the road, 90-acre Lake Columbia (same phone number), offers skiing Wednesday, Saturday, and Sunday afternoons along with boat rental, camping with hookups, concessions, pavilion, picnic tables, and restrooms.

Lake Bogue Homa, at 1,200 acres the state's largest fishing lake (601-425-2148), is 6 miles east of Laurel off Highway 84. It has boat rental, camping with hookups, concessions, picnic tables, and restrooms. Skiing is allowed daily from noon to sunset.

Lake Claude Bennett, 71 acres (601-727-3561), lies to the north of Lake Bogue Homa, 20 miles east of Bay Springs off Highway 18. It has boat rental, camping with hookups, concessions, pavilion, picnic tables, and restrooms. Skiing is open Wednesday and Sunday afternoons.

Lake Dockery, 55 acres (601-835-3050), in Hinds County is located west off Interstate 55 at Byram. No skiing is permitted, and there are no facilities except a ramp.

Lake Jeff Davis, 164 acres (601-792-8225), is 3 miles south of Prentiss off Highway 42, with boat rental, camping with hookups, concessions, nature trail, pavilion, picnic tables, and restrooms. Skiing is allowed Tuesday and Sunday afternoons.

Lake Lamar Bruce, 330 acres (662-869-2009), lies in northeast Mississippi 1.5 miles northeast of Saltillo off Highway 45. It's got beach, boat rental, camping with hookups, concessions, pavilion, restrooms, and swimming. Skiing is permitted Sunday and Thursday afternoons.

Lake Mary Crawford, 135 acres (601-587-7853), is located 5 miles west of Monticello off Highway 84. It has boat rental, camping with hookups, concessions, pavilion, picnic tables, and restrooms. Skiing is allowed only on Sunday afternoons.

Lake Mike Connor (sometimes spelled Conner), 83 acres (601-765-4024), is 8 miles west of Collins off Highway 84 in southeast Mississippi. It offers boat rental, camping with hookups, concessions, pavilion, picnic tables, and restrooms. Skiing is allowed on Wednesday and Sunday afternoons.

Lake Monroe, 111 acres (662-840-5172), is on Coontail Road off Highway 45 between Aberdeen and Amory in northeast Mississippi. It has boat rental, camping with hookups, concessions, pavilion, picnic tables, and restrooms. Skiing is permitted on Sunday afternoons.

Lake Perry, 125 acres (601-784-6119), is 3 miles south of Beaumont off Highway 98 in southeast Mississippi. It has boat rental, camping with hookups, concessions, picnic tables, and restrooms. Skiing is allowed Friday and Sunday afternoons.

Lake Ross Barnett, not to be confused with Ross Barnett Reservoir, 87 acres (601-733-2611), nestles 4 miles southwest of Mize off Highway 35. It has boat rental, camping with hookups, concessions, picnic tables, and restrooms, with skiing on Friday and Sunday afternoons.

Lake Tom Bailey, 234 acres (601-632-4679), is 8 miles east of Meridian on Highway 11. It has boat rental, camping with hookups, concessions, picnic tables, and restrooms. Skiing is permitted Tuesday, Thursday, and Sunday afternoons.

Lake Walthall, 62 acres (601-835-3050), lies 8 miles southeast of Tylertown off Highway 48. It has only a boat ramp. No skiing is allowed.

Lakeland Park Lake, 12 acres (601-692-2776), is located off Highway 84 in Waynesboro. It has no facilities and no skiing.

Neshoba County Lake, 225 acres (601-692-2776), is 6 miles southeast of Philadelphia off Highway 486, with boat rental, camping with hookups, concessions, picnic tables, and restrooms. No skiing.

Oktibbeha County Lake, 479 acres (662-323-3350), is 9 miles west of

Starkville off Highway 82. It has boat rental, camping with hookups, concessions, picnic tables, and restrooms. Skiing is allowed daily from noon to sunset.

Simpson County Lake, 94 acres (601-692-2776), is 5 miles north of Magee on Highway 49. It has boat rental, camping with hookups, concessions, picnic tables, and restrooms, with skiing allowed Thursday and Sunday.

Tippah County Lake, 165 acres (601-837-9850), 2.5 miles north of Ripley off Highway 15 in north Mississippi, has boat rental, camping with hookups, concessions, pavilion, picnic tables, grills, restrooms, and swimming. Skiing is allowed Saturday and Sunday afternoons.

State Parks

If you adjust your expectations, state parks can offer an unparalleled paddling experience. By adjust expectations, I mean put aside notions of wilderness and backcountry, and instead think family and nature. Example: I had a family gathering at a state park with about a dozen members whose ages ranged from one to seventy. Activities for this group included picnicking, sandbox-playing, monkey-bar crawling, strolling, golf, and canoeing. Guess who was in charge of the latter. I brought a canoe and took people out in shifts. On one jaunt, with my eight-year-old nephew in front, we paddled to within a few feet of a group of nutria rats. Add to that the flocks of ducks, the sunshine, the languorous water, and the mild exertion of paddling, and it was an outdoor experience hard to top—and certainly easier than a standard river float, which would have been unfeasible with such a group.

State park lakes also feature some good river trips on the creeks that feed the lakes (which is true of virtually all man-made lakes). The Tangipahoa River at the north end of the lake at Percy Quin State Park, for instance, is a curvaceous avenue into the heart of a swamp. Unlike some streams, it is not plagued by problems of landowners, liability, or difficult access. Just put your canoe in the water—the park will even rent you the canoe—then head up to the narrow passages where the Tangipahoa enters the lake. Granted, you can scarcely go a mile before the stream is blocked by logs, but what a mile! The creek winds among huge oak, cypress, and pine trees as well as open marsh. The swamp is full of the subtle scents of flowers, grasses, wind, and water. In places the river is so still that it mirrors the forest and sky. Paddlers may easily spend five or six hours paddling, drifting, and exploring. Though a few fishermen in flat-bottom boats with motors venture up the river, their size puts them at a disadvantage for exploring side passages. The silent, close-to-the-water canoe does not disturb wildlife easily, and you may see such creatures as beavers, otters, and nutria rats. Great blue herons may startle you when they explode in slow-motion flight from some grassy nook, and their deep-throated croaks will make you look twice. Ospreys sometimes put on a fascinating show, hurtling down to the surface of the water and flapping up with fish impaled on their talons—bass big enough to make even experienced lake fishermen envious.

Fishing, of course, is the prime reason many people venture onto state park lakes. Canoers are at a disadvantage, lacking electronic fish locators and depth finders and motors to zip from one spot to another. However, some park offices have maps of the lake bottom, and park officials as well as nearby bait shop operators are usually glad to offer tips. With patience, lakes can yield good results. All state park lakes are stocked with game fish, but some have acquired reputations for certain species. Natchez State Park is legendary for its rod-bending Florida hybrid bass, holding the state record largemouth at 18.15 pounds. Pickwick Lake, which adjoins J. P. Coleman State Park, is the top spot for smallmouth bass, having produced the 7.9-pound state record. Enid Reservoir (George Payne Cossar State Park) holds the world record for white crappie at 5 pounds, 3 ounces. Lake Lincoln is known for producing chinquapin bream. Sardis Reservoir (John W. Kyle State Park) is a prime bass fishery, while Grenada Reservoir (Hugh White State Park) produces crappie over 3 pounds and is also popular with catfish hand-grabbers. And those are just some highlights.

State parks tend to be crowded, especially on weekends, so you'll want to take extra precautions to avoid areas frequented by speedboats. Unless noted, all the parks offer campgrounds with hookups as well as many other amenities. Canoe rentals are available at Clarkco, Golden Memorial, Paul B. Johnson, Percy Quin, Tishomingo, Tombigbee, and Wall Doxey. Fees are $3 per hour or $15 per twenty-four hours. Of Mississippi's twenty-nine state parks, here are the twenty-one with lakes big enough to canoe:

Clarkco State Park (601-776-6651), 20 miles south of Meridian off Highway 45 at Quitman, has a 65-acre lake.

George Payne Cossar State Park (662-623-7356), 5 miles east of Interstate 55 off Highway 32, is situated on a peninsula at 28,000-acre Enid Reservoir.

Golden Memorial State Park (601-253-2237), Highway 492, 5 miles east of Walnut Grove off Highway 35 in central Mississippi, has a 15-acre spring-fed lake. There are no campsites at this park.

Great River Road State Park (662-759-6762), off Highway 1 at Rosedale 35 miles north of Greenville, has a 30-acre lake.

Holmes County State Park (662-653-3351), 4 miles south of Durant off Interstate 55 at Exit 150 north of Jackson, has an 88-acre lake and an adjacent 22-acre lake.

Hugh White State Park (662-226-4934), 5 miles east of Grenada off Highway 8, is located at 64,000-acre Grenada Reservoir.

J. P. Coleman State Park (662-423-6515), 13 miles north of Iuka off Highway 25 in extreme northeast Mississippi, is located on the Tennessee River at Pickwick Lake.

John W. Kyle State Park (662-487-1345), 9 miles east of the town of Sardis off Highway 315, accesses 58,500-acre Sardis Reservoir as well as the 400-acre Sardis Lower Lake.

Lake Lincoln State Park (601-643-9044), 4.5 miles east of Wesson on Sunset Road, has a 550-acre lake.

Lake Lowndes State Park (662-328-2110), 6 miles southeast of Columbus off Highway 69, has a 150-acre lake.

LeFleur's Bluff State Park (601-987-3923), off Lakeland Drive in Jackson (Exit 98-B on I-55), has a 50-acre lake.

Legion State Park (662-773-8323), 2 miles north of Louisville on North Columbus Avenue (Old Highway 25) in east-central Mississippi, sports a 12-acre lake. There are cabins and tent sites but no campsites with hookups.

Leroy Percy State Park (662-827-5436), 5 miles west of Hollandale off Highway 12 near Greenville, offers a 60-acre lake.

Natchez State Park (601-442-2658), 10 miles north of Natchez off Highway 61, has a 230-acre lake.

Paul B. Johnson State Park (601-582-7721), 10 miles south of Hattiesburg off Highway 49, has a 296-acre lake.

Percy Quin State Park (601-684-3938), 6 miles south of McComb on Highway 48, sports a 700-acre lake.

Roosevelt State Park (601-732-6316), Highway 13 south of Morton east of Jackson, has a 150-acre lake.

Tishomingo State Park (662-438-6914), located at Mile Marker 304 on the

Natchez Trace in northeast Mississippi, has a 45-acre lake. (Also see chapter 4 for a description of Bear Creek, which runs through the park.)

Tombigbee State Park (662-842-7669), 6 miles southeast of Tupelo off Highway 6, offers a 55-acre lake.

Trace State Park (662-489-2958), 10 miles east of Pontotoc off Highway 6 in northeast Mississippi, has a 565-acre lake.

Wall Doxey State Park (662-252-4231), 7 miles south of Holly Springs off Highway 7 in north Mississippi, has a spring-fed 45-acre lake.

For general information on Mississippi's state parks, call 1-800-GO-PARKS.

National Forests

Mississippi's six national forests contain some real jewels for canoeing: scenic lakes tucked away in dreamy, piney-woods hollows. There are woods, hills, silence, and solitude, the reflection of sky on water, the sun shining through Spanish moss—and you might even catch some fish. A typically unheralded example is 14-acre Pipes Lake in the Homochitto National Forest. Unlike many lakes in Mississippi, Pipes Lake is natural, apparently constructed by beavers years ago. The lake spreads in long fingers among forested hills, with depths up to 8 feet. Though it's not a great fishing spot, Pipes has a decent population of fish, including largemouth bass, bluegill, redear sunfish (shellcrackers), channel catfish, a few crappie, and some gar. The largest bass reported from the lake is 7 pounds. The size of the lake makes it ideal for a canoe or small flat-bottom boat with trolling motor; it's just not big enough for a bass boat with a large motor. And it's narrow enough in most places to make it convenient for bank fishermen. It's a good fly-fishing lake, ringed with bream beds that are productive in the spring. No swimming is allowed, but the area features picnicking areas and portable toilets.

At the other end of the spectrum is Choctaw Lake Recreation Area in the Tombigbee National Forest near Ackerman, which boasts a 100-acre lake, first-class campground, and hiking trail. Though the $13 fee may be off-putting to tent-campers, the luxurious beauty is worth it. The main lake is separated by a chute from a smaller section along which campsites are laid out, so motor noises remain at a distance. Small peninsulas reach out into the water for bank fishing. Pine trees tower overhead. And sweetest of all are the huge stacks of split cedar and red oak for campers' use. When I visited at midweek

Tombigbee National Forest near Ackerman offers campsites on a secluded arm of Choctaw Lake.

in March, I had the entire campground to myself. That was bliss indeed, for the main drawback to campgrounds is the fact that some people equate the outdoors with making noise. I prefer to let nature provide the soundtrack. And does it ever. All night long the ducks and geese chattered and cackled while frogs sang and the wind blew the pine trees like a juice-harp choir. Just before dawn the herons wakened with croaks, grunts, and snorts. The lake itself is three-quarters of a mile long with a gorgeous shoreline of open pine forest. No wake is allowed on the entire lake, which is good news for paddlers. Choctaw is a popular fishing spot and is good for all species: bass, bream, crappie, and catfish. When you get tired of canoeing, a nice trail runs around part of the shore, good enough for an hour or two of moseying. You can also hike up the lake's main tributary, a tiny creek, to its birth from springs seeping through fern and moss. These hills, said to be a remnant of the Appalachians, provide sweeping views under the forest canopy, with occasional glimpses of deer, squirrels, and quail.

Those are just two fine examples of national forest lakes. The Forest Service charges fees for a wide range of activities, so it's wise to bring plenty of small bills for dropping in pay boxes at places like campgrounds, boat launches, and trailheads. It's also smart to get a national forest map to seek out some of the more remote places. Here's an overview of the forests and lakes:

The 155,000-acre Holly Springs National Forest (662-236-6550) south and east of Holly Springs in north Mississippi is loaded with lakes. There are campgrounds at 259-acre Chewalla Lake and 96-acre Puskus Lake; Chewalla boasts several miles of hiking trail as well. Most of the lakes were built by the U.S. Soil Conservation Service (now the Natural Resource Conservation Service) for flood prevention or erosion control. Some are accessible only by woods road requiring four-wheel drive. Lakes include 18-acre Autry, 19-acre Bagley, 119-acre Big Snow, 23-acre Bluff Springs, 50-acre Brent's, 16-acre Buck Rucker, 47-acre Chilli, 34-acre Cox, 35-acre Curtis Creek, 36-acre Cypress, 26-acre Denmark, 16-acre Drewery, 9-acre Duncan, 77-acre East Cypress, 13-acre Kettle, 20-acre Little Snow, 17-acre Mild, 43-acre Mount Olive, 189-acre Muddy, 47-acre North Chilli, 30-acre North Cypress, 6-acre Oak Grove, 42-acre Renick, 7-acre Shelby, 66-acre South Chilli, 20-acre Upper Pechahallee, 43-acre Wagner, 26-acre Wood Duck, and 16-acre Yellow Rabbit. Some of the lakes partially border private land: Bagley, Big Snow, Little Snow, Muddy, Oak Grove, Renick, Shelby, South Chilli, and Upper Pechahallee. The forest also borders Sardis Reservoir.

The 66,500-acre Tombigbee National Forest (662-285-3264) lies in two widely spaced units, one near Ackerman, the other south of Tupelo. It has campgrounds at 200-acre Davis Lake and 100-acre Choctaw Lake. Other canoeable lakes include the 23-acre Chestnut, 13-acre Curry, 76-acre Goodfood, 34-acre Little Owl, 35-acre Organ, 15-acre Pendergrass, 19-acre Ross Hill, 63-acre Texas, 60-acre Tillatoba, and 25-acre Walker.

The 178,000-acre Bienville National Forest (601-469-3811) along I-20 east of Jackson is noteworthy for its 23-mile Shockaloe horse trail, wildflower-rich Harrell Prairie, and Bienville Pines Scenic Area and Trail offering a view of a virgin pine stand. But the flat terrain is not conducive to lake-building, so there are relatively few. Campgrounds exist at 55-acre Marathon Lake and 6-acre Shongelo. Other lakes are 35-acre Beaver Pond, 30-acre Greentree, and 40-acre Tishkill.

The 60,000-acre Delta National Forest (662-873-6256) near Rolling Fork is touted as the nation's only bottomland hardwood national forest. It features a virgin sweetgum stand as well as the Big and Little Sunflower rivers (see chapter 3) and several greentree reservoirs. There's a campground at Blue Lake, but at 3 acres it's scarcely big enough to paddle. Other lakes are 4-acre Barge, 29-

acre Clark, 6-acre Lost Lake, and 10-acre Ten Mile Bayou. Since the forest floods seasonally, acreage varies; during high water, huge areas of the forest are submerged.

The 190,000-acre Homochitto National Forest (601-384-5876) covers rugged piney bluffs in southwest Mississippi. Clear Springs Recreation Area has a 15-acre lake, fully-equipped campsites, swimming area, short nature trail, and 20-plus-mile hiking-biking trail. Primitive camping is permitted at 14-acre Pipes Lake and 1-acre Nebo Lake. Nebo is too small for canoeing, and while it is located next to the Homochitto River (see chapter 3), access to the river is difficult down a steep, weedy bank. Under construction at this writing is a 1,000-acre lake on Porter Creek, scheduled to open in 2005 with campgrounds, cabins, trails, and other amenities.

Though by far the state's largest national forest, the 501,000-acre De Soto (601-928-5291 or 601-428-0594) in southeast Mississippi has relatively few sizeable lakes. There are campgrounds at 4-acre Airey Lake, 8-acre Ashe Lake, and 250-acre Turkey Fork, plus primitive camping at 7-acre P.O.W. Lake. Other lakes are 5-acre Ashley Pond, 5-acre Blue Pond, 5-acre Leaf Pond, and 6-acre Fruit Lake. What the De Soto lacks in lakes, it makes up for in other ways, including the 41-mile Black Creek Trail and 21-mile Tuxachanie Trail, popular canoeing streams Black and Red Creeks (chapter 5), and the state's only designated wilderness areas, Black Creek and Leaf.

For details on all the national forests in Mississippi, call the Forest Service office in Jackson at 601-965-4391.

Oxbows

Most of Mississippi's large rivers have some oxbow lakes lying alongside them, like the rivers' old footprints. Those along Pascagoula and Pearl Rivers typically lie within a jungle of cypress swamp on either side of the main channel. Mississippi River oxbows inhabit a realm of flat farm fields and willow trees. Nearly all these waters are home to white egrets, plopping turtles, thrashing gar, catfish rolling slowly over in the murk, and alligators silently submerging. Though the lakes are undeniably scenic, they pose some problems for paddlers. Many of them—especially Mississippi River oxbows—are large, windswept, and prone to be buzzing with fishing boats on weekends. Yet there are plenty of isolated pockets, and the fishing can be grand.

On waters like the Pearl and the Pascagoula, the oxbows are most easily entered by paddling into them from the river during high water. The Pascagoula Wildlife Management Area contains more than thirty-six oxbows. Basic maps are available by calling 601-947-6376 for the George County portion or 228-588-3878 for the Jackson County portion. The best bet is to get out on the river and explore. See chapter 5 for more information. On the lower Pearl, dozens of oxbows lie within Mississippi's Old River Wildlife Management Area (601-772-9024), Bogue Chitto National Wildlife Refuge (504-646-7555) and Louisiana's Pearl River Wildlife Management Area (225-765-2800). See chapter 7 for more information.

Most Mississippi River oxbows are accessible by vehicle and boat ramp. While many are miles long, there are some small ones, like 40-odd acre Artonish Lake north of Fort Adams in extreme southwest Mississippi. Though the lake is privately owned, boaters can get access by paying a nominal fee at Fort Adams Grocery. I took an eleven-year-old cousin, Larry Herndon, to Artonish for some late-afternoon bass fishing, and since it was a weekday afternoon, we had the long, narrow lake almost all to ourselves. We slid the canoe in the water and headed across to a flooded stretch of cypress and buttonwoods. A bait shop owner had told me, "Throw a white bandit up against a cypress tree and you're liable to get your arm broke," so I put a white bandit lure on Larry's line and told him to throw it up against a cypress tree. It wasn't long before Larry got the hang of casting, and he wound up catching bream, gar, and a good-sized bass. I occupied my time freeing his lure from button bushes and steadying the boat against the breeze. Most Mississippi River oxbow lakes are considerably larger than Artonish but may still offer some enticing backwaters out of the way of big bass boats.

There are two categories of oxbow: those still connected with the river, if only seasonally, and those that are completely separate. The latter, which are in the minority, are tidier and more stable, often lined with tidy camps and lawns. The former are controlled by the river, so fishing conditions vary according to river stages. Every winter the Mississippi River rises and spills over into the connected lakes, recharging the fish population. While the water is high, catfishing is at its best as anglers set trotlines in areas that are normally dry. In April or May the river drops and water begins to flow out of those lakes, stirring up the white perch, bream, and bass. At least that's how it usually goes; some years the river may stay up well into the summer. River stages, reported in many state newspa-

During high water at Lake Mary, an oxbow lake near Woodville, even bridges can go underwater.

pers, are critical to fishing success in these lakes. Though the oxbows listed below are public waters, the shoreline is typically private, so camping is not advised, nor are there usually any public campgrounds. There are frequently boat ramps, either public or at a bait shop, which may charge a small fee ($3 is typical). Sizes of most oxbow lakes vary since they can expand drastically with floodwater. For information on fishing or hunting guide services to these lakes call 1-800-270-DELTA.

Here's a partial list:

Lake Albermarle, Highway 465 north of Vicksburg, averages 600 acres. This was part of the Mississippi River until the channel changed course in the flood of 1913. It still connects with the Mississippi during high water.

Atchafalaya Bayou, not to be confused with Louisiana's Atchafalaya Swamp, is a Yazoo River oxbow 4 miles south of Belzoni on Highway 49 west of the Yazoo. It spans 350 acres.

Lake Beulah, 5 miles south of Rosedale on Highway 1, covers 1,031 acres. In 1863 Union troops dug a cutoff in the Mississippi River to prevent Confederate troops from ambushing them in Beulah Bend. The river followed the new channel, and the bend became an oxbow, which still joins the river in high water.

Lake Bolivar, not to be confused with Bolivar County Lake, is 12 miles north of Greenville on Highway 1 at Scott. It covers 1,200 acres. This is a good bass lake, with the best action in early spring.

Lake Chotard on Highway 465 north of Vicksburg has 1,000 acres. Fishing is best when the Mississippi River is below 36 feet on the Vicksburg gauge.

DeSoto Lake lies west of Clarksdale south of the junction of Highways 1 and 322. It contains 3,600 acres. The best fishing is when the Mississippi River stage is between 10 and 17 feet at Helena, Ark.

Eagle Lake lies 15 miles west of the junction of Highways 61 and 465 north of Vicksburg. It spans 4,700 acres and is best known for its bass and crappie.

Little Eagle Lake, 10 miles east of Belzoni south of Highway 12, has 700 acres and is mainly a cypress and black-gum swamp.

Lake Ferguson at Greenville is 10 miles long and connects with the Mississippi River. Fishing is best when the river is between 10 and 30 feet at Greenville.

Lake George, on Satartia-Holly Bluff Road 14 miles southwest of Yazoo City, holds 600 acres. This muddy lake is best for catfish and, when it clears, yields crappie.

Lake Lee, 7 miles south of Greenville, has 1,110 acres. Fish it when the Mississippi River stage is between 20 and 30 feet at Greenville.

Lake Mary, 20 miles west of Woodville off Highway 24, averages 2,500 acres. This is the state's only sizeable oxbow lake south of Vicksburg and is a fishing mecca for southwest Mississippi. It's replenished with fish by high water on the Mississippi.

Moon Lake, 4 miles south of the junction of Highways 1 and 49 north of Clarksdale, contains 2,200 acres. Rock riprap lines much of the east bank for erosion control.

Perry Martin Lake at Great River Road State Park, Rosedale, covers 500 acres. The park has campgrounds with hookups, rental boats, and trails.

Roebuck Lake, east of Highway 7 at Itta Bena, has 400 acres. This is an ancient remnant of the Ohio River and is divided into two bodies of water.

Stovall Lake, 7 miles northwest of Clarksdale, has 1,200 acres. The lake connects with the Mississippi River only during extremely high water.

Townsend Lake, 5 miles southeast of Belzoni, holds 70 acres. The Yazoo River flows into this lake during high water.

Tunica Cutoff, 5 miles west of Highway 61, Tunica, covers 2,500 acres. Tunica Cutoff adjoins the Mississippi River on the south end.

Lake Washington, 25 miles south of Greenville on Highway 1, spans 5,000 acres. This is one of the most popular oxbows for its excellent fishing.

Wolf and Broad Lakes, 5 miles northwest of Yazoo City on Highway 49 West, hold 900 acres. These lakes, formerly part of the Yazoo River, are hot spots for crappie when the water is clear enough.

Lake Whittington, 20 miles north of Greenville west of Benoit, has 2,300 acres. Best fishing is when the Mississippi River stage is between 5 and 15 feet at Arkansas City. Three smaller lakes connect with the main lake during high water.

National Wildlife Refuges

National wildlife refuges provide some of the best lake canoeing in Mississippi, particularly if you appreciate the beauties of a swamp environment. Gilliard Lake on the St. Catherine Creek National Wildlife Refuge south of Natchez, for instance, is mostly cypress swamp and little open water, which makes it ideal for paddling, even more so since only electric motors are allowed. The lake booms with bird life: the crunks, groaks, pipes, and spistles of herons, terns, egrets, coots, cormorants, gallinules, and other bulky waterfowl with weird names. Cypress tree trunks may span 15 feet at the base. On one trip I pulled up under a cypress and just watched. Soon I heard a puffing noise, like dolphins surfacing. Then I saw the brown, round, wet heads of otters. There must have been half a dozen. They dove, surfaced, and stared at me poised still as a cypress knee in my shadow-dappled wood-trimmed green canoe. Otters are playful but secretive. In all my years of canoeing I had never seen one in the wild. This gang puffed, splashed, and generally exuded the happy-go-lucky attitude for which otters are famous. Maybe that's what a wildlife refuge is all about.

National wildlife refuges are tightly regulated, and at times they may host quite a few hunters. Some refuges are subject to flooding, and water levels can vary: Gilliard's ranges from 2 feet in low water to 25 in high. And in the case of Gilliard and its sister lake Butler, four-wheel drive is required in all but the driest of conditions. Fishing opportunities can vary widely too, depending on water levels. For such reasons, it's wise to call refuge headquarters before setting out.

Here's a look at lake paddling opportunities in national wildlife refuges:

Bogue Chitto National Wildlife Refuge (504-646-7555), headquartered

Cypress trees dominate at Gilliard Lake in St. Catherine Creek National Wildlife Refuge south of Natchez.

at 1010 Gause Blvd., Building 936, in Slidell, La., straddles the Mississippi-Louisiana state line (lying mostly in Louisiana) along the lower Bogue Chitto River and lower Pearl. It encompasses a host of natural lakes, sloughs and bayous in a river-swamp environment. (See chapter 6 for details on this area.)

Mathews Brake NWR (662-235-4989), 10 miles south of Greenwood west of Highway 49 East, has a 2,000-acre oxbow lake open to fishing year-round and good for bass and crappie. During low water the lake can become choked with lotus weeds, so best time for paddling is early spring or after frost. Mathews Brake is administered by the Yazoo NWR office.

Noxubee NWR (662-323-5548), 17 miles south of Starkville, has two lakes, 1,200-acre Bluff Lake and 600-acre Loakfoma Lake. Bluff Lake includes stands of cypress. No wake is allowed.

Panther Swamp NWR (662-746-5060), on River Road between Yazoo City and Holly Bluff, accesses Lake George, a branch of Big Sunflower River approximately 7 miles long. The refuge borders the northern edge of the lake. Lake George joins the Big Sunflower just southeast of Holly Bluff.

St. Catherine Creek NWR (601-446-8990) lies west of U.S. Highway 61 south of Natchez and is divided into three units: Cloverdale, Butler Lake, and

Sibley. Gilliard Lake, 400 acres, is in the Sibley Unit. Butler Lake, roughly 800 acres, is in the Butler Lake Unit. St. Catherine Creek flows through Butler Lake and can also be paddled. Four-wheel drive is frequently required to reach these lakes.

Tallahatchie NWR (662-226-8286) west of Grenada has Tippo Bayou, a winding, narrow cypress swamp about 5 miles long with a boat ramp just south of Highway 8 west of Holcomb.

Yazoo NWR (662-839-2638) boasts 5,000-acre Swan Lake, which is mostly cypress swamp. The refuge office is located on Yazoo Refuge Road 26 miles south of Greenville off Highway 1.

Reservoirs

Paddling reservoirs can be tough. These vast lakes can be hazardous because of boat traffic, especially on weekends and during the summer. Even at quiet times, the wind across a miles-long, miles-wide lake can be daunting. What feels like a cool, refreshing breeze on shore can shove a lightweight canoe sideways and slam waves against—or over—the hull. At such times, unless you're in a sea kayak, it's wise to stay ashore. But when the wind is light, as often occurs at dawn and dusk, paddling can be delightful. You can poke into quiet coves where young water-loving cypress provide a bright green apron for tall pines and hardwoods. The wind can pick in a hurry, but coves provide shelter. And if you've ever seen Bill Mason's documentary video *Waterwalker* about his solo canoe trips on Lake Superior, it's hard to be too intimidated by a Mississippi breeze. Paddling a streamlined canoe on open water in the cool morning or late evening is close to flying, close to walking on water. In *Waterwalker*, Mason recalled the Bible story where the apostle Peter hiked on the lake—until he remembered humans aren't supposed to be able to perform such feats. Mason speculated that we've all just forgotten how to walk on water.

Mississippi has five major reservoirs, not counting the Tennessee-Tombigbee Waterway. Though flood control is their primary purpose, recreation is a major draw. As a result, all of the reservoirs are loaded with boat ramps, campgrounds, picnic areas, and other recreational facilities. Acreage can vary greatly according to rainfall conditions, especially on the four Delta reservoirs. Here's a look:

Arkabutla Lake, 4 miles east of the town of Coldwater 10 miles south of Hernando, is an 11,240-acre impoundment of Coldwater River.

Enid Lake, 12 miles south of Batesville off Interstate 55, averages some 28,000 acres behind a dam across Yocona River.

Grenada Lake, northeast of Grenada on Highway 8, consists of 64,000 acres of water from Yalobusha and Skuna Rivers.

Ross Barnett Reservoir, northeast of Jackson between the Natchez Trace Parkway and Highway 25, covers 33,000 acres and is formed by damming the Pearl River.

Sardis Lake, 9 miles east of the town of Sardis off Highway 315, covers 58,500 acres and is formed by damming the Little Tallahatchie River.

Water Parks

Most water parks in Mississippi fall under one of two state agencies, the Pearl River Basin Development District and the Pat Harrison Waterway District. The former handles mainly river parks on the Pearl River and its tributaries (chapter 7), while the latter consists of lake parks, mostly in the Pascagoula River basin. Example: Little Black Creek Water Park between Purvis and Lumberton. I was in the vicinity with a boat in my truck one fall weekday (weekdays are simply the best time to canoe lakes if you want to avoid crowds) and decided to check it out. I found a beautiful, quiet, enchanting lake surrounded by woods and camping areas. An abandoned johnboat stranded in shallows at the upper end of the lake provided an artistic look to the scene. Not all the water parks are so peaceful. Three of the lakes—Okatibbee, Maynor Creek, and Flint Creek—have water slides, which might be great if you have children along. Skiing is allowed at all of the lakes except Little Black Creek, Big Creek, and Dry Creek. All have developed campgrounds, and Okatibbee even has a motel. Pick and choose your times and places, and you can probably find what you're looking for at some of these spots. Here's a look:

Archusa Creek Water Park (601-776-6956), just off Highway 18 East at Quitman, has a 450-acre lake.

Big Creek Water Park (601-763-8555), off Highway 84 between Laurel and Collins, has a 150-acre lake.

Dry Creek Water Park (601-797-4619), just off Highway 49 at Mount Olive, has a 150-acre lake.

Flint Creek Water Park (601-928-3051), on Highway 29 North at Wiggins, has a 600-acre lake and features "Water Town" with four giant slides.

An abandoned johnboat sits stranded in shallows at Little Black Creek Water Park between Purvis and Lumberton.

Little Black Creek Water Park (601-794-2957), on Little Black Creek Road between Purvis and Lumberton, has a 600-acre lake.

Maynor Creek Water Park (601-735-4365), 1 mile west of Waynesboro on Highway 84, has a 450-acre lake and features "Swampy Hollow" with three giant water slides.

Okatibbee Water Park (601-737-2370), just off Highway 19 north of Meridian, has a 3,800-acre lake and features a motel and "Splashdown Country" with giant and kiddie slides.

Turkey Creek Water Park (601-635-3314), 5 miles southwest of Decatur off Highway 15, has a 250-acre lake.

For information on any of the parks, call 1-800-748-9618.

Equipment Checklist

Day Trips

Day pack containing:
Poncho
Sunscreen
Insect repellent
Iodine water purification crystals
Lighters
Fire starters
Eyeglass holders
Compass
Toilet paper in plastic bag
Snakebite kit
Canteen
Sunglasses
Lunch
Wool shirt or sweater in cold weather
Also, a waterproof dry bag for wallet, keys, watch, film, camera
Optional: ice chest

Extended Trips

Loaded day pack (see above)
Sleeping bag
Sleeping pad
Cooking utensils (coffee pot, cook pot, aluminum skillet, spatula, filter for coffee, can opener)
Eating utensils (plate, bowl, fork, spoon, cup)

First-aid kit (all size bandaids, bandage, tape, gauze, tweezers, sewing kit, witch hazel, diarrhea medicine, antacids, pain medication, sunburn lotion, poison ivy lotion, antifungal powder, lip balm, personal medicines, etc.)
Flashlight
Ground cloth
Tent
Light tarpaulin
Machete (or hatchet)
Water jugs
Canteen
Knife
Lighters
Map
Notebook, pen
Toiletry items (toothbrush, toothpaste, comb, ear plugs, etc.)
Toilet paper
Hammock
Biodegradable liquid soap, scrub pad
Stove, fuel
Towel
Trash bags
Book
Duct tape
Fishing tackle (optional)

Clothes

Camp shoes
River shoes
Extra pants
Extra long-sleeved shirt
Two pairs socks
Bandannas
T-shirt
Shorts
Hand towel
Cold-weather clothes as needed (wool shirt, longjohns, wool gloves, etc.)
Wide-brimmed hat with optional cap

Boat Gear

Extra paddle
Bailer (top half of bleach bottle)
Sponge
Life vest
Seat back (optional)

Sample food list

Coffee or tea
Instant oatmeal
Honey
Raisins (or dates or prunes)
Fresh fruit
Crackers
Cheese
Peanut butter
Sardines (or similar)
Carrots
Nuts
Rice
Canned tuna (or chicken)
Soup mixes
Onions
Pasta
Tomato paste
Salt
Red pepper sauce
Oil and cornmeal (optional, for frying fish)
Spices
Cookies
Hot chocolate

Recommended Reading

Anderson, Agnes Grinstead. *Approaching the Magic Hour: Memories of Walter Anderson.* University Press of Mississippi, 1989.

Barnett, Jim. *The Natchez Indians.* Mississippi Department of Archives and History, 1998.

Barry, John M. *Rising Tide: The Great Mississippi Flood of 1927 and How It Changed America.* Simon and Schuster, 1997.

Botkin, B. A., ed. *A Treasury of Mississippi River Folklore.* American Legacy Press, 1955.

———. *A Treasury of Southern Folklore.* American Legacy Press, 1977.

Brown, Calvin S. *Archaeology of Mississippi.* 1926; rpt., University Press of Mississippi, 1992.

Claiborne, J. F. H. *Life and Times of Gen. Sam Dale, the Mississippi Partisan.* 1860; rpt., Reprint Company, from the edition in the Mississippi Department of Archives and History, 1976.

DeCell, Harriet, and Prichard, JoAnne. *Yazoo: Its Legends and Legacies.* Yazoo Delta Press, 1976.

Desowitz, Robert S. *The Malaria Capers.* Norton, 1991.

Duncan, David Ewing. *Hernando de Soto: A Savage Quest in the Americas.* Crown Publishers, 1995.

Estes, Chuck, Elizabeth F. Carter, and Byron Almquist. *Canoe Trails of the Deep South.* Menasha Ridge Press, 1991.

Hansen, Gunnar. *Islands at the Edge of Time: A Journey to America's Barrier Islands.* Island Press, 1993.

Harrar, Ellwood S., and J. George Harrar. *Guide to Southern Trees.* Dover Publications, 1962.

Herring, Mack. R. *Way Station to Space: A History of the John C. Stennis Space Center.* National Aeronautics and Space Administration, 1997.

Higginbotham, Jay. *The Pascagoula Indians.* Colonial Books, 1967.

Iberville's Gulf Journals. University of Alabama Press, 1981.

Kirkpatrick, Marlo Carter. *Mississippi: Off the Beaten Path.* Globe Pequot Press, 1999.

Kosciusko-Attala History. Kosciusko-Attala Historical Society, 1976.

Mason, Bill. *Song of the Paddle: An Illustrated Guide to Wilderness Camping.* Firefly Books, 1988.

McCafferty, Jim. *Holt and the Teddy Bear.* Illustrated by Florence S. Davis. Pelican Publishing, 1991. (Children's book about Teddy Roosevelt's bear hunt near Big Sunflower River.)

McGinnis, Helen. *Hiking Mississippi: A Guide to Trails and Natural Areas.* University Press of Mississippi, 1994.

Mississippi Atlas and Gazetteer. DeLorme, 1998.

Mississippi Road Atlas. University Press of Mississippi, 1997.

Redd, Lorraine. *Only in Mississippi: A Guide for the Adventurous Traveler.* Quail Ridge Press, 1993.

Schueler, Donald G. *Adventuring Along the Gulf of Mexico: The Sierra Club Travel Guide to the Gulf Coast of the United States and Mexico from the Florida Keys to Yucatan.* Sierra Club Books, 1986.

Sevenair, John P., ed. *Trail Guide to the Delta Country.* New Orleans Group of the Sierra Club, 1997.

Smith, Frank E. *The Yazoo River.* Rinehart and Company, 1954.

Smith, Patrick. *The River Is Home and Angel City: A Patrick Smith Reader.* Pineapple Press, 1989.

Thigpen, S. G. *Next Door to Heaven.* Kingsport Press, 1965.

———. *Pearl River: Highway to Glory Land.* Kingsport Press, 1965.

Timme, S. Lee. *Wildflowers of Mississippi.* University Press of Mississippi, 1989.

Twain, Mark. *Life on the Mississippi.* 1883. Reader's Digest edition 1987.

Wells, Mary Ann. *Native Land: Mississippi, 1540–1798.* University Press of Mississippi, 1994.

Acknowledgments

In addition to the people listed in the dedication at the beginning of this book, many others provided help as well, among them: Debbie Best and Pat Howard, who introduced me to Seetha Srinivasan of the University Press of Mississippi; my son Andy Coy, brother Robert Herndon, and paddling buddies Dan Banks, Greg Bond, Steve Cox, Billy Gibson, Eddie McCalip, Robert Spillman and his kids Trey and Krystal, for putting up with me on assorted float trips; Mike Williamson, who introduced me to Mississippi canoeing; Randy Reed of the Mississippi Department of Environmental Quality for water quality data; Bobby McGinnis of Dry Creek Marine in Tylertown for fishing lore; Jamie Cummins of Mississippi Wildlife Foundation in Stoneville for Mississippi River fishing techniques and oxbow lake information; John Ruskey of Quapaw Canoe Company in Clarksdale for help with the Mississippi and Yazoo Rivers; Scott Williams for Mississippi River, Bowie River, and barrier islands; wildlife conservation officer Terry Miles for Bayou Pierre; Steve Diffey of Holmes County Community College for upper Big Black; Stanley Simpson of Flora for middle Big Black; Bill Wright for upper and middle Big Black; wildlife conservation officer Mike Ouzts for lower Big Black; Claire May of Grand Gulf Military Park for the park; Ralph Pearce of Delta National Forest for Big and Little Sunflower; Dr. Don Jackson of Mississippi State University for Yalobusha and Little Tallahatchie; my mother, Maude Riales, and stepfather, Darrel Riales, for Coldwater River; Gary Bridgman of Wolf River Conservancy for the Wolf River of north Mississippi and Tennessee; Don Waldon of the Tennessee-Tombigbee Waterway Authority in Columbus for Tenn-Tom, Buttahatchee, and Luxapalila; Don Burns of Columbus for Buttahatchee; Bill Brekeen of Tishomingo State Park for Bear Creek; Al Wimberly for Noxubee; Reverend Jerry Gressett for Chunky; Dr. Stephen Ross of the University of Southern Mississippi for Okatoma, Bowie, and Bayou Pierre; state fisheries biologist Dave Robinson for the Pascagoula system; Bob Andrews of Sunshine Canoes in Mobile, Alabama, for Escatawpa; Wayne Stone of DeSoto National Forest for Tchoutacabouffa and Red Creek; U.S. Park Service ranger Mike Hobbs for Gulf Islands National Seashore; Joe Feil of Wolf River Canoe and Kayak for the Wolf River of south Mississippi; John Tindall of the Department of Wildlife, Fisheries, and Parks for Nanih Waiya Creek; Mike Davis of Pearl River Basin Development District for Pearl River; Will Sullivan of the *Picayune Item* newspaper for lower Pearl; Alan Huffman of Huffman and Rejebian in Jackson for lower Pearl; Sandy Entrekin of D'Lo Water Park for Strong; Walter Neil Ferguson for Bogue Chitto and Topisaw; Jimmy Young for Bogue Chitto and Yazoo; Danny Breaux and James Harris of Bogue Chitto National Wildlife Refuge for lower Bogue Chitto; Tommie Thomas for Topisaw; Patrice Junius of the U.S. Forest Service for national forest lakes; Terri Jacobson of the U.S. Fish and Wildlife Service for national wildlife refuges.

Index